The Curriculum for 7–11 year olds

The Curriculum for 7–11 year olds

edited by

Jeni Riley and Roy Prentice

P·C·P

Paul Chapman
Publishing Ltd

Selection and editorial material © Copyright 1999 Jeni Riley and Roy Prentice
Chapter 1 © Copyright 1999 Jeni Riley
Chapter 2 © Copyright 1999 Pauline Adams
Chapter 3 © Copyright 1999 Richard P. Bailey
Chapter 4 © Copyright 1999 Roger Beard
Chapter 5 © Copyright 1999 Lynne Broadbent
Chapter 6 © Copyright 1999 John Cook
Chapter 7 © Copyright 1999 Caroline Heal
Chapter 8 © Copyright 1999 Rob Johnsey
Chapter 9 © Copyright 1999 Sarah Martyn
Chapter 10 © Copyright 1999 Roy Prentice
Chapter 11 © Copyright 1999 Tim Rowland
Chapter 12 © Copyright 1999 Dorothy Watt

First published 1999

 Paul Chapman Publishing Ltd
A SAGE Publications Company
6 Bonhill Street
London EC2A 4PU

SAGE Publications Inc
2455 Teller Road
Thousand Oaks, California 91320

SAGE Publications India Pvt Ltd
32, M-Block Market
Greater Kailash - 1
New Delhi 110 048

British Library Cataloguing in Publication data
A catalogue record for this book is available from the British Library

ISBN 0-7619-6461-4
ISBN 0-7619-6462-2 (pbk)

Library of Congress catalog card number available

Typeset by Anneset Ltd, Weston super Mare
Printed and bound by Athenaeum Press, Gateshead

Contents

Notes on Contributors

Pauline Adams is a part-time lecturer in music education at the Institute of Education, University of London and teaches on the MA course at Trinity College of Music. She is responsible for the music education component of the primary PGCE course at the Institute. Wide experience has been gained teaching music in primary and secondary schools and working with teachers in an advisory role in London. In addition she is a member of the editorial board of the *British Journal of Music Education*.

Dr Richard P. Bailey is a lecturer in the School of Education at the University of Reading where he is subject leader for physical education. He has previously taught in primary and secondary schools and is currently writing a book on the teaching of physical education in the primary school. His current research reflects his interests in pupils with physical disabilities in a context of physical education and philosophical issues in education, in particular the application of the theory of knowledge and moral philosophy to educational practice.

Dr Roger Beard taught in primary schools and a college of higher education before moving to the University of Leeds where he is now Reader in Literacy Education. His publications include *Developing Reading 3–13, Teaching Literacy: Balancing Perspectives* and *Rhyme, Reading and Writing* (all published by Hodder & Stoughton); *Reading by Apprenticeship?* (with Jane Oakhill, published by the NFER); and *Reading Development and the Teaching of Reading* (also with Jane Oakhill, published by Blackwell). He has also written the *National Literacy Strategy: Review of Research and Related Evidence*, published by DfEE.

Lynne Broadbent is Deputy Director of the British and Foreign Schools Society National Religious Education Centre at Brunel University. Before taking up this post she was a lecturer at Goldsmiths College, University of London. In a variety of capacities she has gained extensive experience working with both primary and secondary teachers and student teachers in the areas of religious, personal and social education.

John Cook is a part-time lecturer in primary education at the Institute of Education, University of London. He has been a primary school headteacher in London and was a humanities inspector and assistant chief inspector for the London Borough of Tower Hamlets. His long association with the development of the humanities curriculum includes involvement in the preparation of resource material for teachers to support 'distant locality' work with particular reference to Jamaica and the Netherlands.

Caroline Heal is a lecturer in primary education at the Institute of Education, University of London, where she has gained experience as a teacher educator at both primary and secondary levels. Within the primary PGCE course she has responsibility for the development of the history and geography components. Her main research interest is in the development of teachers' thinking and practice through professional dialogue, especially in the context of 'mentoring'.

Rob Johnsey lectures in primary school design and technology and science in the Institute of Education, Warwick University. He has taught in secondary and primary schools both in this country and abroad and has led a wide range of teacher in-service courses in science and design and technology. His research interests include exploring how primary children use procedural skills to design and make products and how teachers might encourage children to progress in using these skills. More recently, he has carried out curriculum development trials in schools in which strategies for teaching science through design and technology topics were explored.

Sarah Martyn is a part-time lecturer in primary education at the Institute of Education, University of London. For ten years she worked in primary schools in the London Borough of Tower Hamlets as a class teacher, curriculum co-ordinator for science and deputy headteacher. Currently she co-ordinates information communications technology (ICT) across the Institute's primary PGCE course, on which she teaches. Her main research interest is the auditing of primary teachers' subject knowledge with particular reference to ICT and mathematics.

Roy Prentice is head of art and design education at the Institute of Education, University of London. Formerly he was the art adviser for East Sussex Education Authority and head of art and design at a London comprehensive school. He has developed the art and design education component of the primary PGCE course at the Institute over the past twelve years and he is course leader for an MA programme in art and design and museum and gallery education. His main research interest is the relationship between subject knowledge and pedagogy in art and design. He is a practising painter.

Dr Jeni Riley is head of primary education at the Institute of Education, University of London. For the past ten years she has been course leader for the primary PGCE course within which she teaches on the English component. Formerly she taught in primary schools and was a member of the schools' advisory service in Oxfordshire. Her main research interest is the development of literacy with particular reference to the early years of schooling, on which she has lectured and published extensively.

Dr Tim Rowland is a senior lecturer in primary education at the Institute of Education, University of London, with particular responsibility for mathematics education. He has taught in schools and formerly lectured in mathematics at Homerton College, Cambridge. His research focuses on analysis of classroom discourse, process aspects of mathematics, generic examples and proof, together with investigative approaches and teaching styles. He is also an active mathematician in the field of Number Theory.

Dr Dorothy Watt is a lecturer in primary education at the Institute of Education, University of London. She teaches on the primary PGCE course and is the course leader for the MA course in primary education. Initially a primary teacher, she has gained wide experience as a researcher into primary science, most notably through the Primary SPACE Project. Her current research interests are effective teaching and learning in primary science and the social context of science education.

List of Abbreviations

CACE   Central Advisory Council for Education
DATA   Design and Technology Association
DES   Department of Education and Science
DFE   Department for Education
DfEE   Department for Education and Employment
DNH   Department of National Heritage
ERA   Education Reform Act
NCC   National Curriculum Council
NFER   National Foundation for Educational Research
OFSTED   Office for Standards in Education

Introduction

Roy Prentice and Jeni Riley

The uniqueness of human existence consists, above all, in our capacity to appraise and communicate with each other about our various experiences of the world. We do this in many different ways, through many different modes of understanding and communication – not just one. (Gulbenkian Foundation, 1982: 18)

The starting point for the book

This book is a response to a curious paradox, namely that a restricted and rigid educational experience should be so confidently promoted by the government as the most fitting preparation for the kind of creative and flexible thought and action the future will demand of children and teachers. We adopt the view that in practice the curriculum in a large number of primary schools has become unacceptably narrow, in terms of both what children experience and how they experience it. Certain aspects of 'high status' subjects, the structures of which promote discursive thought and propositional knowledge, have become dominant. Vital as they are, they do not have a monopoly on learning, neither are they synonymous with what it means to be an educated person. The present situation encourages increasingly prescriptive approaches to teaching, based on a model of knowledge (or information) transmission, at the expense of opportunities for pupils to engage actively in learning. A parallel prescriptive approach to initial primary teacher education gives further cause for concern. In combination these developments reflect an increasing political commitment to invest in the production of what resembles a nineteenth-century map with which to negotiate the uncharted landscape of the twenty-first century.

The government's determined efforts to increase its direct control over curriculum content and teaching methods employed in primary schools culminated with the introduction of the National Literacy Strategy in 1998 and the National Numeracy Strategy in 1999. The former is driven by a traditional view of literacy (rather than by a concept of multiple literacies) while the latter is concerned with numeracy (rather than with a wider mathematical language). The government's 'relaxation' of the National Curriculum requirements for each of six subjects from September 1998 enabled schools to place even greater emphasis on literacy and numeracy.

Clearly, strategies *are* needed to strengthen the teaching of English and mathematics nationally through a consistent approach informed by research evidence. However, the present strategy, to achieve success in two subjects at the expense of the rest, is not only shortsighted; it runs counter to the philosophy of a broad-based curriculum entitlement on which the National Curriculum was founded. It might be argued that in order to implement national programmes of literacy and numeracy it is necessary to focus the attention of teachers more sharply on these priorities for a limited period of time in order to develop specific areas of expertise. Unfortunately, it is all too easy for a temporary measure set up to achieve a particular objective, over a short period of time to become accepted as normal practice. In our view it is the extent to which the current curriculum has become distorted at a time when the nature of the whole curriculum for the next century is under review that is most disconcerting.

The current situation

A growing body of evidence based on the experiences of teachers and student-teachers supports the claim that already in many schools the curriculum has become lop-sided. In particular the arts and humanities, potentially the most powerful humanizing elements of the curriculum, are very often marginalized. Inevitably, reduced opportunities for pupils to engage in different ways of experiencing the world result in the development of a restricted repertoire through which they are able to both make sense of it and respond to it. Given this situation in schools it is logical for the government to insist that the overriding priorities of courses of initial primary teacher education should be the preparation of teachers equipped to address the National Literacy and Numeracy Strategies. This is a limited view of what is involved in being an effective teacher of seven- to eleven-year-olds. It is also in conflict with the need to recruit and retain intellectually curious and creative primary teachers who between them represent a range of subject knowledge in sufficient depth to function as effective subject leaders.

The rationale for the book

It is against this background that the present volume attempts to reaffirm the need for all children to have a broad educational experience in their primary years of schooling. By 'broad' we mean an approach to teaching and learning that embraces the rich diversity of ways in which it is possible for individuals to organize thought, communicate ideas, express feelings and engage in purposeful action. In order to demonstrate intelligence in the distinct ways it is possible to become intelligent, it is necessary for children to understand and use with increasing confidence and fluency a range of different 'languages'.

> As well as the 'language' of number, of empirical observation and record, of induction and deduction, of morals or religion there are . . . the 'languages' of gesture, posture and visual expression.
> (Gulbenkian Report, 1982: 19)

In slightly different ways frameworks for conceptualizing these different ways of understanding the world are presented by a number of philosophers who have had an influence on education. An acknowledgement of the existence of different ways of knowing is advanced by Reid (1986) while Langer (1957) identifies two major modes of knowing: 'the discursive and the non-discursive'. Six 'realms of meaning' are identified by Phenix (1964) and Hirst (1974) refers to eight 'forms of knowledge'. From a psychological perspective the theory of 'multiple intelligences' advanced by Gardner (1983, 1993) reinforces these philosophical positions.

The scope of the book

Each of eleven chapters addresses issues central to teaching and learning in relation to a given subject in such a way that its essential nature and its particular contribution to the primary curriculum is made explicit. Each one was commissioned from a subject specialist with extensive experience of primary schools and teacher education. As a member of an individual subject constituency each contributor is well placed to directly relate up-to-date knowledge in a particular subject to the pedagogical implications for teachers of seven- to eleven-year-olds. Thus all chapters focus on the dual concerns of subject content and subject application, albeit from individual perspectives and with varying degrees of emphasis placed on theoretical issues and classroom practice. In addition, Chapter 1 discusses the nature of thinking and learning with particular reference to the development of children between seven and eleven years of age to provide a shared theoretical context for the arguments advanced in subject-specific chapters.

The organizing framework

Any discussion about the curriculum relies on an appropriate organizing framework to give ideas coherence. This in itself is problematic as all frameworks are open to misinterpretation. Thus, in the interest of clarity, it is important to establish at the outset the rationale for the structure and scope of the present volume.

By focusing on a different subject in each chapter, this book unashamedly echoes the subject-based system of categorization of the National Curriculum with which teachers are now familiar. Furthermore, at the time of writing, it is clear that this subject-based structure, with minor modifications, will be retained as the basis of the 'revised' National Curriculum for the year 2000. To introduce an alternative structure for the purpose of the present discussion would, in our view, be an unnecessary distraction from our purpose. Our main aim is to heighten teachers' awareness of that which is *particular* to a given subject, and its *potential contribution* to children's learning. It is beyond our scope to consider the merits and demerits of alternative ways of conceptualizing ways of knowing and of implementing the curriculum. It is for headteachers, subject-leaders and class teachers to share and apply their professional judgement to determine how best to convert the ideas under discussion into action in each school setting. The order in which chapters are arranged is significant. It is based on the alphabetical order of the contributors' names to avoid reinforcing a hierarchy of subjects.

The nature of the contributions

An overview of the twelve chapters that comprise this book reveals a number of recurring themes that are fundamental to the nature of learning and teaching. In its own way each chapter makes explicit the unique contribution the subject under discussion can make to children's evolving understanding of the world and of themselves. Ideas are developed within and reverberate between chapters. These include challenges to orthodoxies that polarize thinking and feeling, work and play, intrinsic values and instrumental functions. The key

concepts of 'chronology' and 'a sense of place' provide powerful jus-
tifications for the exploitation of those humanizing qualities that history and geography respectively provide. This is regarded as
particularly significant for children living in an era in which 'a sense
of self' shaped by time and place is often difficult to grasp. It is in
helping children understand the origins of values, beliefs, attitudes
and emotions and the ways they influence behaviour in a culturally
diverse society that religious education has a vital contribution to
make towards citizenship. Sometimes contributors adopt approaches
that puncture cherished and long-standing belief systems. Some surprises are sprung, such as the claim that until recently the teaching
of English has been short-changed in the primary curriculum! In addition the attitude towards competition expressed by the writer on
physical education causes stereotyped associations to be disrupted.
Whilst the importance of a synthesis of old and new technologies to
serve personal creative ends is stressed in the contexts of information
communications technology and design and technology, it is curious
that the use of the humble calculator remains a contentious issue. This
point is explored in depth in the mathematics chapter. The ways in
which non-verbal modes of communication and expression are
referred to as 'thinking in sound' and 'visual thinking' in the context
of music and art respectively reinforce the arguments advanced in
Chapter 1. Here the diverse nature of thinking and learning is outlined along with the implications for the primary curriculum if children are to maximize opportunities to learn how (not what) to think.

Above all there emerges from all chapters an acknowledgement of
the relationship between a teacher's subject knowledge and the quality of the learning experiences in which pupils participate. Teachers
of children between seven and eleven years of age have a responsibility to make available to them experiences of quality that encompass the spectrum of possibilities through which diverse intelligencies
are fostered. This volume seeks to make its contribution by inform-
ing and inspiring teachers, by raising expectations and by extending
their subject expertise.

1

Thinking to Learn: Learning to Think

Jeni Riley

Learning to think must itself be learned. While nearly all children have the capacity to learn, not all make, or are enabled to make, equal use of it.

(Cullingford, 1990: 2)

Introduction

It can be argued that the invention of the computer has made it largely unnecessary for schools to be concerned with memorizing factual information, such as 'the longest river in Africa is . . .' or 'the kings and queens of England between 1200 and 1467 were . . .'. Alternatively and crucially, primary teachers have the prime responsibility to develop children's thinking so that they are able to cope confidently with the intellectual and technological demands of the next century. The development of flexible and creative cognitive abilities is vital if individuals are, for example, to operate within the advanced communication systems of language, mathematics and technology. This chapter will explore the level of professional awareness that teachers need in order to be able to support children's thinking in the years seven to eleven in the primary school.

The child as thinker

'You don't know what you know until you say it,' remarked a nine-year-old child (Fisher, 1995). Anyone who seeks to influence the intellectual development of another individual will need some sort of mental map in order to understand what the nature of that task might be. When the person wishing to promote thinking is a primary teacher

1

it is essential that he or she possesses a theoretical model of thinking and its processes.

Perhaps, then, the first question is 'What *is* thinking?' When addressing this question, Fisher (1990) quotes a conversation with a six-year-old child:

RF: What do you think with?
Tom: What do you mean?
RF: When you think . . . where do your thoughts come from?
Tom: I don't know, everywhere I suppose.
RF: When you think of something what do you think with?'
Tom: I know . . . your brain.
RF: How do you know?
Tom: I've seen brains.
RF: What brains?
Tom: In a book. The brains of animals . . . like guinea pigs.
RF: Can you see thoughts?
Tom: No, they were dead. But you can think with your brain, I know that.
RF: Is a thought something that you can see?
Tom: Yes.
RF: What thought?
Tom: An ice cream.
RF: You can see a thought of an ice cream?
Tom   Yes I'll show you. (Fetches paper and pencil. Draws a man with a bubble coming out of his head, containing an ice cream.)

(Fisher, 1990: 3).

Tom, most likely in common with the primary teacher already mentioned, has a notion of what it is to think and which part of the body is responsible for thinking. However, quite understandably, he does not know a great deal about intellectual functioning. Tom is unaware of the processes involved in cognitive development and what precisely promotes intellectual competence. It is less than straightforward to comprehend why psychologists are neither crystal clear on, nor in complete agreement about, the development of thinking.

Our present-day knowledge of the child's mind is comparable to a fifteenth-century map of the world – a mixture of truth and error . . . vast areas remain to be explored.

(Gesell, cited in Fisher, 1990: 1)

Cognitive processes

Cognitive functioning (or thinking) is not a unitary construct. Within cognition there are several information-processing mechanisms. These mechanisms are perception, memory and language; and they also subsume numerous sub-categories of processes. At its simplest level, a process operates on information represented in memory and yields an output. These processes are the basic cognitive skills that underlie the ability to reason, the capacity to learn and the ability to solve problems. Educational research has enabled us to be informed about these processes to include the fact that, layered further on to these different mechanisms of cognitive functioning, are levels of individual variation. The differences between people are the result of each person's intellectual ability, capacity or aptitude, and also her motivation, emotional state, life experience and the expectations of the culture in which she lives. These individual differences influence what can broadly be described as intellectual behaviour or intelligence. This is before we even begin to consider whether there are distinct stages of intellectual development.

Stages of cognitive development

The fact that there are changes in cognitive behaviour over the years of childhood and adolescence is indisputable. The child acquires new concepts and skills, and she is able to apply more and more refined strategies of thinking with increasing age. What psychologists are not agreed about is whether these changes follow a consistent and sequential pattern in all individuals, or whether, in fact, the changes are qualitative or quantative. Major theorists have viewed cognitive development and its sources of influence very differently.

Piaget

Piaget (1896–1980), who has had, perhaps, the most impact on the way in which learning is viewed by teachers, regards thinking in terms of an essentially biological mechanism. Cognitive development occurs as a result of the dynamic interaction of two processes within the individual. These are assimilation, in which new information is taken into the pre-exising concepts, and accommodation, in which these concepts change to fit new information. This notion of the interaction between the child and her environment is critical and has greatly influenced the views of developmental psychologists and primary teachers. The suggestion for which Piaget is most well known is that cognitive development occurs in stages, during the succession of which the child's thinking changes qualitatively.

Donaldson

Through her more recent work, Donaldson (1978) challenges Piaget's interpretation of the cause of difficulty with certain tasks. Donaldson proposes that a child's thinking can be enhanced through both the nature of problems and the way that the problems are presented to her. The essential feature of the tasks that appear to facilitate intellectual performance occurs when the problems make 'human sense' to the child. The tasks that the young child finds very difficult are those that require a type of thought that Donaldson calls 'disembedded' thinking, an idea that is complementary to the Piagetian notion of the young child's ability to operate only in concrete, first-hand experience. In Piaget's view, the ability to think in the abstract occurs relatively late in adolescence. Donaldson (1992), in common with Piaget, suggests that children's thinking moves through qualitatively different stages, developing from what she describes as 'point mode', through 'line mode' and 'construct mode' to finally 'transcendent mode'. In 'point mode' the infant is limited to thinking in the here and now, but in 'line mode' the child can operate in the past and in the future in terms of time. In the 'construct mode' the child is able to generalize from events, albeit still in the concrete mode, and later still, with the 'transcendent mode' the child, with even more advanced thinking, can distance herself in time and space.

Vygotsky

What the child does in co-operation with others, he will learn to do alone.

(Vygotsky, 1978)

Vygotsky (1896–1934), the Russian psychologist, views the adult as fundamental to the child's development. Educators in the West see his work as hugely important for educational practice. Vygotsky, like Piaget and Donaldson, views cognitive development as a series of stages, during which the individual's thinking becomes increasingly flexible and powerful. However, he suggests that the greatest influence on this development is the support offered to the learner by an experienced practitioner. The social situation of the developing child, whilst it is acknowledged by Piaget, is considered by Vygotsky to be the key influence on the thinking of the maturing individual.

Vygotsky suggests that children's thinking develops through their social interactions, particularly interactions conducted through the medium of spoken and written language, which in turn enable them to form their own understandings, or in Vygotsky's words, to 'internalize the concepts' (Hargreaves and Hargreaves, 1997: 29). This view of intellectual development places great value on the role of the adult (the teacher) in supporting thinking and learning. This notion is immortalized by his proposal that the knowledgeable adult (or experienced practitioner) can support the novice into functioning at a level of her 'zone of proximal development' (ZPD).

Bruner

Bruner (1966), whose ideas over three decades have inspired educational thinking, also suggests a stage theory and sees the child as increasingly able to represent her world in more and more complex ways through the three stages of:

- *enactive* representation, during which the individual can only think in a way that is based on actions

- *iconic* representation, during which the child can employ the use of images to think without the objects having to be present (Tom, with his image of the ice-cream thought bubble, in the Fisher quote earlier, is still in this stage of thinking)

- *symbolic* representation, during which stage the child is able to think in terms of symbols to represent the world; an example of this is the essential ability to use spoken and written language.

Unlike Piaget, Bruner developed a theory of instruction to accompany his stages of cognitive development and harnessed the Vygotskian notion that thinking can be facilitated. Through a collaboration between experienced and less experienced practitioners, Bruner proposes that a fruitful, learning relationship can exist, and that it is one in which the novice is 'scaffolded' to attain higher levels of intellectual competence (or ZPD) than otherwise would be achieved.

Applying the theories

It is beyond the scope of a single chapter to do justice to the ideas of these and many other important theorists who have made significant contributions to our understanding of the nature of cognitive development and the ways in which it can be supported. It has been stated that Piaget, Bruner and Donaldson suggest that the thinking of the individual becomes increasingly complex, flexible and subtle as the intellectual functioning advances through the various stages of development. This is demonstrated by intellectual feats, such as the ability to operate with thoughts in the absence of the concrete object, possession of a concept of the past and the future, being able to account for a different perspective from one's own and understanding that something can stand in place of an object. These literally mind-changing levels in the capacity of thought are acknowledged in a child's assertion that 'If we didn't think there wouldn't be an us' (Fisher, 1990: 2, 3).

Vygotsky, Bruner and Donaldson also give us the starting points for thinking about the ways in which teachers can promote intellectual development, but still we are left with the question, 'Are there indeed stages or universal patterns of cognitive development, through which all must pass?' On this Meadows says:

> The degree to which Piaget's stages can be seen in children's cognitive behaviour has been the matter of fierce debate and considerable uncertainty, such that John Flavell, one of the best informed people in the field, published two incompatible decisions in the same year and called himself 'undecided to the point of public self-contradiction'.
>
> (1993: 348)

Perhaps for the present purpose the most useful aspect of this discussion is that through infancy and childhood the individual demonstrates marked changes in cognitive behaviour and during the years seven to eleven children's thinking advances substantially. It is useful, therefore, for primary teachers to be aware of, firstly, the qualitative shifts in thinking that occur; secondly, how they might be developed through the different curriculum subjects; and thirdly and most crucially, the ways in which thinking can be promoted in order to maximize the level of intellectual functioning of pupils.

Changes in thinking

The four theorists already identified share the common belief that the child's thinking develops with maturity, with the appropriate experience and with relevant adult support. Thinking moves from a preoccupation in infancy and early childhood with the physical, the sensory and the immediate, towards being able to operate at a greater distance from the concrete presence of the context of thought. This achievement in mental operations, during the years of middle childhood, has as its ultimate goal the ability to think in the abstract. Not that all mature thinking is abstract, nor is it necessary for all the intellectual functions required of an adult, but without the ability to shift gear into abstract thought, an individual is relegated to the bottom rungs of the educational ladder.

The qualitative shifts in intellectual functioning are demonstrated, for example, by the ability to conduct mathematical and scientific mental operations of reversibility; to be able to divide numbers accurately, and most importantly, to know *when* to use division as a means to solve a problem. Another crucial cognitive leap is the ability to operate within a symbolic system, the obvious demonstration of which is the ability to use the alphabetic code to represent spoken language and to employ a mathematical language and its conventions in order to conduct numerical operations.

Donaldson (1993) clearly states that the ability to read and write offers the opportunity to use a symbolic system, and that through operating within it, thought is made more systematic and ordered. The interactive nature of learning in and through the different curriculum subjects requires a certain level of cognitive functioning, but it is through being able to operate in the sophisticated communication systems of an advanced society that the individual has, in turn, the level of her thinking enhanced. Donaldson says:

> the thinking itself draws great strength from literacy whenever it is more than a scrap of an idea, whenever there are complex possibilities to consider. It is even more obvious that the sustained, orderly communication of this kind of thinking requires considerable mastery of the written word.

> (1993: 50)

In addition, thinking is enhanced by being able to read texts in which the meaning is, of necessity, 'disembedded'. Donaldson writes again:

> But the kind of written language we are now concerned with is also more impersonal in the details of its form. It entails the use of phrases like; 'It is possible that . . .' or 'The causes of this seem to lie . . .' or 'One reason is . . .' or 'What this means is . . .'.

> (Ibid: 51)

Through exposure to these kinds of written texts, the child learns how to reason, to argue and to justify; she is learning how to think in a qualititatively different and more advanced way.

The various mechanisms of cognitive functioning

Thinking is enhanced (or diminished) by the various mechanisms of intellectual functioning, and these mechanisms become increasingly important for the cognitive development of pupils in the years seven to eleven.

Memorizing strategies

Children before the age of seven appear to have few strategies that enable them to memorize material. An adult faced with learning a list of French vocabulary, for example, will employ a range of strategies for attempting the task. Words might be searched for similarities with the English or any distinguishing features that might help summon an image to the mind, perhaps an aspect that resembles the object the word represents. For example, the French word *le bassin* looks like the English word *basin* and helps me to remember that it means *the pond*. It is possible to teach young children to employ such strategies that will help them to remember items, but they have to be reminded to use the mnemonic when asked to recall the material! Eleven-year-olds are more likely to employ very similar strategies to adults such as using categorization and rehearsal in order to impose meaning and structure on the material to be remembered. Without the use of strategies to enable memory to be more effective, we are all victims of memory decay (most particularly in the supermarket!). Through this memory loss an individual's ability to process information is severely hindered.

Metacognition

> A central task of learning how to learn is to develop an awareness of oneself as a learner and of the degree of one's own understanding.
>
> (Nisbet and Shuckman, 1986)

Metacognition is the ability to reflect on the way in which one has learned something, or carried out a mental task; it is the ability to think about thinking in order to think more effectively! It is also, and very crucially, knowing what you do not know. An example might be recalling how one remembered the vocabulary list mentioned earlier. Included within the term 'metacognition' is the ability which supports an individual to reflect on her own mental processes, to be able to generalize from a previous circumstance or problem to solve a new one, and so to recognize which strategy is the most appropriate approach for a task. Self-checking, or being able to highlight for one-self those aspects of a learning task yet to be accomplished, is emerging as one of the most valuable skills through which intellectual functioning can be enhanced. Research evidence suggests that to develop this aspect of thinking is very important.

Galloway and Edwards suggest that teachers have a crucial role to play in the promotion of this type of thinking:

> Metacognitive skills do not just develop. They are learned from obser-vation of other children, from the way teachers organise children's learning and the nature of feedback they give children. Teaching is not only about the transmission of facts and never has been. *It is also con-cerned with teaching children how to learn.* An essential element in this is to monitor what they are doing and to adapt their strategies in the light of this.
>
> (1991: 10, my emphasis)

Deductive reasoning

Thinking involves a variety of mechanisms within it, all of which develop at different rates depending on the opportunities offered to the individual that will encourage that aspect of intellectual behav-iour. The cognitive mechanisms of reasoning, that is 'going beyond the information given' (Bruner, 1957, cited in Meadows, 1993: 67) or 'searching through a problem space' (Newell and Simon, 1972, cited in Meadows, 1993: 67), involve a type of thought (logico-deductive) that is essential for mathematical and scientific work as well as read-ing comprehension in the later years of primary schooling.

Analogical reasoning

Another mechanism, analogical reasoning, is considered by Sternberg (1985) to be the core of intelligent cognition and as such is one of the most important mechanisms of thinking. The classic Aristotelian type of analogy, much loved by the constructors of intelligence tests, is 'if calf is to cow so foal is to . . .'. Meadows says that the ability to use analogy

> is seen as critical in bringing existing knowledge and skills to bear on new information and tasks, as central to the processes of learning and transfer and to the construction of mental models.
>
> (1993: 69)

Children in the later years of primary school show the beginnings of being able to use this higher-level cognitive mechanism.

The use of metaphor

A metaphor enables the use of a vehicle to re-interpret a topic which both encapsulates and also extends the meaning. A metaphor stands for something it is not! We are so used to the application of metaphor to complex concepts that they become absorbed into everyday language; for example, 'short-termism is the cancer of today's society' or the brain is described as 'the body's computer'. Metaphor has much potency in the world of art. The visual metaphor is used to portray concepts such as the notion of the passage of time with Dali's molten clocks suspended over clothes hangers. Children in the early years of primary school are unable to understand an implicit comparison and become locked into the literal meaning, often with bizarre effects on comprehension; for example, 'to leave under a cloud', 'to have one's head in the air' or 'to be on pins and needles' all bring to mind, if taken literally, images that are surreal and humorous. Between the years seven to eleven the child increasingly has the flexible, creative thinking capacity both to comprehend and to generate metaphor.

Transfer

This cognitive mechanism allows for the understandings gained in one learning situation to be utilized in another. Some of us fail to use past experience to inform behaviour in a repeated situation. To be flippant for a moment, the number of weddings between people who have been married before gives rise to the quip that 'second marriages are the triumph of optimism over experience!'

The mechanism of transfer is a multi-faceted construct. Memory and metacognition also play their part in successful transfer to other learning tasks and situations. Those individuals who are good at transfer tend to plan problem-solving approaches, seek additional information, search for and use analogies, check their reasoning, monitor their progress, engage in rectifying strategies when they go off task, and so on.

Problem-solving

Solving a problem is a search that occurs when the means to an end do not occur simultaneously with the establishment of an end.

(James, 1890, cited in Meadows, 1993: 87)

The ability to solve problems is the capability to work towards a goal without a routine way of getting there, and, as such, is an essential and composite cognitive mechanism. In order to solve a problem, a number of cognitive processes come into play. The ones usually considered to be involved are memory, perception, transfer, analogical reasoning and deduction. In addition, there is the need for the individual to apply the appropriate knowledge and context-specific strategies, which frequently interact together in a complex way. It is this complexity and the recognition that background knowledge is a prerequisite that makes problem-solving an aspect of thinking that develops qualitatively in the middle years of primary education, through greater experience and knowledge.

It is not so much that young children cannot solve problems: they can and they do. My twenty-two-month-old grandson, William, is very good at jig-saw puzzles (accompanied by his ritualistic and monitoring egocentric speech, i.e. talking for himself alone). 'Does 'dis go here? . . . no. Does 'dis go here? . . . no. Does 'dis go here? . . . yeesss!' (He shouts yes!) He is also ingenious at finding things hidden from his inquisitive eyes and prying fingers. With maturity, greater knowledge, more sophisticated metacognitive strategies and experience of problem-solving, the capacity to find solutions to problems develops powerfully.

Another important developmental change that occurs is the ability to recognize the crucial features of a problem before attempting to tackle it. This depends, firstly, on the way in which a problem is understood, and secondly, on the extent to which the individual can represent it to herself. Physicists might produce a diagram in order to clarify the issues for themselves. The use of written language to transfer mathematical problems into text can also develop problem-solving abilities in ten- and eleven-year-olds. A clear, verbal representation of the problem and its dimensions enables the key features to be identified successfully, and a strategy then can be developed and operated. Experience also enhances performance considerably, although cynics might (and do!) suggest that too much experience dulls innovation and allows only for the repetition of tried and tested methods of finding a solution.

Automatization

Automatization is an additional mechanism that affects the efficiency of thinking. As cognitive skills develop, they become automatized. This makes them faster and reduces the demands the task makes on the conciousness. This, in turn, enables the individual to think about other things. For example, being unsure of the correct letter to represent a sound or not knowing exactly how it is formed wastes mental capacity, leaving little spare for the consideration of the content of the writing. The early stages of learning to use a word-processing application on a computer had just such a depressing effect on my composition skills!

Meadows (1993) makes the point that the advances in cognitive behaviour that occur in later childhood might not be so much due to increased thinking capacity, but are perhaps the result of improved use of the existing capacity. Teachers need to appreciate that these advanced levels of intellectual functioning require nurture, appropriate teaching and opportunity, if they are to develop fully. The appropriate and informed use of information and communications technology (ICT) to support teaching and to develop children's learning is recognized as increasingly crucial in primary classrooms (see Chapter 9).

There is an additional dimension to intellectual functioning, which is crucial to all stages of life-long learning. It is the extent to which emotional state supports an individual's powers of concentration, attitude, perception and application to a given task or problem.

Emotional intelligence

Emotional intelligence is being able to motivate oneself and to persist in the face of frustrations; to control impulse and delay gratification; to regulate one's moods and keep distress from swamping the ability to think; to empathise and to hope.

(Goelman, 1996, cited in the Scottish CCC, 1996: 6)

Everyone has a friend who despite a high level of intelligence has not fulfilled an early potential; conversely, we each can cite a person we know, who despite relative failure at school is extremely successful in adult life. Personal qualities of self-motivation, diligence, resilience, stability, self-confidence and positive inter-personal skills appear to win over an IQ nearing the two hundred mark. Emotional intelligence is an often neglected aspect of cognitive behaviour that enables effective intellectual functioning to develop fully.

The nurture of such an ability is not straightforward. How far teachers can enable children to know and understand their own feelings, and also to know themselves as learners, will depend on the extent to which teachers themselves are comfortable with their own emotions. As adults, we can only function effectively if we are able to recognize, understand and deal with our own feelings. In addition to this, Sylvester (1994) says:

> We know emotion is important in education. It drives attention, which in turn drives learning and memory. But because we don't fully understand our emotional system, we don't know exactly how to regulate it in school, beyond defining too much or too little emotion as misbehaviour.
>
> (cited in the Scottish CCC, 1996: 6)

Perhaps we can only acknowledge the need for an individual to be 'emotionally literate' in order to be able to persevere, and to be self-motivated and self- disciplined in her learning. Teachers should seek to offer children opportunities through which they can recognize what it is to be emotionally intelligent. Too often, it is easier to identify its absence! Good quality literature is one way that we can 'deal with the whole person, including dealing with the "inner self", the self-esteem, the spiritual dimension of one's life and attitudes and values' (McGettrick, 1995). Books such as *I am David* (Holm, 1965) offer models of individuals coping with adversity, loss and pain and overcoming despair in order to gain insight into themselves. This vicarious learning about life has a part to play in meeting one of the great challenges of growing up. This important aspect of development that impacts strongly on learning needs a place of prominence throughout primary school.

We shall now consider the possibilities for cognitive development that the different curriculum subjects offer seven- to eleven-year-olds.

Developing thinking through the different subjects

Gardner (1983) suggests that, not only do the various subjects offer opportunities for the development and use of different thought processes, 'different ways of knowing', but there are at least seven different intelligences. Gardner describes these as linguistic, musical, spatial, logical-mathematical, bodily-kinaesthetic, inter-personal and intra-personal. This proposed theory is without empirical foundation, but as Merry (1997) cites, 'these intelligences are fictions and most useful fictions – for discussing processes and abilities that (like all of life) are continuous with one another' (Gardner, 1983: 70). Within each individual are different and multiple kinds of intelligence, with one or related areas in dominance. This is the result of aptitude, educational opportunity and recognition of the value of certain types of intelligence. This extended view of functioning is surely a powerful argument for children's entitlement to experience a broad-based curriculum in primary schools.

As the child progresses through the later years of primary school, learning in the subject disciplines becomes more differentiated. This is more true of the current situation, in the late 1990s, than it has been in the past. In order to meet the intellectual demands of individual subjects, different types of thinking are required; it is also through operating within these different subjects that the various cognitive mechanisms have opportunity to be employed and developed.

The particular type of thinking that mathematics demands is usually of the logico-deductive, problem-solving category. It is a type of thinking that many people commonly believe to be beyond them (see Chapter 11). The current emphasis on the mastery of mental arithmetic (National Numeracy Project, 1998) is now considered to be a valuable way of giving children access to this kind of flexibility and agility of thought, enabling pupils to operate the mathematical system with fluency and understanding.

Design and technology develops thinking abilities directly and practically, by giving children the opportunity to identify a design task, to generate ideas, to plan, to design, and finally to evaluate their outcome. The problem-solving centres around the necessity to design a task that is useful in the made world and this calls initially on knowledge and experience, to be able to perceive the need for the solution, and on scientific and mathematical understanding. Aesthetic and design awareness, in addition, is required, to be able to design a product with the use of the appropriate materials in mind. Rob Johnsey (Chapter 8) is clear that challenging design-orientated problem-solving is essential for the promotion of the kinds of creative thinking that living in the next century will demand.

It can also be said that science promotes a particular type of cognitive behaviour; to be scientifically literate is the term used to describe the ability to think and operate in this way. This develops the skills incorporated in 'procedural understanding', namely observing, predicting, hypothesizing, raising questions, interpreting, evaluating and communicating. Whilst these skills are not exclusive to science, it is impossible to be scientific without them. It is through their engagement with scientific enquiry that children have the opportunity not only to understand scientific concepts, but also to learn to think in particular ways through the use of the skills within procedural understanding.

Children between the ages of seven and eleven need the opportunity, through learning about places and geographical themes, to develop the advanced thinking ability specific to decoding graphic communication. Cognitive development is encouraged through the use of geographical skills such as observation, measurement, map-making, reading atlases and globes, interpreting photographs and, crucially, posing and answering questions about them.

The case for the enhancement of thinking skills through mathematics, science or even geography does not seriously have to be made, but perhaps this cannot be said of music. Pauline Adams (Chapter 2) cites research evidence on the stages of musical competence that suggests cognitive development is promoted through the mastery, imitation, imaginative play and metacognition involved in music-making. Swanwick and Tillman (1986) link their study to Piagetian theory, and suggest that mental acuity and intellectual funtioning are developed through playing music accurately. Musical awareness, appreciation and competence are acquired through exposure to a rich and broad music curriculum with many benefits, of which improved thinking ability is only one.

Physical activity is essential for health and undertaken for pleasure. Not only do we come to know our physical space through exploration and movement, we are able to communicate meaning through moving our bodies. In the later years of primary education, children become increasingly aware of their developing motor abilities, the space around them in which they move and which they occupy. They are able to refine their physical movement through conscious thought.

Religious education is related to fundamental questions in human experience and provides children with the opportunity to reflect on their own beliefs, values and experiences. Much of this study is focused on the inter-personal and intra-personal. Religious education also provides opportunity for intellectual growth, through the development of knowledge and understanding of the beliefs, traditions, values and practices of the six principal religions. Vigorous and rigorous study and debate on complex moral issues, the differences between and (perhaps more importantly) the similarities of the principles of the various religious beliefs, all add to thinking that is demanding in nature, philosophical, analytical and abstract.

The methods of enquiry available to children when engaging in historical study allow evidence to form the basis of interpretations of the past reconstructed from different perspectives; interpretations which are able to take account of the beliefs, values, customs and habits of the people of the time when the actions were being taken. An understanding of chronology is central to this process to make connections between sequences of events.

Art has a unique contribution to make to the aesthetic development of the individual. The type of thinking that art fosters stems from it being a non-verbal means of communication and expression that utilizes a range of visual codes and conventions. It is necessary to be visually literate in order to make art and to develop meaningful responses to works of art, craft and design.

Conclusion

Through its breadth and richness, the primary curriculum, as it is described in the following chapters of this book, offers immense potential to develop the intellectual functioning of children. For this potential to be realized fully, teachers need to be aware of the ways in which their pupils think and learn and to know clearly what their role is in those processes. As an eight-year-old child says, 'The best kind of teacher is one who helps you to do what you couldn't do for yourself but doesn't do it for you' (quoted in Fisher, 1990, cited by Scottish CCC, 1996: 14).

2

Music: Unnecessary yet Essential

Pauline Adams

I believe in work. I believe in play. On the whole I see no distinction.
Let us not be afraid of work! Play – games – poetry – music – movement – all the Arts, are unnecessary yet absolutely essential. They make
possible the impossible and reconcile the irreconcilable.

(Tanner, 1989: 3)

Introduction

It is well known that babies, whilst still in the womb and when newly
born, respond positively to music. The evident pleasure displayed by
babies and very young children when making sounds and imitating
the sounds created by other children and adults is there for any of us
to observe. We ourselves enjoy the playful aspect of this call and
response, question and answer interaction. It is experimental and fun
and yet it has a serious purpose, introducing the next generation to
the sound-world of a particular culture and demonstrating our social
acceptance of a new member into the group.

Music touches everyone and it is through study and practice that
children can develop their musical gifts and talents (Music Education
Council, 1998: 6). Music-making requires a focused mind and develops keen memory, analytical and critical thinking, co-ordination skills
and physical self-awareness. It encourages creativity, sensitivity,
awareness of others and self-discipline. It promotes collaboration and
communication, as well as encouraging individual responsibility. It
can foster creative expression and waken the imagination. The following words, written by a nine-year-old, encapsulate these features
in a simple and meaningful way:

I was doing an ostinato in assembly with some friends. I was playing the shakers and I went wrong, I shaked the shaker at the wrong time, so Michelle gave me a nudge. When the performance was over I found that I was clapping to myself. Donna giggled.

Music is part of our social fabric and our inheritance. It is therefore important that neither Michelle nor Donna nor any primary child should be denied access to its riches.

An historical account framing a contemporary perspective

The 1870 Education Act marked the beginning of compulsory schooling at elementary level for all children. The curriculum focused on the 'three Rs', reading, writing and arithmetic, and was taught in a didactic way to large classes. Music-teaching methodology also adopted this model with large numbers of children singing in unison to a piano accompaniment. To lead such sessions a teacher required an ability to play the piano and an ability to detect whether or not children were singing in tune. Inspectors of schools, too, were to be satisfied that singing was fairly well in tune, and that words were properly articulated. The content of the music curriculum focused on preparing children to take part in collective worship, both at school and at church, and through a repertoire of patriotic songs promoted a sense of nationalism.

Such corporate activity also served to strengthen school identity. Music in schools at the end of the nineteenth century was primarily regarded as a civilizing and refining force (Cox, 1993: 8). A method of learning to sight-sing, developed by Curwen in the latter half of the nineteenth century (Simpson, 1976: 31), became a fashionable teaching tool and influenced the Hungarian composer Kodaly who developed a similar approach in Hungarian schools by devising a sequential programme of singing activities. In the early part of the twentieth century the singing repertoire broadened to include folk songs from the different areas of the British Isles and by 1925 the descant recorder was being mass-produced and purchased by schools for class teaching purposes, mainly to promote the learning of staff notation (music written on the five-line stave).

The invention of the gramophone enabled musical appreciation to be introduced into the curriculum and with it, passive listening and the 'cultural heritage' perspective, set in a factual historical 'life of the composer' context. Mass manufacturing made instruments like the piano and violin affordable. Many more children now had access to such instruments at home. The instrumental lesson was thus established and having skills, particularly in playing such a versatile instrument as the piano, was regarded as something special and a sign of being qualified as a musician. How many school advertisements for a visiting music teacher still require this skill as a prerequisite for the job?

The 'child-centred' ideas of Rousseau and Froebel were taken up on behalf of music education by Carl Orff in Germany during the 1930s. His work with children resulted in the publication of *Orff Schulwerk* in 1932 (Simpson, 1976: 90). This practically based scheme focused on developing the musical imagination of children through the handling of basic musical material such as rhythmic and melodic patterns. Speech patterns, singing and physical involvement, with clapping and movement, were seen as basic procedures to encourage the memorizing and internalization of musical ideas. The musical arrangements allowed for differing levels of musical development, with opportunities to play simple repetitive parts and to improvise rhythmically or melodically. An English adaptation of the *Orff Schulwerk* course was introduced into Britain in the early 1960s, allowing teachers to experiment with and develop this particular approach. The practical nature of the work needed resources such as tuned percussion which included xylophones, glockenspiels and metallophones of different sizes to cover a wide range of pitch. Good quality tambours (single-headed drums) and floor-standing tunable timpani of different sizes also provided a range of pitched sounds. Different sounding untuned percussion instruments, such as tambourines, cymbals and woodblocks, allowed for exploration of texture and timbre. An emphasis on using appropriate playing techniques and attention to phrasing and dynamics encouraged teachers to think about musical ways of approaching their teaching.

Music lessons could now allow children involvement and active participation. There was room for improvising and composing music, exploring instruments and discovering new sounds, thus fostering expression and enjoyment. Performing skills were developed through group music-making along with general musicianship skills through shaping and analysing various compositions. Although some of the Orff material, including words accompanying rhythmic patterning and songs, will not appeal to the contemporary child, the ideas and musical material are as relevant as ever and the influence of his educational work upon current music educational thinking must not be underestimated.

This thinking was reinforced and further developed in the wake of the Plowden Report (CACE, 1967) which recognized that curriculum development in music was less well advanced in comparison to other subjects such as English or art. In his seminal book *Sound and Silence* (1970), Paynter reaffirms the notion of the child at the heart of the learning and music as a 'creative' art, not to be isolated from other areas of human experience. He compares music to a language; a vehicle for expression. The creative process involved in exploring, inventing, discovering and refining music is a way of articulating what Gamble (1984) calls 'thinking in sound'. For children between seven and eleven years of age such expression raises self-awareness and awareness of the world.

During the 1970s and 1980s the terms 'children as composers' and 'inventors' became firmly established in the vocabulary of teachers committed to offering children practical musical experiences. The notion of children working with the materials of music and thus coming to understand how music actually works (Swanwick, 1988) promoted some rethinking about the way music might be organized in schools. In art lessons children gained experience of handling the materials of the subject and engaged in the physical and mental processes involved in creating a piece of art work. In music this was still a relatively new idea, an alternative perspective to the 'received tradition' model. At last the word 'creativity' had entered the music educators' vocabulary!

By 1985 the Department of Education and Science (DES) was stating that 'Music Education should be mainly concerned with bringing children into contact with the musician's fundamental activities of performing, composing and listening' (DES, 1985b: 2). Music was rightly designated as one of the foundation subjects in the primary curriculum, becoming statutory in 1992. Important work had been achieved by inspectors, music advisers, music lecturers, teacher educators and teachers in developing a philosophical base and clear rationale for a practically based curriculum for music in schools. In addition, the interest and support within the political arena of music professionals, including composers, conductors and artists, was instrumental in influencing the National Curriculum for Music (DES, 1982b; 1992). However, despite the richness of the original discussion document, the music curriculum that finally appeared was somewhat diminished and impoverished.

Nevertheless, a statutory National Curriculum for Music in England and Wales has, for the first time, encouraged schools to formalize their commitment to the teaching of music as an entitlement for all children across the primary age range five to eleven years.

Music in the classroom

It was during the late 1970s that teachers who played instruments other than the piano, or were just interested in music, either as consumers or as amateur practitioners, were encouraged to play a part in the music education of their pupils.

The role of the 'music specialist' was re-cast as 'music curriculum leader' or 'music co-ordinator'. This wording redefined the changing role of the specialist to include that of music supporter and enabler, thus allowing more children to benefit from classroom-based music sessions led by class teachers.

This is not to deny the important role a teacher who is a trained musician can play in the musical life of a school. The school choir, recorder group, special percussion group, instrumental group are all enriching opportunities. There are instances, however, of successful teachers who would not view music as their specialism but who have considerable expertise in some areas of music-making. An example can be cited of a maths specialist, who as a keen amateur singer has experience of choral singing and performance. The children in this particular school sing well, confidently and are secure in part-singing. Such teachers are an asset to any school as they bring to music-making the enthusiasm and joy which are at the heart of many amateur choirs and instrumental groups.

During the late 1970s and 1980s generalist primary teachers were positively encouraged to integrate musical activities within the broader primary curriculum. Many local education authorities appointed advisory teachers for music to provide practical support for generalist teachers. After all, many teachers were teaching art, English and drama. How many of these were professional artists, novelists, poets or actors? The music activities could be integrated into other areas of work and would benefit from natural links across the curriculum. The once weekly music lesson, with the music specialist who released the class teacher for curriculum planning time, could be reappraised. Co-operation between teachers that involved joint planning and team teaching had the potential to raise the profile of music for pupils and ensure an integrated approach with no loss of respect for the discrete skills of each subject involved.

Observation of lessons and discussion with primary colleagues tells us that there is still a reluctance on the part of some teachers to commit themselves to creating musical opportunities in the classroom. *The Arts in Schools* report observed that those teachers who 'feel ill at ease in the arts are unable to organise these essential experiences for children, it may be because they were denied them' (Gulbenkian Foundation, 1982: 57). The report, which argued for the arts as an important feature of any balanced curriculum, emphasized that this situation 'strengthened the argument about long-term dangers of lop-sided educational priorities'. Until the arts feature as a valued component within the curriculum for all pupils, some of whom will be future educators, this vicious circle will remain. A number of teachers are uncertain and unsure about how to approach the arts in their own classrooms. This situation has implications for the arts in education.

The contribution music makes to the development of the child

Many schools have planned and documented their music programmes in the same way as they have those other subjects which are frequently seen to be of more importance in the hierarchy of teaching and learning. OFSTED inspectors noted in their main findings 'that there is much to celebrate about music in schools' (OFSTED, 1998e: 60) but that one of the areas where teachers experienced difficulties was ensuring continuity and progression.

Whole-school planning, which actively seeks ways to build continuity and progression into the music programme, may benefit from considering a sequential model of musical development as suggested by the psychologically based research of Swanwick and Tillman (1986). This research provides an analysis of children's compositions, recorded over a period of four years within the age range three to eleven. It is based on psychological concepts of mastery, imitation, imaginative play and metacognition. Piaget's view of fundamental human processes, how children come to understand their world and the pleasure they gain from exploring and mastering their environment, was influential in the research. This model has more recently been broadened to help teachers focus on other aspects of musical development in performing, listening and appraising. Such a well-defined developmental model has also, in some instances, influenced the monitoring and assessment procedures by which teachers record pupils' progress at seven and eleven years.

Singing is also gaining recognition as being more than singing the teacher's favourite repertoire, choosing the latest popular song to entice reluctant singers to join in, a song for Harvest or one with words that fit a particular cross-curricular topic. A developmental view of children's singing (Welch, 1986) concentrates on identifying 'comfortable' singing ranges and explores ways of allowing pupils to sing in tune through appropriate training and the selection of suitable songs. It is accepted that 'rhythm is one of the foundation structures in all motor skills' (Seashore, 1967: 148) and that pitch awareness emerges later. Songs, chosen carefully, can allow more children success in pitching and thus singing with accuracy. 'Right fit' material can also encourage pitch awareness at different stages of development and can support pupils who experience difficulty with singing in tune. Singing that involves the whole school can indeed be enjoyable as a corporate activity but if we are interested in a developmental model, then class-based sessions are essential. It is also in the classroom that pupils can discuss the interpretation of a song and have some ownership of performance, deciding on mood, tempo, dynamics and the final arrangement. Does everyone sing all the time? Should different groups sing different verses? What is the balance between those singing an ostinato part (a repeated rhythmic/melodic pattern) and those singing the melody? When should everyone take a breath?

Leading a singing session poses difficulties for teachers who are not confident about using their own singing voices in the classroom. Help needs to be at hand either in the form of support from a more confident singer or from appropriately pitched recorded song material. Using the voice does not necessarily mean singing songs but can also take the form of vocal exploration and experimentation; for example, using the voice to slide upwards in pitch from low to high, changing from one vowel sound to another while staying on one chosen pitch, or using comic strip words such as 'bang', 'pop', 'thud' and 'wheeze' to explore loud, quiet, high, medium or low sounds. Such experimentation frees the voice from the limitations of singing only a melodic line.

The teacher as observer of musical behaviour

Observing children working with musical ideas tells us that music is not just about grasping the correct playing technique or being aware of structure. The sensory response of the individual is all important, indeed crucial in developing aesthetic awareness. Young children can be seen to react to extremes in dynamics, pitch and tempo with delight, astonishment, dislike and so on. When they hear a piece of music getting faster and louder they often respond to the build-up of excitement by physically moving, or by giggling at the end. A group of thirty young secondary school pupils, listening to a recording of Strauss's 'Also sprach Zarathustra' were seen to clap spontaneously at the build-up to the end of the first section. This demonstrates the power of music in the realm of feeling, arising from the very essence of the music itself: *sound*.

Who knows what a child sitting playing in an Indonesian gamelan orchestra for the first time may feel about this new and unusual music; the vibrations of the large gongs, the effect created by a different tuning system and the overall sound of so many metal instruments being played together. These personal responses go far beyond the tick box assessment of 'played with accuracy', 'mastered damping technique', 'worked well in a group', important as these aspects of learning and assessment are. The aesthetic or emotional response, the 'language of feeling' as expressed by Langer (1978: 221) and described by Swanwick (1988: 54) as a way of 'knowing the life of feeling' are particular to music and to the arts. Langer believes 'the real power of music lies in the fact that it can be "true" to the life of feeling in a way language cannot' (1978: 243). Music can express different images and moods; it can ebb and flow, have tension and resolve. It can convey opposing moods transmitted simultaneously. It needs no words. It is thinking in the abstract. It is transitory and only the resonance of the performance lingers in the atmosphere and in our minds. Music is thus unique. We all remember some precious moment when music moved us in some inexplicable way.

This concern for feeling and expression, the affective, cannot be isolated or seen as separate from cognitive and skill development. The child experiencing a gamelan session has to have an understanding of the structure of a piece in order to play accurately within the ensemble. Specific playing techniques have to be mastered, aural memory is required in order to internalize the melodic and rhythmic patterns. This level of mastery requires mental acuity, intellectual keenness, and an awareness of the need for problem-solving skill.

Scientific research into the functioning of the brain has long interested music educators. The division of the brain into right and left hemispheric activity enables it to process things in different ways. To put it in the simplest way (and not forgetting that intelligent functioning requires both hemispheres), the left hemisphere allows for rational analysis, sequential logic and verbal language whereas the right hemisphere is the seat of the emotions and of spatial awareness. There is a view that education has been too concerned with promoting left brain activity. Odam (1995: 9) says, 'Western European education gives a great deal of priority to thinking processes and teachers are used to strategies that promote such activity.' Music teaching of quality can ensure a balance of activities which can actively encourage children to engage the functions of both left and right hemispheres of the brain.

Gardner (1993: 122) believes that accomplishments in music demonstrate a distinct form of intelligence. Research on children with various disabilities has shown 'evidence of musical abilities as being distinct from linguistic abilities' (Durrant and Welch, 1995: 8). Gardner (1983: 99) cites an example of the autistic child who can sing back flawlessly any piece he hears. Obvious examples of exceptionally early development are child prodigies such as Mozart and the violinist Yehudi Menuhin. Such beliefs support the notion that all children should receive a musical education.

It is only through practical activity and active appraisal that children begin to internalize and understand the musical procedures and structures composers use to interpret musical ideas. For example, music which increases in dynamic, that is becomes louder as layers of sound are progressively added (e.g. Ravel's 'Bolero') creates a feeling of rising excitement, whilst the tremolo effect played on strings (e.g. Vivaldi's 'Four Seasons') is used to convey the shivering icy cold of winter.

A conceptual framework begins to underpin the compositions of children aged between seven and nine when melodic and rhythmic repetition, metre, phrasing and dynamics start to feature in the music. Children begin to tap into the 'conventions of musical production' with a 'desire to enter the adult scene' (Ross, 1984: 130). They begin consciously to use musical devices to express thoughts and emotions.

Swanwick and Tillman (1986) found that children's compositions at this age are short, are marked by repetition, and use musical conventions, demonstrated in particular by the structure of their musical phrasing. Their music is predictable and draws on musical vocabulary gained from experience in and beyond school. By the time children reach the age of ten they are more concerned with experimenting and deviating from what they already know. They try new ideas such as extending and varying melodies, creating surprises in their compositions and experimenting with structure and form. Group work involves discussion and decision-making about whether to retain or discard ideas. This increasing compositional complexity also demands more technical mastery as children take on the challenge of realizing their new ideas.

Encouraging musical behaviour and critical response

Discourse about the processes involved in composing a piece of music, deciding what makes a good performance, discussing responses and writing about a recorded extract when listening to the music of other composers are all ways of helping children to develop musical behaviour, to refine their own work and appraise the music of others. Refining work allows for initial plans and details to be modified, and what is 'novel' to the child in terms of discovery may become integrated into an ever-increasing musical repertoire. For example, the discovery that some pitches when sounded together create tension or discord and others sound harmonious and resolved may lead to a conscious use of discord to create a piece that is 'spooky' or 'scary'. The terminology of the current National Curriculum, 'listening and appraising', is there to encourage 'active' listening where children are attentive and are able to make critical evaluations bringing to their listening an understanding of musical elements alongside relevant factual knowledge, gained from supportive resources and personal research. The choice of music is crucial and what is chosen has to have some feature which will appeal to both the ear and the imagination of the listener.

Implementing a music curriculum

The National Curriculum for Music approaches music teaching and learning through the elements of music: rhythm, pitch, dynamics, tempo and structure, timbre and texture. It is a framework to be interpreted within the context of the school and different schools will adopt various approaches and devise curriculum content which reflects the musical strengths and skills of teachers and matches the experience and needs of the children they teach. It has to be acknowledged that some children may have more developed skills in, and knowledge of, a particular musical area than the teacher.

Time is seen to be a strong determining factor in structuring a music curriculum. 'There are many schools where the arts flourish. In every case the headteacher and staff appreciate and support them. In those schools where the headteachers think the arts are marginal, they suffer, whatever the economic circumstances' (Gulbenkian Foundation, 1982: 48). The 1990s have made additional demands on schools, not only economically but in terms of the proportion of time to be spent on certain core areas of the curriculum and information and communications technology (ICT). If music is to be a taught subject within the curriculum, regular timetabled provision has to be allocated each week alongside an agreed whole-school scheme of work.

Cross-curricular themes which emerge naturally can enhance children's learning. Historical studies which integrate, for example, children's own medieval music compositions using drones and modes, a medieval song, music linked to dance, listening to the sounds of medieval instruments (and seeing illustrations of them), are all activities which allow for musical learning in its widest sense.

We must not forget that music is a performance activity. Most music is composed or improvised with performance in mind and it is important that children be given a platform for performing their own music and the music of others. Small (1998) uses the word 'musicking' as an active verb to demonstrate that music is something to be participated in. From a shared group composition in a whole-school assembly to a large-scale performance for parents, these are ways of celebrating music outside the classroom. It becomes part of the life of the school.

Extra-curricular clubs and groups allow for voluntary participation in other kinds of musical experiences such as instrumental groups and choirs. All children, including talented musicians, can be given opportunities here to demonstrate their enthusiasm for music and for some children this may be influential in their future artistic lives.

A musical dialogue

Teacher observation and pupil feedback, sensitive and probing questioning, and most importantly, listening to what children have to say, all encourage a deeper level of enquiry and send clear messages to children about the seriousness and interest the teacher has in the work. 'The conversation will succeed best if the teacher (a) is genuinely concerned to interpret, understand and develop the pupils' aesthetic understanding; (b) is personally engaged in the here and now of the conversation and therefore is content to linger, brood and reflect upon this in an open and friendly way' (Bierton *et al.*, 1993: 39).

Such teacher–pupil exchange may seem unrealistic within given curriculum demands to cover so much in so little time, but creative learning is about articulating and reworking ideas, about reflecting and making sense of the learning, about communication between human beings and about the sheer pleasure of a shared discovery.

Intercultural approaches to music

'Music is culture' (Wiggins, 1996: 21). Different cultures have distinct musical voices. Sounds unique to a particular culture are organized into socially accepted patterns (Blacking, 1995). In this context music has a function and a specific meaning for each particular group of people. Once it is transferred and heard within another context it changes meaning for the groups and individuals. In this way music can have many owners and be listened to in different settings and responded to in a variety of ways. For example, a devotional Hindu song may deeply move a Western Christian, or Russian Orthodox Vespers move a devout Muslim.

We should not shy away from introducing unfamiliar music to children, but we need to consider how to approach this. It may be done by listening for similarities or differences between two culturally contrasting pieces. For example, the Australian didjeridoo and the Irish bagpipes both produce a drone. The sound of the tabla (North Indian drums) is very different from the sound produced by the Kodo drums of Japan, as is the style of playing. There is a wealth of recorded listening material to support teachers in this area, including CD-ROM and information on the Internet.

The acknowledgement of intercultural influences within music poses an important question for all those who fear that we are abandoning our 'own traditions'. We may, however, ask 'whose traditions'? 'Crossover' in music is exemplified by the influence of one tradition upon another. Ethnic diversity within Britain has provided opportunities for a broadening of knowledge and the development of skills in music for many musicians and music participators, professional and amateur. Musicians from different cultural backgrounds are working together to create new sounds and styles of music, mixing instruments European, Middle Eastern, Asian and African and exploring composite structures. This is music for an intercultural setting where a number of traditions meet, fuse, and innovate. This widening of musical repertoire and experience can enhance and further illuminate that which is already familiar.

We do have to remind ourselves, however, that children in some of our schools are bringing musical experiences direct from another culture. An example of this was recorded by a trainee teacher when a ten-year-old Somalian refugee was entered on the school role. He had no way of communicating in English and uttered no sound at all within the classroom. He was not relating to others on any level. The teacher had no knowledge about what his previous life experiences had been. During a music lesson the teacher divided the children into groups, giving each group a number of percussion instruments including a xylophone. The task set was a compositional one. It was at this point that this child communicated for the first time. He picked up the beaters and started to play the xylophone in a way that impressed the other children. His considerable technical facility and the sound he created communicated strongly to the other children in his group and they made it clear that they respected these skills, constructing their own music around his playing. During the performance of their composition he smiled and beamed with pride. This boy was happy to share something with which he was familiar and the response of the other children allowed him the experience of contributing something personal for that moment. The teacher must not be forgotten in this story as she offered this pupil the opportunity to share this personal breakthrough and it is evident from his confidence to do this that the atmosphere was both enabling and encouraging. This teacher allowed the child to draw upon his aural memory of a style and tradition he knew well.

This should encourage teachers who are unfamiliar with staff notation and therefore regard themselves as unqualified to teach music in the classroom. Of course, there are certain circumstances where knowledge of staff notation is essential. All orchestral players must read staff notation fluently in order to be able to play the orchestral repertoire. There are, however, a number of notation systems throughout the world which provide appropriate symbolic representation as a cue for recalling music. The aural tradition depends on developing a keen aural memory and is strong within many cultures. Musicians who develop aural memory are in close contact with sound itself rather than having to interpret symbols. To enable children to develop this aural awareness we must operationalize the maxim 'sound before symbol'. After all, we speak before we write and our writing skills emerge from our understanding and desire to communicate.

Collaborative encounters

In recent years the professional musical world has entered the world of music education, bringing an additional range of skills and expertise into the classroom. Funding from a number of bodies (such as the Arts Council, various Arts Boards, companies and businesses) has provided opportunities for children, young people and teachers to work in collaborative projects with artists, dancers, musicians and poets. This may mean collaboration between a school and a gospel singer, a composer, an African dancing and drumming group or some professional orchestral musicians as part of an integrated project involving other arts subjects.

For teachers and schools this is good news. It is impossible for any teacher to know everything and yet it is possible to increase knowledge through partnerships with others interested in education and in

working with children. The professional musical world is beginning
to take its community role very seriously. Some music conservatoires
are now providing educational components within their training
courses, linked to school-based work and the wider community.
Higher education degrees are attracting professional musicians who
wish to deepen their understanding of educational theory and practice, so that they can bring not only a musical perspective to their
work but an educational one, underpinned by an understanding of
pedagogy and of children's musical development.

Orchestral projects have introduced pupils to live music, to compositional ideas, to the sounds of individual orchestral instruments,
to professional players and to the concert hall. Previously unknown
instruments, such those found in the Javanese gamelan, are to be
found in many areas of Britain, from Scotland to Sussex. Children not
only have first-hand experience of playing such instruments but they
gain an understanding on a simple level of how the music works and
also become familiar with cultural procedures, like removing shoes,
not stepping over instruments or not resting beaters on bars. This is
experience outside anything a school can offer and is an important
development in the structuring and resourcing of musical opportunities for children.

Conclusion

How then can such positive and productive activities be incorporated
into the developing curriculum? We read in yet another statutory document that for seven- to eleven-year-olds the proposal is, 'to teach
singing regularly but provide opportunities for composing less frequently' (QCA, 1998c: 17). But will the inspectors spend most of their
time, like their Victorian counterparts, listening for singing to be fairly
well in tune and words properly articulated, or will they also be
moved by listening to the original and unique compositions of individuals and groups and asking questions which reach to the heart of
children's music?

Further reading

Mills, Janet (1998) *Music in the Primary School*. Cambridge University Press.
2nd edition. This book is intended to support all teachers in the classroom.
It provides theory linked firmly to practice and gives guidance on planning and curriculum content.

3

Physical Education: Action, play and movement

Richard P. Bailey

Play, not work, is the end of life. To participate in the rites of play is to dwell in the Kingdom of Ends. To participate in work, career, and the making of history is to labor in the Kingdom of Means ... Work, of course, must be done. But we should be wise enough to distinguish necessity from reality. Play is reality. Work is diversity and escape.

(Novak, 1967: 40)

Introduction

Physical activity is an essential element in the lives of children. It is also a medium through which they can join with their peers, their family and the wider community in meaningful, enjoyable experiences. This chapter considers the appropriate content of a physical education for seven- to eleven-year-olds, and goes on to examine certain aspects of child development that are significant for teachers of this age range.

The physical child goes to school

Infans ludens – child the player

Children love to move. An observation of primary school playtimes reveals most children physically playing for a great deal of the time, whether it is chasing a ball, chasing another child, skipping, dancing or the numerous other activities that we all recognize as normal, healthy behaviour. Physical play is the first appearing and most frequently occurring expression of play in children. This is a fact that has not escaped Bruner (1983: 121), who suggests that action, play and movement constitute the 'culture of childhood'. Yet, it is a cul-

31

ture that each new generation of children re-create for themselves. In light of the fact that all children in all cultures physically play, that children will play without encouragement, and that much exhibited play cannot be accounted for by copying others, it may well be the case that there is some sort of 'play instinct' with regard to movement (Bailey and Farrow, 1998).

At the same time, games and other more formal physical activities hold a special place within our society. The fate of a favourite football team, the latest athletics hero or the seemingly inevitable collapse of the England cricket team are topics of conversation for many children and their families. The range of sports and activities available is such that almost everyone can find something that gives challenge, fulfilment and joy to them. Sport and similar activities are important to children and they will remain important to many of them for all of their lives, whether as players or spectators.

Not only do physical activities hold a special place within society, but research suggests that competence in such activities is a significant factor in the quality of children's social experiences at school. Children would rather take part in physical activities than any other endeavour in their experience (Roberts and Treasure, 1993). They would also prefer to succeed in these activities than in classroom-based work. A number of studies have highlighted the central place that physical competence has in the developing social relations of childhood. In his classic study of social status in teenagers, Coleman (1961) found that sporting prowess was the major factor affecting popularity in boys during adolescence. More recent research (Weiss and Duncan, 1992) has supported Coleman's findings, whilst extending their application to all ages of children and to both sexes. Children, it seems, gain acceptance by being perceived as 'good' at activities that are highly valued by their peers. At the same time, children who have not developed a base level of physical competence suffer from poor social relations, which has a consequent impact upon their developing self-esteem (Evans and Roberts, 1987).

It is not only children's psychological and social well-being that is associated with physical activity. A mass of evidence is being collected that strongly endorses the common-sense view that regular exercise is a vital factor in the maintenance and improvement of children's levels of health and fitness (Armstrong and Welsman, 1997; Fentem, Bassey and Turnbull, 1988). A number of positive outcomes have been associated with habitual physical activity, including efficiency of movement, greater endurance, strength and flexibility, as well as contributions to mental and emotional health. At the same time, the consequences of low levels of activity can be severe, and despite the fact that childhood constitutes the most physically active part of human life, it seems that many children today are just not active enough. A number of researchers have started to raise concerns regarding low levels of activity, prompting one leading paediatric physiologist to describe the current situation as 'cause for concern' (Armstrong, 1990: 13). Public concern for habitually sedentary lifestyles is most often directed towards adults. However, studies have begun to highlight such lifestyles among even the youngest children. Sleap and Warburton (1992; 1994) have carried out a number of studies of primary school children's levels of physical activity and have found that many go through their day without ever experiencing adequate levels of intensity or duration. Diseases associated with low levels of physical activity are being witnessed in increasingly younger children, including Coronary Heart Disease (CHD), obesity, high blood pressure and weak bones (Bailey, 1999).

The place of physical education

An anthropologist observing our culture, aware of the privileged place of physical activities, as well as the health consequences associated with lack of participation, might be led to assume that movement experience (in one form or another) would occupy a central place within the curriculum for every child. That physical education adopts a position that could accurately be described as 'marginal' might, then, come as a surprise. Children in the United Kingdom already receive fewer hours of physical education than any other comparable country in Europe (Armstrong and Welsman, 1997). That recent government guidance (DfEE, 1998c; QCA, 1998c) seems set to further marginalize its place in the curriculum (in England and Wales, at least) may come as a shock. This is not the place to make an extended plea for physical education's place in the curriculum. However, it is important that every teacher of children in the seven to eleven age-range fully recognizes the importance of this area of experience for their pupils. This is, in part, a matter of professional understanding. But, in a climate of a broad, balanced and over-crowded curriculum, 'seeing the point' of the subject would also seem to be a necessary condition for its full promotion.

Of course, teachers have a far better understanding of the needs of their pupils than the policy-makers, and readily acknowledge the important role that physical education can play in the education and development of children. One study found that teachers of seven- to eleven-year-olds ranked physical education as the third most important curricular area, after English and mathematics (Williams, 1989). Interestingly, precisely the same ranking was awarded to those subjects in a study of the attitudes of primary and secondary pupils (Birtwistle and Brodie, 1991).

A physical education

So, what would be the content of a physical education? What subject knowledge would make it up? How can a physical education contribute to the overall education of children between the ages of seven and eleven?

It has been suggested that physical activities, both formal and informal, form significant elements within our culture, as well as within the very notion of being a child. As such, a physical education of some sort would seem to be a valuable and necessary part of the primary school curriculum. However, the importance of physical education has not always been recognized. The philosophically minded might attribute this predicament to an exaggerated separation of the mind and body, in which matters physical are placed a poor second. This lies at the heart of Williams' (1989: 19) perceptive statement: 'The paradox with which we are faced is that while it is the physical nature of the subject which gives it its distinct identity and its unique place in the curriculum, it is this very physical nature which places it at the periphery of the curriculum.'

The suggestion here is that physical education has a unique and significant contribution to make to the overall education of every child. Moreover, if the potential and range of the physical education experience is not fully realized, then that child cannot be said to be properly educated. The following sections consider the purposes and possibilities of physical education, and go on to suggest specific applications for children in the seven to eleven age group.

Arnold (1979) provides a useful framework for the classification of the different elements that might make up a physical education:

- education *about* movement
- education *through* movement
- education *in* movement.

This model will be adopted and adapted for the present discussion. However, it ought to be admitted straight away that the employment of these terms is purely one of convenience; the interpretation of the terms offered here is not that of Arnold.

Education *about* movement

As a highly valued and central aspect of our culture, it is important that children come to understand the range and importance of purposeful physical activities. This is the focus of an education *about* movement. It introduces children to a range of activities, as well as the concepts, rules and procedures associated with them.

Of course, there are very many activities that children might experience, and each can make a specific contribution to their development and understanding. The National Curriculum for England and Wales (DFE, 1995d) offers a useful, but not exhaustive, list in its 'areas of activity':

- games
- gymnastics
- dance
- swimming
- athletic activities
- outdoor and adventurous activities.

Traditionally, competitive games have formed the dominant feature of the physical education curriculum, and there are some who seem to wish that it is still the case (DNH, 1995). These activities have a great deal to recommend them, since they offer the chance for children to experience challenge and achievement, in a 'mutual quest for excellence in competitive situations with others' (Almond, 1989: 20). As long as competition, itself, is not raised up as the sole aim of the enterprise, but rather as a medium for participation, games offer a structured but flexible environment in which children can test their skills and physical abilities. Moreover, the different types of games – invasion-type games (like football and netball), striking and fielding-type games (cricket and baseball), net and wall-type games (tennis and squash) – present distinct and exciting challenges to children's understanding and physical competence. In order to participate, children must learn the different rules, roles and tactics that make up each type of game.

Athletics shares some of the same possibilities as games. Both encourage the acquisition of new skills and their application in different settings, and both encourage children to take on responsibility for their own development. Indeed, the core elements of athletics –

running, throwing and jumping – also reappear in a number of games contexts. Many of these skills require only limited resources, yet offer children the all-too-rare opportunity to excel in situations that are really meaningful to them. By focusing upon personal achievement – How far can you run in ten seconds? How long can you jump? How far can you throw? – (rather than upon crude and unnecessary comparisons – Who can run fastest?), and by offering the children frequent opportunities to improve upon their results, the teacher is able to create an environment of personal challenge, in which children recognize themselves as agents of their own improvement (Almond, 1989).

Gymnastics, like athletics, builds upon skills that children seem to acquire naturally. Through a variety of apparatus, as well as none, it leads children to extend and articulate their movements, with greater control and poise. At the heart of gymnastics in schools is the notion of body management, and since each child's body is unique, this leads to actions that are truly distinctive and original. This is what separates educational gymnastics from Olympic gymnastics. While the latter might be characterized by the pursuit of the mythical, perfect move, the former involves the child's creation and expression of movement. Of course, there is a need for the development of particular skills – ways of rolling, balancing and travelling safely and effectively – but these skills are not ends in themselves, but rather vehicles for greater creation and expression. This seems to be the essence of a statement by Wright (cited in Smith, 1989a: 76), an influential teacher of educational gymnastics:

> In however transient and modest a way, gymnastics, rightly conceived and taught, can be a means for the 'release of individuality' of some of our pupils; we should at least hold to the ideal that we should be trying to make it happen for all our pupils.

The 'release of individuality' also lies at the heart of dance. Like gymnastics, dance is not inherently competitive: it focuses upon the *quality* of movement performed, not simply the outcome. This is an important distinction, as it adds an aesthetic element to the child's physical experience. As such, it can develop the capacity for imagination, innovation and appreciation. Through a combination of stylized and improvised actions, the dancer is able to develop her movement vocabulary. She is initiated into a long and rich tradition of practices that have a valued place in the culture, and encouraged to extend those practices through her own individual exploration.

To a large extent, *all* structured physical activities are co-operative:

children co-operate whenever they follow the rules of a game or work together in a gymnastic sequence or a dance. Outdoor and adventurous activities extend this premise of co-operation still further by creating situations in which no child can succeed unless others succeed. Trust games, problem-solving, climbing and a host of other activities all encourage children to work together towards a common goal. The teacher who is sensitive to the different personalities and strengths of the children in her class can strike a balance between boredom and anxiety, and create an atmosphere of challenge and adventure that is often missing from our protected and comfortable lives. Moreover, opportunities can arise in numerous environments, from a windy hillside or rock-face to the school hall or playground.

In learning *about* movement, it is important that children come to know the range and character of the forms of physical activity. Performance of these activities constitutes a vital aspect of this knowledge. By taking part in different structured activities, pupils can come to know *how* to move in particular situations to achieve certain outcomes. They learn how to position their bodies to comfortably roll or change direction, and how to stand in relation to others to create space in games. At the same time, however, children also need to come to know *that* some ways of moving offer more success or are more aesthetically pleasing than others. An adequate physical education encompasses both kinds of knowledge: knowing how and knowing that.

To constitute a physical education, rather than a mere physical training, children need to think about their actions; they need to plan ahead and reflect upon their physical activity. A continuous cycle of planning, performing and evaluating contributes to the development both of pupils' physical skills and of their understanding of the procedures underlying these activities. Gordon Clay (1997) cautions against viewing these processes as essentially sedentary, intellectual operations. The processes of planning and evaluating are not add-ons to performance; they inevitably occur at the same time as performance. Planning takes place as a pupil prepares for a gymnastics action or weighs up the possibilities in a problem-solving task. Pupils evaluate whenever they assess the outcome of a movement, the success of a strike or the fluidity of a sequence. Nevertheless, the teacher may think it is appropriate in certain circumstances to focus upon the intellectual aspects of the activity. Some children may find it difficult to excel in the performance of some skills, but can reveal high levels of knowledge and understanding in choreographing a dance routine or in observing and 'coaching' others. This may, particularly, be the case for those for whom a severe physical disability limits their ability to perform certain actions.

Different children enjoy and succeed in different activities, and the breadth of the physical education curriculum is a recognition of this fact. A narrow conception of a competitive team-games-centred curriculum threatens to alienate a large section of the school population, as well as rob them of valuable learning opportunities in different contexts. Girls, in particular, seem to shy away from overtly competitive games, and often prefer individual or co-operative activities, such as dance or gymnastics (Sports Council, 1993). An adequate education about movement, therefore, introduces the full range of movement experiences and offers each pupil the opportunity to excel.

Education *through* movement

Education *through* movement refers to the use of physical activities as a means of achieving educational goals which are not intrinsically part of those activities. An important part of this concept, and one that is particularly significant during the primary years of schooling, is the contribution physical education can make to work in other areas. Movement is particularly well placed to act as a medium for learning across the whole curriculum, since it plays so fundamental a role in children's overall learning and development: in Bruner's words, quoted before, it represents the 'culture of childhood'.

Bjorkvold (1989) has emphasized the role that physical activity (and music) play in the lives of children, and goes on to suggest that any schooling that disregards such experiences creates a harmful and dispiriting tension. He expresses this view as a clash between 'child culture' and 'school culture', an abbreviated model of which is given here:

Child culture	School culture
Play	Study
Being in	Reading about
Physical proximity	Physical distance
Testing one's own limits	Respecting boundaries set by others
The unexpected	The expected
Sensory	Intellectual
Physical movement	Physical inactivity
I move – and I learn!	Sit still!

Teachers aiming to offer continuity between infancy and later years should acknowledge the valuable place movement holds in children's development. Movement-based activities can create an environment that is enabling and 'fun'. Daley (1988) has claimed that such activities are capable of generating empowering situations, in which children relax and enjoy learning. By presenting learning situations as games and play, teachers can encourage children who have built up defences to lower their 'affective filters' (Gildenhuys and Orsmond, 1996: 105), their frustrations and anxieties, and develop their skills and understanding incidentally as the physical activity is explored and mastered. Moreover, as movement is universal, children become involved in experiences that bridge differences in social or cultural background, ability or intelligence.

Every area of a child's education can benefit from a movement-based approach, through introducing concepts, or reinforcing them, or giving practical examples. Nowhere is this more apparent than in children's language development. In fact, movement does not simply support the development of language, it is an inherent aspect of it. Teachers working with pupils in the seven to eleven age range can capitalize upon the movement and language development achieved by young children in their earlier experiences, without which there would be a needless discontinuity (Maude, 1998).

A number of authorities agree that language is acquired and decoded through the integration and subsequent relationship of language and bodily movement (Gildenhuys and Orsmond, 1996). Children act out their conversations, and talk about their actions, as part of an inseparable symbiosis. As Asher (1983: 4) poetically puts it: 'Language is orchestrated to the choreography of the human body.' Bruner (1983) suggests that within physical play and movement, all utterances have relevance, as the game becomes the topic and the situation provides a contextual conversation:

> Movement-based interactions provide an environment in which the learner is immersed in understandable messages, where language can be placed in context naturally and meaningfully.
>
> (Ibid.: 23)

The scope of language usage implicit within physical education is vast. The activities likely to be experienced by the seven- to eleven-year-old child, for example, each contain their own specific terms and concepts, and cutting across these is a language of description, quality and expression. Maude (1998) offers a useful taxonomy of vocabulary within physical education. It includes vocabulary of body awareness (*stretching arms and legs, exercising heart and lungs*), of space (*moving forwards and backwards, high and low, near to your partner, over the top of them*), of time (*travelling slowly, accelerating, stopping*) and of the quality of movement (*running lightly, jumping explosively, changing direction gracefully*). Movement and participation provide an environment in which children are led to use language naturally and purposefully. They read instructions on a task card, record scores and devise notation systems to represent dance or gymnastic sequences, and in each case the activity occurs in a meaningful context. Moreover, it is a context with which children are familiar from early childhood.

The relationship between movement and language are strong and far-reaching. Moreover, many of the benefits associated with a movement-based approach – contextualized learning, enjoyment and relaxation, first-hand experience – are applicable to any aspect of children's learning. The potential list of activities is almost endless, but a sample is offered below:

- *mathematics (shape)* – children can hold balances or represent two-dimensional shapes with their bodies; they can follow patterns as they travel around an area

- *mathematic (number)* – children practise arithmetic as they keep score during games; they measure the distances objects are thrown in athletics

- *science* – gymnastic balances reinforce concepts of force and centre of gravity; the effects of exercise on the body are examples of bodily processes

- *geography* – children can plan their own gymnastic apparatus layouts; they can develop their understanding of distance, direction and the relationship between map and territory through orienteering.

Education *in* movement

Education *in* movement is the third and most fundamental dimension of the physical education curriculum. Through actively engaging in physical activities and through exploring the possibilities and the limitations of those activities, the child comes to experience them from 'inside', rather than as a disinterested observer. Therefore, whilst coming to a greater understanding of the skills and concepts that make up the subject, it is vital that children also learn to love the activities for what they are. It is essential that teachers, too, realize that physical activities are much more than ways of keeping children fit and healthy, or useful 'tricks' through which to teach less palatable parts of the curriculum. They are activities and experiences that are valuable and worthwhile in their own right. Undoubtedly, there are valuable extrinsic benefits to be gathered from physical activities, but their ultimate importance, as well as their educational justification, lies in their intrinsic worth:

> If we believe in the value of education in physical activity for the junior school child then we believe that, by giving the child the experience (and the skills necessary for the experience) of movement activities, we are introducing him/her to a 'physical' dimension which should be included in education for its intrinsic value and for the satisfaction which such movement experience can bring.
>
> (Williams, 1989: 21)

Without denying the contributions that physical education can make to a host of other educational objectives, their ultimate educational justification lies in the distinctive nature of the physical activity itself. Games, dance and other forms of activity represent experiences that are valuable aspects of our culture, and as such deserve a place within the overall education of children. If children cannot come to see the activity from the perspective of an insider, they will never recognize the full potential or beauty of that activity. If they are denied the opportunity of these experiences, their education would not be complete; they are part of the process of becoming a civilized human being:

> Now anyone who has managed to get to the inside of what is passed on in schools . . . will regard it as somehow ridiculous to be asked what the point of the activity is. The mastery of the 'language' carries with it its own delights . . . But for a person on the outside it may seem difficult to see what point there is in the activity in question. Hence the incredulity of the uninitiated when confronted with the rhapsodies of the mountain-climber, musician, or golfer. Children are to a large extent in the position of such outsiders. The problem is to introduce them to a civilised outlook.
>
> (Peters, 1966: 255)

The skill hungry years

The seven to eleven years age-range makes up, by general agreement, the 'skill hungry years' (Maude, 1996; Williams, 1996). It occurs between the periods of rapid development in infancy and puberty, and represents a time of relative stability for children, during which they can significantly extend their physical competence in numerous contexts. This is the period in which most children have established the generic movement patterns – running, jumping, throwing, kicking, climbing – and are now keen to develop their expertise in new and challenging situations. It is, therefore, a particularly exciting time to teach physical education. Having acquired a reasonable level of competence in the 'basics', children of this age-range seek out opportunities to increase the range and quality of their movement.

One way in which the child's understanding of movement is developed is in the area of relatively formalized activities. Whilst younger children will have experienced simple games, these children are now ready for greater structure, more explicit rules and more clearly defined roles. Of course, these elements of activity should only be introduced progressively and incrementally, but children's greater understanding of form means that they are better able to cope with the responsibilities of more formal play. The active desire on the part of most children between seven and eleven years of age to develop their skills means that motivation is rarely a problem for teachers. At the same time, the fact that this is an optimum time for learning physical skills means that teachers must not waste the opportunity. Failure to capitalize upon children's desire and readiness to improve can lead to long-term underperformance and even disenchantment with physical activity.

Starting with the child

Sharp has stated that 'children are not simply small adults. Indeed, they differ from adults qualitatively as well as quantitatively' (1991: 70). In order to maximize learning and achievement, it is vital that teachers acknowledge the different ways that children behave and respond, and adapt their teaching accordingly. One of the problems that has bedevilled physical education since its beginning has been the well-meaning, but ultimately damaging effects of enforcing adult values and expectations upon young children's physical activities. Small children playing within large teams, with inappropriate equipment, on huge playing areas, to adult-designed rules is a recipe for frustration and failure. All the evidence (and common sense) suggests that simply importing adult games or similar activities into the curriculum is bad practice. It is also likely to exclude a great many pupils, especially those who do not fit in with the narrow conception of the activity, such as girls and children with disabilities.

Understanding the player

One significant way in which children differ from adults is that of information processing. Whereas teenagers and adults are selective in the way they scan the environment and identify relevant features, children are far more exploratory and unselective. Ross (1976) characterizes infants' attention allocation as *over-exclusive*, as they tend to focus ferociously upon one object (for example, a ball) with relative disregard for other features (other children). A significant change takes place during the seven to eleven period. Now, children become *over-inclusive* in their attention, considering a huge range of factors as they play. They are easily distracted, they attend to sounds too heavily and often find it difficult to focus upon important visual cues.

It is important that the teacher develops the pupils' ability to identify and act upon information from their environment. A simple way of doing this is to limit the information the child is expected to handle. In almost all cases, it is better for children to work in small rather than large groups. The precise number of children in a group is variable, depending upon the point of the activity, the space and the available resources. Small group work makes them much better placed to recognize relevant cues for action. It also ensures a far greater level of activity and participation, and, therefore, greater opportunity for challenge and improvement.

Small-sided activities are also a solution to the inherent complexity of much of the physical education curriculum. Although seven-year-olds are ready to take part in activities with a previously agreed rule structure, such as a game, many present quite complex social problems – What is my role? What are their roles? What are they likely to do? How will they respond to my actions? (Lee, 1993) – which can cause them difficulties. Small-sided activities reduces the variables, so that children are better able to develop an understanding of an activity's requirements. By gradually developing work in pairs, then threes and fours, and by offering the chance to play in different positions, teachers can initiate children into the rules and roles of an activity in a way that is manageable, yet challenging.

Almost every aspect of physical education requires children to deal with a number of tasks at the same time. In dance, pupils might be moving their bodies in time with others; in gymnastics, they might be performing a travelling pattern, whilst crossing a bench. Some children will find it too difficult to perform multiple tasks properly, especially if each task requires their thought and attention. It is important, therefore, that as well as introducing new skills and activities, the teacher does not forget the development of basic movement competence. The child needs time to practise and 'play' with the basic movement skills. Repetition is rarely considered in terms of primary practice, but in physical education (and, it is suspected, many other areas of the curriculum) it is vital if children are to develop their full potential. By practising and repeating these actions, they become relatively automatic, and the child's mind is freed to give attention to more complicated aspects of the game that require greater attention or decision-making (Bailey and Farrow, 1998).

Another factor of child development that is of relevance to the present discussion is motivation. A large number of studies have suggested that two perspectives on achievement can influence children's behaviour and work in the school environment (Nicholls, 1984; Roberts and Treasure, 1993). A *mastery perspective* (sometimes called a task orientation) occurs when a child focuses upon demonstrating her ability or competence at a task, and where the emphasis is upon self-improvement or self-comparison. A *competitive perspective* (a.k.a. ego orientation), on the other hand, is characterized by a child seeking to compare her ability or performance with others. A common assumption seems to be that the competitive orientation is the norm for children, especially in the physical education environment. However, research suggests that this is not necessarily the case. Whilst teenagers often exhibit a competitive goal orientation, younger children seem to be far more influenced by mastery goals (as well as social approval) than competition (Roberts and Treasure, 1993). Although boys are generally more competitive than girls, in the junior age-range both tend to be more concerned with the improvement of skills and the overall development of physical competence than being favourably compared with their peers.

Some writers have stressed that the 'motivational climate' created by adults can have a powerful effect upon the way children perceive a task (Ames and Archer, 1988; Roberts, 1992). Teachers' responses to the child's activity can initially conflict with and then begin to sway the child's assessment of the situation. By giving certain cues and rewards, and making explicit expectations, significant adults structure the sport context so that task- or ego-involved conceptions of ability are the criteria by which performance is evaluated (Ames and Archer, 1988).

This motivational climate deserves serious attention by teachers, as it relates closely to the behaviour of children. Children who have adopted a mastery orientation seem to be better able to select challenging tasks, persist despite set-backs and remain interested in the activity. They also seem able to develop positive relationships with peers. Some of this may also be true for children with a competitive perspective. However, evidence suggests that there are greater risks of problematic behaviours emerging. If a child has a high perception of their competence, then she tends to exhibit the same qualities as the child with a focus upon mastery. However, for the child with low perceptions of ability, her behaviour tends to be characterized by poor motivation, avoidance of challenge and lacking in persistence (Hayward, 1993). The negative reaction to competitive situations may be more apparent in girls than boys (Sports Council, 1993). Also, the competitive frame can be very fragile and a child's confidence in her own ability can be damaged by failure or difficulty (Dweck, 1986). Whatever the perceived ability, children with a competitive orientation to their participation are the ones most likely to give up sport once they leave the primary school (Roberts and Treasure, 1993).

None of the above should be understood as a criticism of competitive elements within physical education. On the contrary, competition forms a distinctive feature of the subject, and one that many children enjoy. The key point, however, is one of emphasis. Competition might form the environment of participation, but it ought not be the goal; it is the medium not the message. An unwarranted emphasis upon winning can, in the long term, lead to a rejection of the whole enterprise. Ironically, by emphasizing the importance of doing one's best, trying to beat previous performances or improving skills, the teacher is likely to encourage enjoyment of the competitive element (when it is present and appropriate) in the physical education lessons, as well.

Conclusion

'Why is it that people ignorant of their national heroes, of their monarchs, statesmen, poets and scientists, will nevertheless rattle off the names of the Arsenal eleven and supply each with an adoring biography?' (Scruton, 1998: 2).

This chapter has presented the outlines of a model of physical education for children aged seven to eleven. These children are at a particularly exciting age with regard to their performance of physical activities. They are hungry for new skills and experiences. They are also still infused with the spirit of play, of adventure and of challenge. The successful teacher is one who can address these two needs. The range of subject knowledge is broad, but with support and guidance, teachers are able to present a rich and varied movement curriculum. In doing so, they are able to initiate their pupils into activities that may remain important and fulfilling for the rest of their lives.

Further reading

Bailey, R. P. and Macfadyen, T. M. (eds) (forthcoming) *Teaching Physical Education 5–11*. London: Cassell. Presents an overview of the theory and practice of primary physical education. Includes specific information on the different elements of the physical education curriculum, as well as guidance on issues such as planning, assessment and special educational needs.

Bunker, D. (ed.) (1994) *Primary Physical Education – Implementing the National Curriculum*. Cambridge: Cambridge University Press. A useful, practical guide to planning and implementing a balanced programme of physical activities.

Lee, M. (1993) *Coaching Children in Sport – Principles and Practice*. London: E. & F. N. Spon. Although focusing upon sports coaching, there is a great deal of information of relevance to teaching all areas of physical education.

Acknowledgement

I would like to thank my colleagues Tony Macfadyen, Mike Osborne and Russell Jago for very useful comments upon an earlier draft of this chapter, and the whole team for helping to create the environment in which the ideas expressed were first developed.

4

English: Range, Key Skills and Language Study

Roger Beard

The uses of a language are as varied as life itself.

(Crystal, 1990: 83)

Introduction

Recent years have been unsettled ones for the primary curriculum, as a succession of central government changes have made major new demands on what is taught and assessed. The outcomes from these developments have not always been positive ones and the teaching of Key Stage 2 English has sometimes suffered as a result. The first version of the National Curriculum was massively overcrowded, leaving Key Stage 2 teachers potentially grappling with several hundred statements of attainment *per pupil*. The English curriculum itself had several structural weaknesses, including its parsimonious details on how reading skill could be extended beyond the initial stages (Raban, Clarke and McIntyre, 1993).

The revised version of the National Curriculum was intended to be more manageable, although its more explicit details of 'key skills' gave the new Order added complexity which teachers found hard to translate directly into practice (Stannard, 1997). There also remained the perennial ambiguity of English as a separate subject and English as a medium through which other subjects are taught. This was an ambiguity which left English in danger of being marginalized by the demands of several other subjects whose more content-based programmes of study made them easier to 'deliver' and to warrant specific curriculum space. As the programmes of study of the foundation subjects were slotted into curriculum plans alongside those for the detailed content areas of mathematics and science, Key Stage 2 English remained at risk.

The implementation of the National Literacy Strategy (NLS) in England, with its *Framework for Teaching*, its dedicated Literacy Hour and its national targets of achievement for 2002, has at last put English centre-stage. The NLS also makes additional demands on how English is taught, with a more conscious use of direct teaching, with classes and groups, and focused plenary sessions (Beard, 1999). Its emphasis on direct teaching is in marked contrast to the more child-centred, individualized approaches which have been associated with 'good practice' in primary schools for over thirty years. Thus the NLS brings with it a broader cultural change which may require some time to take hold in teacher education.

However, as the need for more teacher-centred approaches becomes appreciated, the new millennium promises to be a time when the educational potential of years of research and scholarship in primary English can be more effectively realized in Key Stage 2 classrooms. This chapter will discuss several aspects of this potential, in relation to the place of the subject, the learning environment, cross-curricular approaches, pupil grouping and language and learning in general.

An underlying theme in the chapter will be that the NLS may help to rectify some long-standing imbalances. There is growing recognition that the Key Stage 2 curriculum was inadequately conceived by the Plowden Report in 1967, which did little more than project 'infant practice' upwards into the junior school (Peters, 1969).

Twenty-two years later, the writers of the first National Curriculum over-reacted to the Plowden legacy by imposing a secondary subject-based model on the primary curriculum, when a transitional curriculum framework may have been more appropriate. The NLS may help to resolve some of these kinds of polarized tensions which have beset those who teach in the seven to eleven age-range, although several questions remain to be resolved in the years ahead.

The place of English in the Key Stage 2 curriculum

To consider the place of English in the primary curriculum, it is necessary to look at the purposes it fulfils. These purposes were particularly carefully discussed in the Kingman Report (DES, 1988), both in the main report and in an Appendix by Henry Widdowson. The report outlines some of the main purposes of English in adult life in a way which helps to remind us of what schools have to prepare pupils for:

- the world: creating a symbolic model of the world in our heads, in which past and present are carried forward to the future

- democracy: participating in a democracy: defending rights and fulfilling obligations
- everyday life: coping with 'functional' language and literacy
- work: dealing with the language of work
- community: non-standard and standard features
- change: adapting to social and technological change
- literacy: accommodating new forms of literacy.

The report also outlines the parts played by language in children's development:

In intellectual development
- representing their perceptions of the world and making sense of their experience
- allowing children to go beyond their own limited experience and to encounter the thoughts of others, including the greatest minds
- using language to speak of things independently of the context, of things in the past and of possibilities in the future
- using language to acquire new and difficult concepts

In social development
- becoming aware of the legitimacy of the different accents, dialects and languages of family, peer groups and wider world

In aesthetic development
- developing an ear for language and a full knowledge of how thoughts and feelings are made accessible through language and literature.

Oracy

These ideas can be seen at work in the sections of the National Curriculum on speaking and listening. There is an emphasis on 'range' (explaining, investigating, describing, presenting) and on 'key skills' (clear expression, organization, ways of contributing to discussions). The National Curriculum section on 'Standard English and Language Study' also encourages understanding of the differences between spoken and written language and between standard and non-standard dialects.

All this recognizes the ubiquity of oral language and its centrality in life and learning. Such a recognition runs through effective teaching of English in Key Stage 2. This is underlined in annual reviews of inspection evidence by HMI and OFSTED. These reviews also provide indications on how far the central place of oracy in the Key Stage 2 curriculum is being realized.

In the early 1990s oral English seemed to benefit very quickly from the introduction of the National Curriculum (HMI, 1992: 9). This may have been because the new document provided an explicit indication of the kinds of talking and listening which it would be valuable to promote. More recent reports associate high standards in speaking and listening with 'adaptability' in speech, the use of standard English when appropriate, the ability to listen attentively to explanations and questions (OFSTED, 1997a: 2).

There are also recurrent weaknesses identified in the inspection evidence, suggesting that the central place of oracy is not being totally accommodated. Chief among these is the need to develop children's listening skills (OFSTED, 1997a; 1998). This means providing opportunities for them to listen carefully and to demonstrate what they have heard in discussion. Drama, including role play and improvisation, can be used more in many schools to strengthen skills in speaking and listening (OFSTED, 1998c: 5).

Literacy

Literacy builds upon oracy and helps children to think in certain ways. In particular, reading and writing promote 'systematic' thought. Vygotsky (1962: 180–1) referred to writing as 'written speech' and as having a separate linguistic function, differing from oral speech in both structure and mode of functioning. Donaldson (1993: 50) has developed this view by arguing that language written down is 'cut loose' or disembedded from the context of ongoing activities and feelings in which speech functions and on which speech thrives.

Written language is a permanent kind of communication. It doesn't disappear into thin air, like speech (unless speech is tape-recorded). This gives written language particular advantages for communicating across space and time, including to ourselves in various kinds of memos, prompts and diaries. Reading enables us to learn from people we cannot personally know. Writing helps us to communicate with people we are unlikely ever to meet. By its very nature, what we write needs to fulfil its purpose without us being present to provide additional clarification or supporting detail. As a result, composing written language can help to sustain and order thought (Olson, 1994).

Again the National Curriculum recognizes these insights. There is an emphasis on independence and reflectiveness in reading. There is encouragement to read a range of literature, some long-established, some modern, and texts from a variety of cultures and traditions. The details on information reading also encourage the reading of non-fiction not specifically designed for children. In writing there is an emphasis on writing for varied purposes and on helping pupils to understand that writing is essential to thinking and learning.

Once more, HMI and OFSTED evidence provides indications of how far the potential of literacy in the Key Stage 2 curriculum is being capitalized upon. As was mentioned earlier, there was a weakness in the first version of the National Curriculum itself in not promoting reading for information as much as was recommended in the Cox Report, which gave it a separate attainment target (DES, 1989; Raban, Clarke and McIntyre, 1993). As early as 1992, HMI were reporting that, in Key Stage 2, research and study skills frequently needed more systematic attention. This aspect of literacy has evolved into an enduring legacy. As recently as 1996, OFSTED reports that, in one school in ten, development of pupils' reading is left too much to chance (OFSTED, 1996: 19). By 1998, it was felt that the lack in many schools of a structured programme of reading for Key Stage 2 pupils was unacceptable (OFSTED, 1998: 19).

If anything, there is even more concern expressed in the accumulating inspection evidence on writing. For one thing, it is consistently reported that standards of writing (in all of the first three Key Stages) are lower than those in speaking and listening and reading (OFSTED, 1993: 2; OFSTED, 1998c: 3). For another, there are indications that Key Stage 2 pupils are sometimes given writing tasks which lack authenticity and that the English curriculum is unduly influenced by decontextualized and undemanding exercises (OFSTED, 1995a: 8).

Overall these are disappointing comments on Key Stage 2 English ten years after the introduction of the National Curriculum and nearly twenty-five years after the publication of the Bullock Report (DES, 1975) in which many well-informed ideas for teaching English to seven- to eleven-year-olds were carefully discussed and strategically laid out. It is timely, then, to take stock of the place of English in the Key Stage 2 curriculum, to revisit some major principles and to remind ourselves that there is still much to do in bringing the most effective practice to many more primary school pupils.

The learning environment

As was mentioned earlier, the National Literacy Strategy may be instrumental in changing widely held views about what constitutes 'good primary practice'. For the last thirty years, this notion has often been associated with individualized approaches, in which classes of children have tackled several different subject areas at the same time in various kinds of 'integrated day'. A succession of research findings have warned about the related quality control issues: it is very difficult for teachers simultaneously to monitor so many different aspects of learning across several subject areas (Alexander, 1992; Galton, Simon and Croll, 1980; Mortimore *et al.*, 1988). Yet alternative approaches have been slow to gain status.

In recent years, international studies of school effectiveness have shown what alternatives might include (Creemers, 1994; Scheerens, 1992) and the National Literacy Strategy is very much a response to this more informed thinking (Beard, 1999; Stannard, 1997). Central to school effectiveness is the idea of 'direct, interactive teaching' in which the teacher plays a much more pro-active role than the kinds of supervisory and individualized teaching which characterized post-Plowden models of 'good practice'. OFSTED (1997a) has commented that there is too little direct teaching in many primary schools and that too much teaching time is sometimes wasted on unduly complex organizational arrangements.

So what kind of role is the Key Stage 2 teacher to take in English? Mortimore *et al.*'s (1988) research into the effectiveness of over fifty schools gives helpful pointers:

- structured sessions, involving a teacher-organized framework but allowing pupils to organize a degree of independence

- intellectually challenging tasks, with teachers using higher-order questions and statements and with pupils using creative imagination and problem-solving

- a work-centred environment, with high levels of pupil industry and low levels of noise

- a limited lesson focus, on one curriculum area (or, at the very most, two) with some differentiation, as needed

- maximum communication between teachers and pupils, with some whole-class teaching.

The above findings also indicate that there is no one way to teach with optimum effectiveness and researchers have warned about such findings being used to create 'blueprints' for schools.

Within primary English in Key Stage 2, other research and publications have given further nudges towards fine-tuning the learning environment so that various kinds of 'fitness for purpose' can be explored within the scope of the field as a whole. This fine-tuning can be better understood – by pupils and teachers – by the deceptively simple means of exploring how one language mode can be used to enhance performance in another. Speaking, listening, reading and writing are in themselves important resources for improving competence in each other. There is only space for a few of these links to be explored, but they are related to some aspects of recurring concern in research and inspection evidence which were discussed earlier.

Talking and writing

'Expressive' writing (personal narratives) may be particularly fostered by an informal relationship between teacher and pupils, in which personal experiences are regularly shaped and shared, in speech and in writing, in a secure and trusting context (Beard, 1984; Britton, 1970; DES, 1975).

Reading, listening and talking

The reading of literature may be particularly supported by the teacher making careful selections about what to read aloud and discuss with a class. In addition to the shared reading of the Literacy Hour, the class story is for many children a unique kind of serialized and supported experience of their literary heritage (Fox, 1995; Morse, 1995). Children who are read to by sensitive and enthusiastic teachers and parents are more likely to read themselves (Hall and Coles, 1999).

Reading and writing

Some of the most explicit ways of linking reading and writing have been explored in the 'genre theory' non-fiction projects in Australia (Callaghan and Rothery, 1988; Cope and Kalantzis, 1993). The intention of this approach is to make visible what has to be learned in factual writing genres.

- Shared reading is used to model the uses and features of factual genres (reports, explanations, procedures, discussions and recounts).

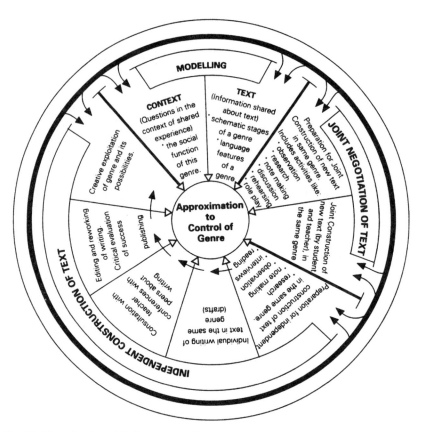

Fig. 4.1 The wheel model of genre teaching
Source: Callaghan and Rothery, 1988: 39.

- A new text in the same genre is constructed in shared writing by teacher and pupils.

- Pupils then construct another new text in this genre independently.

This approach is taken up in a number of ways in the National Literacy Strategy *Framework for Teaching* (DfEE, 1998g). The framework also draws upon the work of the EXEL project (Lewis and Wray, 1995) in highlighting how pupils' factual writing can be supported by the use of 'frames': sentence starters, connectives and modifiers, which are typically found in certain genres.

Writing and reading

It is a curious paradox that, in helping Key Stage 2 pupils develop as readers, especially of non-fiction, they need to be encouraged to look *on*, to get a sense of the length and structure of a text. In contrast, in helping them develop as writers, they need to be encouraged to look *back*, to review what they have written in the light of their intentions and what they were trying to say. Reviewing a text by re-reading is an integral part of the complex process of writing. This goes far beyond the fastidious details of proof-reading. Extensive research in Canada suggests that reviewing and re-reading are most effective when the reading is done 'with a writer's alertness to technique' (Beard, 1991; Bereiter and Scardamalia, 1987). Bereiter and Scardamalia together undertook over a hundred investigations into the writing of pupils and students in the 1980s. Their conclusions underline how growth and development in writing are fostered by modelling and discussing the composing processes of writing. This helps to build the 'discourse knowledge' within which content knowledge is selected and shaped (Bereiter and Scardamalia, 1987).

These modest suggestions are a reminder that the learning environment is more than classrooms, displays or resources. A central element of the learning environment in Key Stage 2 English is the teacher's knowledge and expertise in linking direct teaching to pupil activity and in making mutually supportive links between the four modes of language.

Themes and cross-curricular approaches

Thematic and cross-curricular approaches were another legacy of the Plowden Report, which saw subjects as rather artificial and contrived ways of viewing the world. The report did not appear to consider the implications of the words of one of the main influences on the child-centred thinking, John Dewey, who suggested that early years education should be concerned with providing experiences which 'live fruitfully and creatively in *subsequent* experience' [my italics] (Dewey, 1938: 27–8). Dewey did not discount the significance of subject areas as much as the Plowden Report seemed to assume (Peters, 1969). However, the report created a legacy of relatively loose thinking on a number of thematic aspects in primary education. The choice of a topic for thematic work was sometimes influenced more by calculations of which topic could most comfortably accommodate the optimum number of subject areas, rather than by criteria related to optimum growth and development in pupil learning (Blyth, 1984).

The 1970s and 1980s saw recurrent concerns about the limitations of thematic approaches in Key Stage 2, as they were then undertaken.

An HMI Primary Survey (DES, 1978) raised questions about the relationship between themes; Richards (1982) pointed out that the inconsistency between schools in curriculum coverage was not compatible with genuinely 'comprehensive' education; Alexander (1984) argued that the curriculum beyond the basics was in danger of being *ad hoc* and whimsical. Such arguments prepared the way for a National Curriculum. This, despite its overloaded nature, did bring greater consistency to the Key Stage 2 curriculum. However, inspection evidence suggests that there is still a tendency for topic work to be planned which covers too many aspects or subjects under such titles as 'Change', 'Travel', 'Autumn' or 'Food' (OFSTED, 1993: 9; 1998c: 13).

The relaxation of the National Curriculum programmes of study should help to reduce the pressure on teachers to squeeze so much detailed content into their curriculum planning. Coupled with the National Literacy Strategy, this relaxation should also help to ensure that the first years of the new millennium see the most effective teaching of English in whatever themes and cross-curricular approaches schools choose to use. The different aspects of the Literacy Hour provide several areas of promise:

Shared reading and writing

These are promising ways of helping Key Stage 2 pupils to improve the ways they organize less familiar kinds of texts. As Cope and Kalantzis (1993) suggest, shared reading and writing are ways of realizing the 'powers' of literacy. These approaches help pupils to see, hear, discuss and model the genre features of text, the less obvious syntactical and organizational features. When these features are brought under conscious control, they give their users access to certain realms of social action and interaction and certain realms of social influence and power (Cope and Kalantzis, 1993). Martin (1989) has shown how the genre features of a range of non-fiction genres can be used in teaching approaches which can draw upon subject knowledge from across the curriculum.

Guided reading and writing

These are teaching approaches which have been specifically developed to extend direct teaching to groups of pupils (Fountas and Pinnell, 1996). Group work has long been something of a paradox in primary schools. It has been *de rigueur* to seat children in classroom groups, but observational research has consistently shown that it is rare for pupils to engage in sustained collaborative work. It is salutary to note that changing classroom layout so that pupils all face the teacher significantly improves the time on task and the attainment of Key Stage 2 pupils (Hastings and Schwieso, 1995). Guided reading and writing are some of the few teaching approaches in literacy which make strategic use of group seating arrangements.

The Literacy Hour is designed to have a brisk, cyclical momentum to help teacher and pupils to work purposefully and productively each day. The rolling programme of group and independent work, perhaps shown on a classroom task board, can provide a clear reminder of what each group will be tackling with a teacher. Guided oral or silent reading can be tailored to any type of text. The teacher can 'top and tail' each group session so as to provide a sense of common purpose and foster the social dynamics of the group. The group seating arrangements are utilized in ways rarely achieved in other approaches to teaching English.

Independent reading and writing

These provide the most open-ended elements of cross-curricular and thematic aspects of English. They can also lead to some of the most inconclusive curriculum approaches. Independent cross-curricular work can, as Dearden (1971) once observed, range from something resembling an 'embryonic university' to something resembling a 'wet playtime which lasts all day'. OFSTED's (1993) annual reviews of inspection evidence have consistently warned of the pitfalls of project work. Much time and effort can be wasted if pupils are given too little guidance about what they should be looking for and the purposes for which they are collecting the writing information from reference books.

A great deal of practical guidance on the teaching of information skills has come from the EXEL project at Exeter University (Wray and Lewis, 1997). Table 4.1 shows how the information-retrieval process can be broken down into several interrelated stages, with associated questions and teaching strategies.

The table is significant in the way it links reading, writing and other kinds of representation. It is also noteworthy how clearly it specifies the teacher's role, in what is the most individualized aspect of literacy across the curriculum.

In addition to the Literacy Hour, the use of Information and Communication Technology (ICT) provides important potential for developing other cross-curricular approaches in English:

Table 4.1   EXIT: Extending Interactions with Text

Process stages	Questions	Teaching strategies
1. Activation of previous knowledge	1. What do I already know about this subject?	1. Brainstorming, concept mapping, KWL grids
2. Establishing purposes	2. What do I need to find out and what will I do with the information?	2. Question-setting, QUADS grids, KWL grids
3. Locating information	3. Where and how will I get this information?	3. Situating the learning
4. Adopting an appropriate strategy	4. How should I use this source of information to get what I need?	4. Metacognitive discussion, modelling
5. Interacting with text	5. What can I do to help me understand this better?	5. DARTs, text marking, text restructuring, genre exchange
6. Monitoring understanding	6. What can I do if there are parts I do not understand?	6. Modelling, strategy charts, grids
7. Making a record	7. What should I make a note of from this information?	7. Modelling, writing frames, grids
8. Evaluating information	8. Should I believe this information?	8. Modelling, discussing biased texts
9. Assisting memory	9. How can I help myself remember the important parts?	9. Revisit, review, restructuring
10. Communicating information	10. How should I let other people know about this?	10. Writing in a range of genres, writing frames, publishing non-fiction books, drama, 2D/3D work, other alternative outcomes

Source: Wray and Lewis, 1997: 41.

ICT use in information-retrieval

The need for explicit and direct teaching in individualized work is especially highlighted in the use of CD-ROMS for information-retrieval. Sparrowhawk (1995) has observed the use of CD-ROMS in over fifty primary schools, as part of a National Council for Educational Technology study. Her observations suggest that teachers need to undertake the following:

- Helping pupils 'narrow down' their questions: 'What animals live in Africa?' could be answered by 18,000 items in one CD-ROM.

- Ensuring that pupils persist in accessing the information they require: one child looking for a picture of a tiger settled for printing one of a leopard.

- Helping pupils to identify accurately words to try: when 'Motzart' [*sic*] failed to find any information about music, the pupil concluded that this CD-ROM did not have anything on music (the subject head 'Performing Arts' meant nothing to him).

- Encouraging children to appreciate the special features of the CD-ROM (speech, pictures, animations, video, as well as the text).

- Raising pupils' awareness about the mismatch between their interest and publishers' classification systems. Typical pupil questions from the study included:

  What does a spider eat?
  Did Tchaikovsky know Mozart?
  Was Van Gogh good at art at school?

It would be a mistake to dismiss such questions as immature and inappropriate. They warrant careful consideration and provide interesting opportunities for review and reflection in whole-class plenary and shared-text sessions.

ICT use in word processing

There is less clear-cut evidence on word processing in KS2. Several meta-analyses of research have failed to demonstrate that word processing improves the quality of pupils' writing, despite the understandable optimism when computers were first used in primary schools (Bangert-Drowns, 1993). The only gains in 'before and after' studies of the effects of helping primary pupils become reasonably proficient at word-processing skills have been where pupils' initial pencil and paper skills were low (Cochran-Smith, 1991; Bangert-Drowns, 1993). However, the number of published studies of systematically analysed evidence is still relatively small.

Moreover, inspection evidence suggests that word processors are still being widely used as an amanuensis to help produce more presentable end products (McFarlane, 1997). As computers become more readily available in schools and as shared and guided writing become more established, then the full potential of the word processor may become more widely understood. As Bangert-Drowns (1993) suggests, the key to enlightenment here may be simple editing, addition and deletion, rearrangement and rewriting. Such experience helps pupils learn about the fluidity of text and the higher-order processes of composition by removing many of the mechanical difficulties of changing text, whatever the subject matter being tackled. This subject matter can create opportunities for interpretation, evaluation and exploration in mathematics and science; analysing causal factors in history; exploring geographical phenomena and relationships; interpreting and evaluating religious language and symbolism, and so on (OFSTED, 1998c: 32).

Grouping pupils

Perhaps the most far-reaching change to affect English primary schools at the beginning of the new millennium is a change in how pupils are grouped for teaching. Particularly since the Plowden Report (CACE, 1967), a view of 'good practice' has pervaded teacher education which has been associated with individualized and group work. The role of whole-class teaching in good primary practice has been an uncertain one. As Alexander (1992) points out, the term 'good practice' can reflect a number of dimensions, reflecting pragmatic, empirical or political statements or statements of personal belief.

At the end of the 1980s, publications began to appear which re-examined the role of teacher instruction. Edwards and Mercer (1987) analysed video-recordings of primary school lessons to show how classroom communications take place against a background of implicit understanding, some of which is never made explicit to pupils. Edwards and Mercer departed from individualized accounts of teaching and learning and offered instead a study of classroom dialogue as the creation of socially constructed 'common knowledge'.

Mortimore *et al.*'s (1988) major study of school effectiveness provided valuable insights into how the social processes of primary schooling were linked to various elements of school effectiveness in promoting pupils' learning. It notes that, where there was little whole-class teaching, communication with individual pupils was often brief and routinized. More importantly, higher-order communications occurred more frequently when the teacher talked with the whole class.

The difficulties created by excessive individualization are compounded if several different subjects are running concurrently. Pupil industry is lower, noise and pupil movement greater, teachers spend more time on routine matters and behaviour control, communications between teachers and pupils are reduced and pupil progress is less. Mortimore *et al.* suggest that teachers were too often unable to cope satisfactorily with the myriad of demands made upon them. It is interesting to note that the authors report that their findings were often welcomed by heads and teachers. Experienced and skilful teachers, whose normal practice was to limit the curriculum focus of their lessons, had been made to feel guilty about their failure to manage more diverse activities.

The authors also stress that they are not advocating traditional class teaching. Their data indicate the value of a flexible approach that can blend individual, class and group interaction as appropriate. Nor does the focus on one (or at most two) curriculum areas imply that the pupils should do exactly the same work. Effects were most positive when the teacher geared the level of work to pupils' needs but not where all pupils worked individually on exactly the same piece of work. These findings have subsequently been confirmed and extended in meta-analyses of international research evidence (Creemers, 1994; Scheerens, 1992; Teddlie and Reynolds, 1999).

The Literacy Hour will provide extensive opportunities for teachers and pupils to use and reflect upon the blend of whole-class, group and individual teaching approaches in primary English. Their complementary effectiveness will also be thrown into a clear light by the cyclical rhythm which underpins the National Literacy Strategy *Framework for Teaching*. The success of its forerunner, the National Literacy Project (Sainsbury, 1998), may be partly related to its use of objectives which help teacher planning, can be shared with pupils (on task boards) to give a common sense of purpose, and can structure plenary sessions. Although the Literacy Hour presents considerable challenges to schools, once widely established, it will help improve consistency between schools, and enable schools to sustain an effective English curriculum as teachers come and go.

It is also important to note that there are other key areas of English which are taught outside the Literacy Hour and which are discussed in the next section:

- reading to the class and individual reading
- extended writing
- many aspects of speaking and listening, including drama.

Each provides more open-ended possibilities for grouping pupils in ways which seem appropriate in the classroom 'milieu' and which maximize effective learning time.

Recent OFSTED evidence has highlighted a need for particularly careful attention to be given to Year 3 and 4 pupils. Progress is inadequate in too many lessons (OFSTED, 1998c: 18). As Figure 4.2 shows, in 1996–7, pupils' progress was weakest in Year 3, which had the lowest percentage of good lessons in English and the largest percentage of unsatisfactory lessons. The reasons for this are not clear, but it does suggest that this age-range is targeted for additional support in many schools. It may also be an age-range where the Literacy Hour may make one of its largest impacts (Sainsbury, 1998).

Progress by year

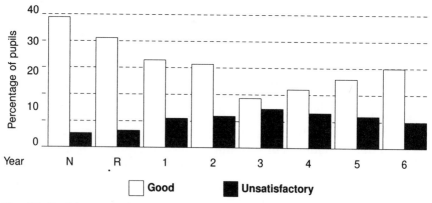

Fig. 4.2. Pupils' progress by year.
Source: OFSTED, 1998c.

Language and learning: beyond the Literacy Hour

As was said earlier, the National Literacy Strategy brings with it a great deal of potential on a number of fronts: for raising standards of children's literacy; for improving teacher knowledge; and for making more of English in the National Curriculum. Yet there is more to Key Stage 2 English than that. The broader potential of English in the new millennium lies with what is done outside the Literacy Hour, partly informed by it but also developing alongside it. Effective teaching and learning is related to what happens throughout the school day and year, much of which is permeated by various aspects of language and learning. This section will look at three such possibilities: in reading to the class (and promoting individual reading); in extended writing; and in some aspects of speaking and listening.

Reading to the class

As was noted earlier, the National Literacy Strategy *Framework for Teaching* (DfEE, 1998g: 14) provides useful pointers to some of these aspects. The list of suggestions includes reading to the class and promoting individual, voluntary reading, building on the National Curriculum emphasis on provision for range in reading:

- a range of modern fiction by significant children's authors
- some long-established children's fiction
- a range of good quality modern poetry

Procedure: The following activities are intended to support your work in beginning an action plan for eventual use in (i) your class (and year group), (ii) your Key Stage: (iii) your school:

Planning

1. Make an initial list of 10–12 children's novels which you feel your pupils will especially benefit from reading. Are all these books easily available? Are there any categories of literature missing (real-life, humorous, fantasy, myths/legends, historical realism)? Are any celebrated or cult authors omitted (Roald Dahl, Anne Fine, Dick King-Smith, Penelope Lively, Philippa Pearce)? Is there a place for any of the 'classics'? Discuss your list with the other colleague(s) in your year group and come up with your final 'desert island books' list

2. Which books will you definitely read aloud as class serials during the year? How would you sum up their distinctive qualities? Can other curriculum work be linked to them?

3. How will you promote the voluntary reading of the other books, perhaps by:

- *reading aloud excerpts to the class*
- *displaying book/author posters (some designed by children in the school)*
- *sending home short annotated lists to help the family at birthdays, Christmas etc.*
- *organizing short 'Do try this' sessions (summarizing the plot and recommending the book) etc.*

4. Over time, try to extend your lists to (i) the rest of your Key Stage and (ii) all the Primary phase.

- some classic poetry
- texts drawn from a variety of cultures and traditions
- myths, legends and traditional stories.

Such a list provides for interesting possibilities for year group and whole-school planning around a 'desert island books' theme. Guidance from a school co-ordinator might include that above, which is based on recent work in a Local education authority in the North West of England (Beard, 1997).

Similar exercises can be undertaken for poetry, focused on shorter time cycles.

Extended writing

The Literacy Hour can only provide so much opportunity for extended writing and much will need to be done through the other subjects of the curriculum. Inspection and research evidence suggests that writing in Key Stage 2 is now far less of a single session, 'one-off' experience than it once was. There is now far more writing with a real audience in mind, with an emphasis on composing and planning, the seeking of advice from teacher and peers, perhaps some redrafting and, when appropriate, some form of 'publication'. The collaboration which this brings can invigorate and enliven the communicative contexts of classrooms. Interest has now centred firmly on the reviewing of what children have written, far more than in the past, and on the use of a draft (in a variety of forms) as a resource for teaching and learning. The main point is that these processes naturally cut across the day and that teaching and learning in the Literacy Hour can contribute to them but not always accomplish them all.

Speaking and listening

It is a truism that speaking and writing pervade the Literacy Hour. Its whole-class direct interactive teaching, its plenary, its group and independent work, all have deep-seated possibilities for promoting a range of talk for teaching and learning. But again there are kinds of talk which may be more fruitfully fostered from the context of other themes and issues and which may benefit from other kinds of structure and support, through drama, history or moral and religious education.

Mercer's research has shown that, without the establishment of 'ground rules', Key Stage 2 children often interact in uncooperative, competitive ways, which generate 'disputational' talk. Where they do co-operate, they tend to share and build information in an uncritical way, in 'cumulative' talk. The natural incidence of 'exploratory' talk, in which small groups engage critically but constructively with each other's ideas, is very low (Mercer, 1995; 1996).

Mercer's subsequent research shows how the quality of children's reasoning and collaborative activity can be improved by developing their awareness of language use and by promoting certain ground rules for talking together in small groups of two or three pupils. The ground rules drawn up by one group, for instance, included the following (Mercer, Wegerif and Dawes, 1999: 100):

- Discuss things together. That means:
    ask everyone for their opinion,
    ask for reasons why,
    listen to people.
- Be prepared to change your mind.
- Think before you speak.
- Respect other people's ideas – don't just use your own.
- Share all the ideas and information you have.
- Make sure the group agrees after talking.

These suggestions provide useful indicators of how collaborative speaking and listening may be more productively encouraged in many primary classrooms.

Conclusion

The future holds much for Key Stage 2 English. This chapter has shown how the future can be informed by the successes of the past as well as by the experiences of when educational polices may have taken a wrong turn. The work of the primary classroom can have a very special kind of 'milieu'. The direct interactive teaching of the Literacy Hour is now changing that milieu for part of the day, but other parts can still connect with some of the more productive elements of the individualized past, especially in providing for extended writing and some information-retrieval work. The particular atmosphere of the end-of-day story should endure, based on a more informed judgement on what is being read and why. The success of Key Stage 2 English in the new millennium will depend, as always, on curriculum planning and classroom organization. It will also depend on the teacher's recognition of the educational significance of direct teaching and of the possibilities of the occasional *ad hoc* and inspirational response to unplanned events and ideas. However, more than ever before, this success will depend on the teacher's professional knowledge of primary English, which this chapter has tried to explore at length.

Further reading

Beard, R. (1999) *The National Literacy Strategy: Review of Research and Other Related Evidence*. London: DfEE.

Mercer, N. (1995) *The Guided Construction of Knowledge: Talk Amongst Teachers and Learners*. Clevedon: Multilingual Matters.

Wray, D. and Lewis, M. (1997) *Extending Literacy: Children Reading and Writing Non-Fiction*. London: Routledge.

5

Religious Education: A Challenge for Religion and for Education

Lynne Broadbent

Aside from religion, teaching and learning is as close to the meanings of life as one can get

(Fullan, 1993: 147)

Introduction

Religious Education offers a challenge to teachers and pupils alike. For teachers, it presents the demands of gaining knowledge and understanding of a range of religious traditions. It demands the confidence to allow pupils the space and time to explore the questions and issues that are stimulated through encounters with religious beliefs and practices, without the fear that this is dangerous ground for there are often no easy answers to pupils' questions. To encounter 'Lucy', for example, (see below) describing her dog's grave can be daunting for teachers who themselves may not feel comfortable discussing issues such as death.

For pupils of seven to eleven years, Religious Education can offer a vigorous learning experience. It offers opportunities to develop knowledge of the local and wider community, to explore religious beliefs and practices, to raise questions and to develop a sense of personal identity. It offers opportunities to become researchers and investigators, to become skilled in moral decision-making, and confident in social interactions with peers and adults.

Setting the context

Current documents on the curriculum appear to present a view that curriculum planning in the United Kingdom began in 1988 with the Education Reform Act and the introduction of the National

Curriculum. Recent educational texts rarely refer to the period before 1988 or, if they do so, it is to question the supposedly unfocused teaching and learning which accompanied the child-centred approaches of the post-Plowden era. However, the teaching of Religious Education in schools has been a legal requirement since the 1944 Education Act, and to totally disregard the period prior to 1988 is to disregard a period of fertile debate and development, the legacy of which underpins the concept of Religious Education within the curriculum today. But on what educational grounds is Religious Education to be included within a curriculum for the primary school?

The 1944 Education Act made it compulsory for schools to make provision for what was then termed 'Religious Instruction' for all pupils except those whose parents exercised their right of withdrawal under the Cowper Temple clause. Religious Education had to be taught according to a locally agreed syllabus: syllabuses were determined locally rather than nationally in order that they might respond to the context of the local community. In the early period following the Act, syllabus content tended to be focused on the study of the Bible and Christian practice and morality. Teaching was confessional and designed to lead children to a belief in God. Religious Education, in law and in practice, closely reflected the needs of a predominantly Christian society which, emerging from a world war and the threat of Nazism, sought to secure a form of religious and moral rearmament through its educational system. However, by the early 1970s, British society had dramatically changed. The country had become prosperous and confident, educational research contributed to an understanding of how children learn, and the presence of Hindu, Muslim and Sikh children in city classrooms rendered a confessional approach to the teaching of religion unacceptable.

With the 1988 Education Reform Act, Religious Education encountered few but significant changes. Provision for Religious Education remained a requirement for all schools, and the right of parents to withdraw their children from the subject was retained. Religious Education was still to be taught in accordance with a locally agreed syllabus, only now each syllabus had to 'reflect the fact that the religious traditions in Great Britain are in the main Christian whilst taking account of the teaching and practices of the other principal religions represented in Great Britain' (ERA, 1988: 2.1a). The multi-faith nature of society was now recognized in legislation through the provision for Religious Education in schools.

The Education Reform Act (1988) established the National

Curriculum with its core and foundation subjects, its programmes of study and its procedures for assessment. Religious Education was not, and could not, be included in this National Curriculum. Historically Religious Education had been locally rather than nationally determined, and parents' right to withdraw their children meant that the national programme of assessment which accompanied the National Curriculum could not apply. Religious Education became part of the 'basic curriculum', that is the National Curriculum together with Religious Education, constitutes the basic curriculum for all schools.

There were to be further changes, when in January 1998, the Secretary of State for Education announced a relaxation of the statutory requirements for non-core subjects in order to accommodate an increased focus on literacy and numeracy. The curriculum for children between five and eleven years of age was now to focus more sharply on five subjects: English, mathematics, science, information and communications technology and Religious Education. The balance of the curriculum had shifted and Religious Education became part of what was known as the new 'core'.

Religious Education has had an established place within the school curriculum since 1944, a place confirmed and strengthened through the 1988 legislation and by curriculum change in 1998. Its subject content and methodology have reflected the changing nature of society.

A rationale for Religious Education

A rationale for Religious Education must draw upon a range of sources, from the work of educational philosophers to the wider social context in which learning takes place.

The educational philosophers Hirst and Phenix offer clear justification for the study of religion to be included in the curriculum. Hirst (1974: 32) refers to education as a 'deliberate, purposeful activity directed to the development of individuals', an activity which also involves consideration of the values underlying education. He notes 'a demand for an education whose definition and justification are based on the nature and significance of knowledge itself, and not on the predilections of pupils, the demands of society, or the whims of politicians' (Hirst, 1974: 32).

Hirst identifies eight distinct disciplines or 'forms of knowledge', one being religion and the others mathematics, the physical sciences, history, literature, the fine arts and philosophy. Each form of knowledge is seen not so much as a body of knowledge to be conveyed from teacher to pupil, but as 'a distinct way in which our experience becomes structured round the use of accepted public symbols' (Hirst, 1974: 44). He asserts that through exploring these symbols, the personal experience of individuals can be more fully structured and thus be more fully understood. In terms of religion, Hirst relates the symbols to central concepts such as God and sin, but in a broader context, they might include the concepts of religious commitment or sacred symbols. This raises an interesting question in relation to Religious Education: that is, how far and in what way can the study of religion provide a structure through which pupils between seven and eleven years of age might explore, structure and understand their life experiences? This does not presuppose the fitting of one's life experiences into a Christian, Muslim or Buddhist framework but that through the study of religious places, rites of passage, celebrations and rituals and the experiences of others, pupils might come to understand their personal experiences in a deeper way.

There are broad similarities between Hirst's view of the purposes of education and those of Phenix. Phenix's thesis is that 'Human beings are essentially creatures who have the power to experience meanings' and that education is 'the process of engendering essential meanings' (Phenix, 1964: 5). Phenix analyses the nature of meaning and identifies six patterns or realms of meaning, each with distinctive features yet each relating to the other realms. These realms he terms symbolics, empirics, esthetics [*sic*], synnoetics (from the Greek meaning 'meditative thought'), ethics and synoptics (which included history, religion and philosophy). Religion, Phenix deems, is concerned with ultimate meanings and concepts such as the Transcendent. Phenix suggests that, if these six realms cover the range of possible meanings, then they might be considered to comprise the basic competencies which the curriculum should develop. He claims that such a curriculum would be designed to satisfy the essential human need for meaning and result in a person who is

> skilled in the use of speech, symbol and gesture, factually well informed, capable of creating and appreciating objects of esthetic significance, endowed with a rich and disciplined life in relation to self and others, able to make wise decisions and to judge between right and wrong, and possessed of an integral outlook.
>
> (Phenix, 1964: 8)

A comprehensive set of outcomes to challenge any National Curriculum!

However, if education is concerned with engendering meanings, then, Phenix asserts, there are various threats to meaning, one of which is the volume of knowledge to be learnt. Phenix presents four principles for selecting and organizing curriculum content. It should be drawn from a specialist field of enquiry, be representative of that field (a relatively small volume of knowledge would develop effective understanding of a far larger body of material), exemplify the modes of understanding associated with the particular field, and arouse the imagination of the learner.

The principle that a relatively small body of knowledge should be selected to represent the field of enquiry has significant implications for teaching and learning in Religious Education. The selection of knowledge might be based on the six dimensions of religion identified by Smart (1971), namely ritual (worship, prayers), mythological (the stories of faith traditions), doctrinal (the beliefs and teachings), ethical (codes of ethical behaviour), social (the communal organizations) and experiential (the experience of both key figures and individual adherents). The material dimension is a more recent addition to this list (Smart, 1996).

While Hirst justifies the inclusion of the study of religion on the grounds that religion is a form of knowledge, Phenix identifies religion as a way of focusing on ultimate meanings. Both, however, indicate that a study of religion will have a profound impact on personal development.

There are further arguments for the place of Religious Education within the curriculum. Firstly, religion has been a distinctive feature of history, for good or ill, and continues to be a distinctive feature of human experience. The Durham Report on Religious Education (1970) identifies this in the following way: 'There are many millions of men and women throughout the world who find through their religious beliefs a deep meaning and purpose for their lives and a system of values by which their lives can be lived' (cited Swann Report, p. 469). To exclude the study of religion therefore would be to exclude the possibility of understanding a key form of motivation within personal, social and political life.

Secondly, there is an argument which stems from the first, that in a multicultural and multifaith society such as Britain, an insight into the beliefs, values and practices of the different religions represented within society is a crucial element in both recognizing and celebrating diversity and acknowledging commonality. Such a process can be a means of fostering positive relationships within the local community and extending awareness of the worldwide community. The Swann Report (1985) identifies the contribution that Religious Education could make in preparing pupils for adult life: 'religious education can play a central role in preparing all pupils for life in today's multi-racial Britain, and can also lead them to a greater understanding of the diversity of the global community' (Swann, 1985: 518). The report also suggests that Religious Education has a role to play in 'challenging and countering the influence of racism in our society', a current and pertinent issue.

Thirdly, while religion does not have a monopoly on morality, it cannot be denied that religions contain clearly defined moral codes and make powerful statements on the responsibilities that humans have within personal and societal relationships and towards the natural world. A study of moral codes within the teachings of holy books could introduce pupils to moral frameworks, while an exploration of the moral issues contained in religious and secular stories could sharpen pupils' skills of moral decision-making and, indeed, exemplify a method of applying belief to practice found within religion itself.

A rationale for Religious Education in schools would seem to encompass five areas:

- religion as a form of knowledge

- religion as a distinctive form of human experience

- religion as having a role to play in any discussion on morality

- religious understanding as crucial in preparing pupils for life in a multifaith and multicultural society.

- religion as making a significant contribution to structuring and understanding personal experience.

Current aims for Religious Education

In 1994, the Schools Curriculum and Assessment Authority (later the Qualifications and Curriculum Authority), published two model syllabuses for Religious Education. The syllabuses were not statutory documents but designed as 'models' for local education authorities developing new syllabuses. The model syllabuses contained aims for Religious Education which subsequently have been widely adopted.

The aims focus upon three areas: the development of knowledge and understanding, the development of skills and attitudes, and the contribution made by Religious Education to pupils' personal development. The aims state that Religious Education should help pupils to develop their knowledge of Christianity and the other principal religions represented in Great Britain, and should develop their understanding of the influence of beliefs, values and traditions on individuals, communities, societies and cultures. This firmly establishes a knowledge-base for the subject and one which might be seen to support an understanding of a multifaith society. It is, however, interesting to note that for Hirst and Phenix, it was 'religion' itself that was to be studied, rather than 'religions'. Thus, instead of studying aspects of religion, the syllabus presupposes that aspects of each religion (the principal religions are taken to mean Buddhism, Hinduism, Islam, Judaism and Sikhism which, with Christianity, total six) will be studied. This indicates a considerable amount of content.

The aims also seek to develop pupils' abilities to make reasoned and informed judgements about religious and moral issues and to foster in pupils a positive attitude towards others, respecting those who hold views different from their own. To make a reasoned and informed judgement is a complex operation involving the gathering of evidence, the recognition of prejudice and preference within that evidence and the ability to offer a personal perspective based on the evidence. Placed within a context of, for example, a religious reponse to environmental issues, this would offer a real challenge to seven- to eleven-year-olds!

The third aspect of the aims requires Religious Education, alongside other subjects, to enhance pupils' spiritual, moral, cultural and social development by relating religious teachings to fundamental questions of human experience. This would seem to have strong links with Phenix's view of religion as being concerned with ultimate meanings. This contribution to pupils' personal development specifically does not include any bid for their religious affiliation. Any desire to convert children or to nurture them in any particular religious tradition is prohibited. This is the role of the home, the faith community and, where appropriate, the denominational school.

The aims for Religious Education are thus strongly focused on the intellectual and personal development of children within the context of the society in which they will grow.

Religious Education for seven- to-eleven-year-olds

Sam is eight years old, sociable and likes action! He delights in the successes of Manchester United and collects information books on the England football team. His passion of a year ago, collecting and identifying fossils from the local beach, an interest shared with his father, has been replaced by his newly discovered skills in identifying the birds which descend on his bird table, his Christmas present. At times, Sam reads quietly in his room, he goes to Cubs, fights with his sisters and asks exactly what his step-sister had to promise at a wedding he did not attend, and whether humans are ever 'put to sleep' like animals when they are sick.

In Sam, we can see evidence of his intra-personal and inter-personal development (Gardner, 1983). Through his delight in investigating fossils and birds, and his questions about death, he is not only developing intellectually but also developing his personal identity and sense of self. Through his membership of the Cubs, and even his fights with his sisters, he is learning to live as a member of society. Sam needs an approach to learning which is vigorous and challenging, an approach which allows him to extend his knowledge about religion and create a mental 'fact-file' within a strongly interactive context while also providing him with opportunities to reflect upon and make sense of his inner world. Even his desire for argument needs to be channelled into dialogue and debate!

These two areas of Sam's development correspond with the two approaches currently applied to teaching and learning in Religious Education. The first of these, 'learning about religions', relates to the development of knowledge about religions through a study of their writings, people, forms and places of worship, festivals and celebrations. The second, 'learning from religion', encourages pupils to reflect on what can be learnt from religion in the light of their own experiences and to respond to the questions of meaning and purpose which religions highlight. The two approaches in practice should be closely linked and should promote the development of a range of skills such as investigation, interpretation (for example, the ability to draw meaning from religious artefacts and symbols), reflection and expression, that is, the ability to respond to religious questions through a variety of media.

The following programmes of study designed for seven- to-eleven-year-olds exemplify these two approaches to learning and reflect the five areas identified within the rationale for Religious Education.

Religion as a form of knowledge and understanding

The programme of study was the Jewish festival of Passover. The learning objectives were to focus on the symbolism of the seder meal and the significance of the festival to the Jewish community. An introduction to the topic involved discussion about personal celebrations and public festivals. With some prompting, pupils remembered a lesson when the local vicar had explained the celebration of the bread and wine at communion. The pupils now began to explore the idea of food as a symbol linked to a particular event. The teacher set a table for the seder, with the seder plate containing among other things a bone, bitter herbs (horseradish), charoset (a sweet mixture of apples finely chopped with cinnamon and wine), a bowl of salt water and some matzot. This encouraged discussion about the possible meanings of the food. Clues were said to be found in the Bible in the book of Exodus. Consequently, the story was read and was followed by discussion about why this festival was celebrated by Jews. Attention was drawn to the belief that it was God who had led the Hebrews from slavery in Egypt to a new life as freed men and women A member of the local synagogue visited the school to explain how she prepared for and celebrated the festival in her home. Pupils visited the local synagogue and looked at the Torah scrolls, hearing part of the Exodus story read in Hebrew.

The pupils had learned about a key festival representative of the Jewish religion. Their study had involved investigation through story, through interaction with a member of the local faith community and through a visit to a place of worship. They had learned how, through the authority of a holy book, the Torah, belief gives rise to religious ritual and practice, and had begun to explore the concept of religious persecution both in the past and in the present.

Religion as a feature of history and as a distinctive form of human experience

The programme of study was based upon a visit to the local church. Prior to the visit the teacher had collected pictures of the focal points within the church, the cross on the spire, the font at the main door, the altar with its cross, and pictures showing details of the stained glass windows. As this was to be a cross-curricular topic involving geography and history, the route to the church was mapped and the site, fabric and history of the building discussed at length using early photographs from guides to the church.

In the church, one group followed a 'rites of passage' trail, role-playing a baptism at the font and learning about marriage and funeral services held at the altar. Another group followed a candle trail, studying the baptismal candles, the votive candles, candles lit before images of Mary and the saints and the altar candles. A further group looked at stained glass windows (a study of Christian myths), noting the symbolic colours as well as particular images used to tell the stories. A final group investigated the community of the past by listening to stories, using church records and visiting selected graves. The experiences of the community of the present were recorded from interviews with the priest and a member of the congregation and by identifying current church activities from noticeboards and newsletters.

Religion as a source of morality

The programme of study was entitled 'Rules and Laws.' It began with the inevitable study of school rules and rules of the road. Pupils were then asked to identify, in pairs, five guidelines which would make the world a better place. Most found this easy but were challenged by trying to explain how their 'rules' would be implemented and who would 'police' the offenders. In the end they were forced to acknowledge the impossibility of the latter – a lesson in itself for it introduced the idea that not all rules were for external monitoring. Some were solely reliant on the intentions and integrity of the individual. Such are religious rules! Pupils were introduced to the five moral precepts in Buddhism and asked to compare these with their own examples.

From here came the story of the Buddha and his story of riches to rags – which gave rise to much puzzlement and later to quiet reflection. The focus on moral behaviour developed with the story of the boy Gotama (later known as the Buddha or Enlightened One) and his cousin Devadatta. The story tells how a swan, wounded by an arrow, fell before Gotama who instantly began to care for it. Devadatta appeared claiming that as he had shot the swan, it was by rights his. In the story Gotama and Devadatta take the problem to the wise men – and at this point the teacher stopped reading and sent the children into small discussion groups. They were to present the verdict and, more importantly, provide reasons for their judgements.

Religion as a preparation for life in a multifaith society

The focus of this programme of study was a trail to investigate the different places of worship in the locality. The investigation began with a consultation of telephone directories, maps and a range of resource texts on places of worship. Routes were planned and questions for local religious leaders prepared. Instructions were given on appropriate behaviour for each place of worship, for example, the wearing of head covering and/or the removal of shoes. Equipped with cameras, questions and sketchbooks, the children began their investigations.

The outcome of the programme of study was a mini-trail set out at one end of the hall. Roads were identified and each place of worship represented by a model building showing the appropriate shape and external symbols. A wall display of photographs showed internal features and labels identified appropriate behaviour.

While this programme of study involved visiting places of worship, a similarly focused study could have included an investigation through food and festival (the ritual dimension of religion). It might also have involved a series of visits from parents or members of the local community to speak about their beliefs or festivals.

Religion as a means of structuring experience and developing understanding

How do the examples above contribute to the ways seven- to-eleven-year-olds structure and develop their understanding of their own life experience? Provision for this is made through the focus on 'learning from religion' which asks pupils to consider their own experiences in the light of what they have learned about religion. So, for instance, before embarking on a study of the church or of any other place of worship within the community, a teacher would need to establish an understanding that these are special places for adherents. As a preamble, pupils would reflect on and discuss their own special places and the feelings evoked by being in these places. Or a preamble to a topic on symbolic food and celebration meals would relate celebration and special meals to pupils' experiences of food and celebration.

An example might illustrate the potency of such an approach. A class of seven- to-eight-year-olds were beginning a topic on special places. The teacher described her own special place and the feelings it evoked. Then she divided these quite young children into small groups so that they could describe their special places and how they felt when they were there. As the groups began to get to grips with the task, one of the girls, 'Lucy', announced, 'you'll laugh at me when I tell you about my special place.' But when her turn finally came, no one laughed as she told of her special place being by her dog's grave which she visited when she felt sad and lonely, because by that time several children had shared similar experiences of loss and bereavement. The teacher hadn't bargained for such a response but the needs of her pupils to speak about their special places and special relationships had burst forth into that classroom.

It is interesting that a recent school inspection report (OFSTED, 1997b) notes a tendency on the part of teachers to focus more fully on 'learning about religion' rather than 'learning from religion'. To do so is to keep pupils on the edge of learning and turns Religious Education into a collection of facts rather than an exploration of the inner experiences and beliefs made manifest in the outer symbols and rituals.

The programmes of study illustrated here raise further issues. Firstly, how many religions should be studied during each phase of education? The model syllabuses suggest that for pupils between seven and eleven years, teaching should normally focus upon Christianity and two other religions in depth in order to develop a coherent understanding of each religion. This guards against the overabundance of information identified by Phenix which mitigates against meaning-making. Secondly, the programmes of study deserve a word about methodology. Recent research (Jackson, 1997) alerts us to the fact that religion is diverse and changing. Textbooks produced in an earlier period tended to present categoric statements about religious practice (for example, 'Sikhs wear turbans and do not cut their hair') and ran the risk of stereotyping practices. While it is true that many Sikhs do wear turbans, other Sikhs do not. It has become more common for both text-based and broadcast material to present a given religion through the perspective of a specific child from the faith community. This method is ideally suited to learning in the primary phase, where learning takes place between the two children, the pupil and the adherent, and through the eyes of another child's experience, the pupil is encouraged to look again at his or her own experience. This supports the process identified by Phenix, of structuring and understanding experience.

Spiritual, moral, social and cultural development

The 1988 Education Reform Act, in addition to establishing a National Curriculum, made it incumbent upon all schools to address the personal development of pupils.

> The curriculum for a maintained school satisfies the requirements . . . if it is a balanced and broadly based curriculum which –
> (a) promotes the spiritual, moral, mental and physical development of pupils and of society; and
> (b) prepares such pupils for the opportunities, responsibilities and experiences of adult life
>
> (ERA, 1988: Part 1:2)

The inclusion of this requirement suggests that pupils' personal development would not automatically arise from following the attainment targets and programmes of study within the National Curriculum. With the 1992 Education Act and the institution of school inspection under the OFSTED framework, the school's provision for pupils' spiritual, moral, social and cultural development became one of four areas of school life to be inspected. Subsequent discussion papers (NCC, 1993a; OFSTED, 1994b) on spiritual, moral, social and cultural development indicate that all subjects should contribute to these aspects of personal development. It thereby became the responsibility of subject co-ordinators for each subject to identify the contribution that their particular subject could make.

The spiritual, moral, social and cultural can each be regarded from a cognitive and an affective perspective, and in terms of content and methodology each area fits easily into a framework for Religious Education. Eight aspects of 'spiritual' development have been identified (NCC, 1993a). These include developing an understanding that people have individual and shared beliefs, a sense of awe and wonder, experiencing feelings of transcendence (whether of a divine being or related to a sense that one's inner resources allow one to rise above difficult situations), a valuing of relationships and a sense of community, and a search for meaning and purpose. Religious Education with pupils from seven to eleven years explicitly teaches about the beliefs and values of others and encourages pupils to explore and express their own beliefs, whether or not of a religious nature. Discussion about beliefs and practices inevitably encompasses those issues related to questions of meaning and purpose and to questions about experiences of transcendence expressed by religious believers. Pupils learn about religious communities and in the process identify the communities to which they belong, and these too may or may not be of a religious nature.

Reference has already been made to the links between the Religious Education curriculum and pupils' moral development in terms of providing moral frameworks and case studies for discussion and debate. Through visits to places of worship and through receiving members of faith communities into the school, pupils' social and cultural development are enhanced. They learn about a range of social and cultural groups and learn how to behave in different social and cultural settings. Religious Education broadens the context in which they may develop this knowledge and learn these social skills. Other aspects of social and cultural development should include opportunities for working in small and large groups to plan and conduct interviews, to investigate the local area and to explore a range of musical and artistic expression such as Hindu mandalas and Islamic architecture and patterning.

The social and moral dimensions of pupils' development will receive greater attention as the new requirements for 'Education for Citizenship' are addressed. The final report of the Advisory Group in September 1998 identified three strands which should run through all education for citizenship, namely *social and moral responsibility, community involvement* and *political literacy,* The teaching and learning undertaken with seven- to eleven-year-old pupils in Religious Education will support development in at least the first two of these strands.

Phenix claimed that a curriculum designed to satisfy the essential human need for meaning would result in a person 'skilled in the use of speech, symbol and gesture, factually well informed, capable of creating and appreciating objects of esthetic significance, endowed with a rich and disciplined life in relation to self and others, able to make wise decisions and to judge between right and wrong, and possessed of an integral outlook' (1964: 8). As we move towards the end of the century, the question for Religious Education, indeed, for the curriculum itself, might well be its capacity to produce such a person, fitted for adult life in a multifaith society in the new millennium.

Further reading

Bastide, D. (ed.) (1992) *Good Practice in Primary Religious Education 4–11.* London: Falmer. This book contains a series of articles on planning and implementing a programme of Religious Education with seven- to eleven-year-olds and includes articles on the use of artefacts and drama, and the place of story in Religious Education.

Ericker, C., Brown, A., Kadodwala, D., Hayward, M. and Williams, P. (eds) (1993) *Teaching World Religions.* Oxford: Heinemann Educational. The opening section of this book explores the relevance of teaching world religions to pupils within the primary phase of education. Subsequent sections address the teaching of specific faiths within the primary classroom.

6

Geography: A Sense of Place

John Cook

Children of this age are concerned not only about their personal future but also the future of their local community and the global future ... Children are trying to make sense of the world and their role in it and the teacher should be facilitating this process.

(Hicks and Holden, 1995: 100)

Introduction

The aim of this chapter is to reaffirm the importance of geography as a subject in the curriculum. I will argue that, by the later years of primary school, children are able to cope intellectually with advanced concepts and that this developing ability can be extended further through engagement with geographical enquiry and study. This learning is crucial for the overall educational and personal development of pupils between the ages of seven and eleven.

Understanding of the world and one's place in it

Coming to terms with a sense of place in an increasingly complex world, through play and other forms of learning, is an essential part of growing up. Geography fosters this development. It also contributes in many other ways towards a broad and balanced education, from the moral dimension in its treatment of environmental issues to its fundamental concern with the nature and development of places and societies.

By the time they are seven or eight years of age, most children know something about the features of their local environment and of other places with which they are familiar, and will have developed opinions about these places that they are increasingly able to express. They notice changes in environments and they are able to say what they like and dislike about places. This development of awareness, knowledge and understanding happens naturally through the experience of children interacting with the world they inhabit. Geographical concepts and geographical vocabulary are necessary in everyday life and are available to children through their interaction with the people around them.

At school, pupils have opportunities to consolidate and extend this knowledge and understanding as the curriculum for geography sets an agenda of geographical enquiry about particular places and themes chosen for study. Children are introduced to maps, photographs and other secondary sources and they begin to communicate their findings in a wider variety of ways. They extend their geographical vocabulary and contribute their own questions to extend enquiries about places and topics studied. They are taken out into natural and urban environments to gain their first experiences of fieldwork.

As they grow older, it is important that children sustain an intense interest in the world around them. The range and detail of their awareness needs to develop, to absorb information about other places studied in school, places visited or learnt about through books, computer software, television and the media. How children feel in different locations and what they know about places matters.

Geography is a challenging and vibrant subject and young geographers are encouraged to consider a number of key questions:

- Where is this place?
- What is this place like?
- How did it come to be like this?
- What would it feel like to be there?
- How and why is it changing?

For children aged ten and eleven the range of places studied becomes wider and the conceptual demands of their learning become greater. Key geographical concepts and understandings are introduced, such as location, cause and effect, stability and change and notions of underlying systems and processes.

Alongside developing skills and emerging understanding there is every opportunity to foster more tolerant attitudes and promote a greater awareness of a multicultural society through the choice of studies. Geography helps young people to have some understanding of the complex, interdependent world in which they live and some sense of the responsibilities of the 'developed' economies towards the less wealthy. The study of geography has the potential to promote environmental awareness and understanding.

At the outset the three main aims for primary geography described in the National Curriculum were:

- to help pupils develop geographical knowledge and understanding
- to introduce pupils to geographical enquiry
- to help pupils develop a sense of identity through learning about the United Kingdom and its relationships with other countries. (DES, 1991)

Worthy and academic though these aims are, they seriously under-state the particular contribution to pupils' learning that geography can make. In the wider context this can be better summarized under the headings of skills, knowledge, understanding and values as shown in Figure 6.1. In addition, along with the other non-core sub-jects of the National Curriculum for England and Wales, geography has a part to play in the development of the key skills of literacy, numeracy and information and communications technology (ICT) (QCA, 1998c).

The place of local studies

A study of the local environment has traditionally been a strong fea-ture of the primary school geography curriculum, built on work of a practical nature firmly based on the children's interests and direct experiences. Starting points can be various, and usually involve sur-veying, mapping, recording environmental qualities and pursuing environmental issues. Aspects of this are clearly illustrated in an example from a school's inspection report:

> A class of eleven-year-olds was investigating how their local area had changed, studying new economic developments including recent gravel extraction in a river valley. Previously, the pupils had devised a ques-tionnaire in groups and, using parental and other school contacts, sent it and a letter to some local businesses. The teacher had prepared an outline base map which pupils used to identify economic activities in the area, linked to businesses they had written to. During the lesson the pupils located places on the map and reported their questionnaire find-ings to each other, filling in tables about the number of employees, raw materials used, and reasons for location etc. The data generated were put into a database by pupils for future use working in pairs ... The pupils were enthusiastic, using their own local knowledge to good effect and drawing on the teacher's expertise.
>
> (OFSTED, 1998d)

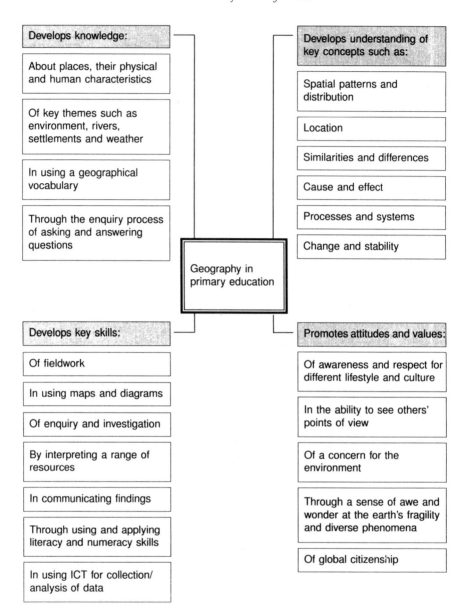

Fig. 6.1 A place for geography in the primary school

The local area is also used as a point for comparison with, and contrast to, distant place studies and as a focus for thematic work such as river or weather studies. As children enter the later years of primary education, so the scope for these studies widens and the questions raised become more sophisticated. One of the challenges in primary geography is to help children come to understand the nested relationship, in which smaller places are located inside larger places; for example, a house within a street, district, town, county, country and continent. Research indicates that this concept is often misunderstood, even by older primary pupils (Harwood and McShane, 1996; Jahoda, 1963; Piaget and Weil, 1951), though learning can be accelerated by systematic teaching using stimulating resources.

A more worrying recent finding (Hillman, 1993) is that the scope of children's play and learning experiences in and around their home area is declining. This is due to much greater parental control and imposed restrictions because of concerns about traffic and fear of strangers. In the 1970s Hillman's surveys showed that 80 per cent of seven- to eight-year-olds went to school unaccompanied by an adult. Twenty years later, the proportion had declined to only 9 per cent. Escorted journeys and restrictions on play areas are now commonplace and within this boys are often given more freedom than girls to explore their surroundings. Schooling cannot easily compensate for the missed opportunities of social play, adventure and direct informal learning experiences. However, focused activities in the school's locality can widen children's horizons, help them to develop their natural curiosity and understanding, and in addition promote their skills and knowledge. Teaching about the locality need not be repetitive, there are plenty of opportunities to take different perspectives including exploiting cross-curricular links with history and with science. What matters is to build up a well-defined picture of *our place* ensuring progression from one year to the next.

Studies of distant places

In the 1980s school inspectors noted an almost complete absence of a global dimension to the work they observed in geography in primary schools (DES, 1989c). This was partly due to an over-emphasis on local studies and also a misplaced view that distant place studies were of little relevance or consequence to the children, and beyond their understanding. Research, however, at the time and certainly recently, points to just the opposite. An awareness of the rest of the world is apparent in very young children. Aboud (1988) noted that children as young as four years of age are capable of expressing negative responses towards ethnic groups. Weigand (1991a) found that by the ages of seven and eight children are generally able to name five or six countries, usually the larger land masses such as America, India and Australia, although some confusion creeps in with fantasy lands

such as Disneyland and Legoland also being mentioned! Their awareness of other places grows steadily from the influence of books, television, video, computer games and software and the fact, also, that
children now travel further and more frequently than in the past. All
this can lead to children in the middle primary years expressing very
stereotypical and biased views of other peoples and places (Spencer
and Stillwell, 1974; Storm, 1984; Weigand, 1992). However, this is also
a time when children are naturally inquisitive and by ten years of age
are likely to be at their most positive towards other nationalities
(Klineberg and Lambert, 1967). It is an appropriate time to teach about
distant places. Both Friend (1995) and Harrington (1998) showed that
children's images of Africa could be widened and more fully developed as a result of balanced teaching programmes. Stereotypic views
cannot be completely eliminated but challenging them at an early age
is the way forward.

Inclusion of distant place locality studies in the National
Curriculum documentation immediately strengthened primary geography and also staked an important claim to geography's wider
responsibilities of education for citizenship and cultural awareness
and understanding. High-quality locality study resources for older
primary pupils have been developed by the Geographical Association
and the Development Education agencies. Good quality resource
materials and support for teaching schemes make use of photographs,
aerial views, video and audio-tape recordings, weather and climate
details, case studies of families and the features of small localities. For
younger children the emphasis is more likely to be on the description
of physical and human features, suggesting reasons for the character
of places and looking for similarities to and differences from the local
area. By the age of eleven, there is an expectation of more sophisticated explanation and description, thinking about cause and effect
and taking into account links with the wider region. Another example from a school inspection report shows the level of understanding
that can be achieved:

> the oldest pupils have a good knowledge and understanding of their
> current locality study, a village in India, and can draw on knowledge
> and skills learnt in relation to previous studies . . . . They can give expla-
> nations for ways in which human activities have affected that environ-
> ment, raise geographical questions and come to plausible conclusions.
> They have a wide geographical vocabulary and can talk of developed
> and developing countries, discuss issues of change in landscapes and
> describe geographical features accurately.
>
> (OFSTED, 1998d)

Environmental education

One of the main findings of the survey of geography in primary schools by school inspectors (OFSTED, 1998d) was that the subject makes a major contribution to children's environmental education. This is encouraging and shows that the key theme of environmental quality, relationships and issues, which runs through both early and later years of the geography programme as outlined in the National Curriculum, is being addressed by schools. Typically, this begins with younger children articulating their views about what they like or dislike about features of their local environment. At a later stage they are able to consider how they think it might be changed or improved. By the age of eleven years, case-study material can be used to illustrate that there are often very different but equally valid points of view held by other pupils on environmental issues and also that different approaches can be adopted for landscape management. Recent research points to children's interest in and natural inclination towards care and concern for the environment. Palmer (1993) found in children as young as four what she called 'an emergent environmentalism', and documented discussions with young children in which they talked about and showed considerable awareness of environmental issues such as the destruction of the rain forest and global warming. As children develop they are able to handle more complex and abstract issues in environmental education. The Liverpool Eight Children's Research Group (1996) studied primary children's views on how to make cities better places in which to live. Leeson, Stenisstreet and Boyes (1997) looked at what a group of older children thought about increased car use and its effect upon the environment. The children's level of interest was high and their ideas wide ranging. This was also noted by Hicks and Holden (1995) when they asked children to write about their hopes and fears for their local area. In this study, for instance, seven-year-olds were concerned that their local area might become subject to the type of violence that they saw happening in other places through television programmes. Eleven-year-olds were concerned for the prosperity of their local area and wanted to see less crime, against both property and people. Many were concerned about pollution and wanted to see increased facilities for recycling waste materials. Interestingly, these older children were concerned about their future and that of the local community and were optimistic that the quality of life would improve. They were less hopeful about the global situation. The study showed that children do want to be better informed about the world around them and to contribute to its future well-being. The geography curriculum has a major role to play in heightening pupils' awareness of environmental issues and relationships.

Geographical skills

It is in the context of teaching about places and geographical themes that advanced skills such as observation and measurement, map-making and the reading of atlases and globes, interpreting photographs and asking and answering questions are developed. Geographers use the term 'graphicacy' to describe this essential skill for communicating information through such means as cartography, photography, computer graphics and the graphic arts (Balchin, 1996). It is, fundamentally, the communication of spatial information that cannot be conveyed adequately by verbal or numerical means alone. The plan of a town, features on a relief map, a drainage network would be typical examples. Geography educators make a strong argument for placing graphicacy alongside literacy, numeracy and oracy to establish the four basic modes of communication. Very young children use pictures and sometimes maps quite naturally to illustrate their personal worlds. Norris Nicholson (1993) sees maps and plans as integral to people's lives and a driving force for children's curiosity about the world. An atlas, a globe, an aerial photograph or a view from space are powerful stimuli in any primary classroom. Catlin (1998: 10) has summarized the likely competencies and understandings of children as map-makers by the age of eleven as:

- using their experience and knowledge of a locality to identify and select features and pathways
- drawing maps of the locality with recognizable spatial accuracy
- depicting features and areas in detail on their local area maps
- increasing use of plan-view style to represent features
- drawing on experience of maps to present information in conventional forms
- recognizing that what they include on their map does not show every detail in an area.

There are gender differences. Boardman (1990) and Taylor (1998) both found that boys tend to outperform girls in most map-making tasks, particularly in the aspect of range of map (type and distance covered) and in choosing to use plan-view representation. The progression in map-making and investigative skills is clearly set out in the current National Curriculum. At the centre of this is the enquiry process within which 'key questions' give direction and focus to the study. The emphasis of this is on a pupil-led rather than on a teacher-led activity (QCA, 1998b). Children should be given opportunities to observe and ask questions about geographical features and issues, collect and record evidence to answer the questions and analyse the results in order to draw conclusions and communicating findings.

Evidence of this type of development was described in the case of one school as follows:

> By the end of Key Stage 2 all the pupils are making good progress, particularly with their skills in making and interpreting maps, using symbols, keys and co-ordinates with growing confidence. They show progress in using and applying the correct terminology to landscape features and are particularly knowledgeable in explaining river processes based on fieldwork they have undertaken locally and then compared with their studies in South America ... the ability of Year 6 pupils to draw together several aspects of previous learning to investigate environmental and conservation issues concerning a proposed by-pass was particularly impressive; they could support their arguments well, could identify conflicts in land use and consider the consequences attached to particular decisions.
>
> (OFSTED, 1998d)

There is good evidence that mapping skills are being developed well, based on practical work related to place and theme studies. This, however, has not always been the case.

The improvement of standards in geographical skills

During the 1970s and 1980s Her Majesty's Inspectors (HMI) were critical of what was being taught in the name of primary geography. At this time the work was often judged to be superficial, repetitive, lacking in progression and often involved 'copying' from books. Standards were 'very disappointing' and in the period 1982–86 were satisfactory or better in just one-quarter of infant and junior departments (DES, 1989c). There has been considerable improvement since then which is summarized in Table 6.1, although even in 1996–97, whilst much of the work is deemed satisfactory, standards are clearly not high enough, especially when compared to other subjects (OFSTED, 1998d). The comparatively slower improvement of geography is partly attributable to the first set of National Curriculum requirements. These were widely recognized as being overly complex and burdened non-specialist teachers with too much content. The geography curriculum did not sit easily alongside other equally over-loaded subjects, in the later stages of primary school. HMI recognized this in 1994, concluding that, 'Many primary schools . . . have found it difficult to interpret the Geography Order, to create a manageable curriculum which focuses on the requirements . . . '(OFSTED, 1994a: 3). Other key strengths now to be found in schools include well-organized and well-managed field studies and the children's positive response to and enjoyment of these studies. There are now more

Table 6.1   HMI/OFSTED evidence showing the development of primary geography in junior schools, 1982-97

National Monitoring Survey 1982–1986	Inspection findings Review 1993–94	Standards in primary geography 1996–97
Standards Satisfactory or better in only 25% of junior schools. An almost total absence of a national or world dimension.	**Standards** Satisfactory or better in 73% of lessons in KS2. Local area knowledge better than distant environments.	**Standards** In nine out of ten KS1 lessons, but in slightly fewer at KS2 pupils make satisfactory progress.
Teaching The amount of time allocated was rarely adequate, in most schools there was a tendency for geography to lose its distinctive contribution. In a minority of schools, there was either no or very little teaching of geography.	**Teaching** Great variability, quality of teaching was satisfactory or better in 67% of KS2 lessons. Almost half of lessons contained unsuitable content and activities with too much inappropriate use of worksheets, copying of text and diagrams.	**Teaching** Satisfactory or better in over nine out of ten lessons, good in one-third. The quality of teaching dips in Year 3 and rises to Year 6 where half of the teaching is good.
Planning, curriculum In few schools effective planning took into account the development of key geographical skills and ideas, there was rarely a rationale for the selection of topics, progression and continuity weak.	**Planning, curriculum** Most schools did not have a scheme of work although they were generally meeting the requirement of the NC order. Geography usually taught as part of broader topics though in years 5 and 6, sharpening of focus often led to improved standards.	**Planning, curriculum** Planning good in 1 in 5 schools, still unsatisfactory in 2 in 5. Many schools still have inadequate schemes of work to show how the key ideas and skills are going to be taught.

appropriate resources of a higher quality and 'model' schemes of work to support schools. Considerable time has been given to in-service training and to strengthening the role of subject co-ordinators in the pursuit of improving the teaching and learning in geography.

At the point when there is growing confidence in the teaching of geography, when more is known about the importance of a geographical education and when standards have been shown to be rising, the geography curriculum has suffered from yet more change and new debate about its status. Like the other curriculum subjects facing time reductions, modifications and the effect of the ongoing mantra of literacy and numeracy, geography appears to be marginalized and devalued. Guidance to OFSTED Inspectors (1998a) now indicates that the non-core subjects should merely add up to a 'worthwhile experience' and relaxes the need to grade and report overall on attainment. Nevertheless, geography is still required to be taught. At this time, it is vital that appropriate, informed decisions are taken about what is to be retained, and celebrated in terms of achievement, in both the short and the longer term. The changes in the content of geography during the period 1991–98 for pupils between seven and eleven years of age are summarized in Table 6.2.

Teaching through skills, places and themes is still at the heart of geographical learning and the subject is, rightly, seen as one in which literacy, numeracy and ICT skills can be powerfully developed. Time reductions have led to 'prioritizing', 'combining' or 'reducing' the curriculum content (QCA, 1998c). Inevitably schools will make choices based upon their levels of curriculum expertise, existing practice, their resources and their sense of their strengths and successes. There is some evidence, at the early stages of this 'deregulation', that much is being left to individual teachers to teach what they can whilst they introduce the literacy and numeracy strategies. At some stage a whole-school approach will be needed to review exactly what is being taught across all year groups in a school. The following checklist highlights the kind of debate which needs to take place in order to review the geography curriculum:

A checklist of key elements in a review of the geography curriculum

- Is there a balanced, integrated approach to the teaching of skills, places and themes?
- Are the studies supported by fieldwork and practical approaches?

Table 6.2   Changes in geography for seven- to eleven-year-olds, 1991-98

Order: 1991 Range of Studies	Order: 1995 Range of Studies	QCA further reductions
Places • the local area • contrasting UK locality • locality in an economically developing country • locality in a European Community country • the home region	*Places* • the local area • an area in the UK • an area from Africa, Asia (not Japan) or South or Central America	There is no longer the requirement to teach the full programmes of study. Schools can:- *Prioritise* Retain the 3 places and 4 themes but give priority to selected parts
Themes • environmental geography • weather and climate • river and seas • landforms • animals, plants and soil • human geography	*Themes* • rivers • weather • settlement • environmental change	*Combine* Select parts of themes to be studied and combine them with a locality study *Reduce* Teach fewer places or themes e.g. 2 rather than 3 localities or an overall narrower range of content.

- Have wider world locality studies been retained as an essential part of the curriculum?

- Do the studies continue to support environmental awareness?

- Is planning for ICT, numeracy and literacy included within the geographical work?

- Is the resulting curriculum seen to support the pupils' spiritual, moral, social and cultural development?

- Do the new schemes of work ensure progression and continuity across the key stage?

As a result of using the above checklist, one school decided to strengthen its cross-curricular links and 'combine' the teaching of skills common to history and geography in a local history study with eleven-year-old children. The theme was 'change', in particular noting the rapid development of an inner city area as a result of the coming of the railway line in late Victorian times. This involved fieldwork in the local area and the use of secondary source materials such as photographs, census data, street directories and early maps. The children's geographical learning included:

- using their mapping skills to build up a picture of the growth of their settlement

- thinking about the strengths and weaknesses of very early maps as a source of evidence

- drawing map overlays to communicate information, including current land-use details

- undertaking surveys of a range of views about improving the local environment

- finding out about and responding to the local council's proposals for redevelopment.

Pupils used ICT to store, analyse and display some of their work. Literacy Hour sessions used examples from documents and the formal language of local borough proposals to support the teaching of reading comprehension of non-fiction text. The curriculum makes sense and is relevant when approached in this kind of way.

The subject knowledge of teachers

The single most effective way of improving standards in primary geography would be to improve teachers' subject knowledge and competence in geography teaching (OFSTED, 1998d). It goes without saying that schools need detailed schemes of work and coherent curriculum planning which identifies progression in geographical ideas and skills. They also need appropriate high-quality resources to support lessons. The development of model teaching schemes to cover National Curriculum requirements has been well promoted by local education authorities and most recently by the QCA (1998b). These re-emphasize the importance of fieldwork, the enquiry process and the use of practical approaches as well as outlining progression and continuity of content coverage, skills, knowledge and understanding. A short guidance leaflet produced by SCAA (1997) highlights the key features of good geography teaching, for older primary children, in order to:

- make geographical work exciting, interesting and relevant to children's lives

- use an enquiring, questioning approach to work and encourage children to ask and answer questions

- use real places at a range of scales to illustrate work on places and themes
- make good use of children's own experiences (e.g. holidays, family links) in studying other places
- give children opportunities to learn about other lifestyles and cultures
- introduce children to a wide range of appropriate geographical vocabulary
- involve children in a range of teaching, learning and assessment activities; for example, fieldwork, discussion and using IT as well as written tasks
- monitor children's progress, assess their work regularly and provide helpful feedback.

Assessment

The issue of assessment and recording is particularly relevant given that it is described as being unsatisfactory in geography in half of the primary schools inspected (OFSTED, 1998a). This is a higher proportion than in most other subjects. Improving methods of assessment is clearly related to coherent curriculum planning and to teachers being sure of why and when particular recording and assessment strategies are to be used. Opportunities to do this in geography may arise from:

- general observations
- reviews of written work
- oral work
- group activities
- fieldwork
- images and perceptions developed through concept-mapping and brainstorming before the unit of study begins
- self-assessment by the children, at the end of the unit of work
- drawing and interpreting freehand maps and using published maps
- focused activity using photographs, pictures, atlas, globe.

Information and communications technology

The National Curriculum requires that each foundation subject should provide appropriate content for children's use of information and communications technology. There is tremendous potential for this in the geography curriculum. Many teachers already make confident use of television, video, film and photography to support their work. Some of the rich possibilities for using computers and the recent information and communications technologies have yet to be fully explored and incorporated. ICT should be an integral part of the subject and opportunities for its use planned into schemes of work. There are a number of ways in which ICT can be used to stimulate and facilitate children's geographical learning, whilst also providing opportunities to enhance their ICT skills. A whole range of geographical evidence can be collected during fieldwork in the environment. This might include traffic counts, land-use surveys, questionnaires and interviews. Additionally, secondary sources might include the census, timetables and maps. Where this information is statistical, or a collection of facts about a locality, a database can be created. Computers can help children to

• store information
• analyse and categorize information
• search for specific answers
• present information.

Sensing equipment, such as that used for recording weather conditions, can be used to monitor aspects of the environment. Where the information is in narrative form, providing descriptions, personal views, responses, or first-hand accounts, the use of word-processing facilities and multimedia presentations offers various opportunities for well-designed visual presentations. Computers can also help with the development of mapping skills through the use of adventure games and simulations. Finally, there is the whole area opened up by email and the world wide web. Sites show, for instance, the progress of a hurricane, the eruption of a volcano, or the day-to-day life of children in other countries. Interactive maps can be used to allow closer and closer inspection of a chosen location or the live coverage of the earth from space.

Conclusion

Over the last ten years, geography has emerged in primary schools as a subject in its own right, having previously been very often subsumed into general 'project' work, the humanities or environmental studies curricula. The argument for linkages is still very strong, but so too is the case for subject distinctiveness.

- Geography has its own skills, knowledge and understanding appropriate for children between the ages of seven and eleven. At the same time it promotes positive attitudes and values across the full range of spiritual, social, moral and cultural development.

- Geography is a subject which is in harmony with children's natural curiosity and psychological outlook about their place in the world now and in the future.

- Geography teaching provides an excellent context in which literacy, numeracy and ICT skills can be learnt and practised as well as a way of fostering links with science, history and other subjects.

It is a subject which has developed considerably in recent years and in which standards are continuing to improve. Having spent a decade confirming what should be taught in geography, training teachers in the appropriate enquiry-based methods of teaching the subject and providing resources, it seems dysfunctional to dismantle the curriculum in an *ad hoc* way. In a recent QCA survey, three out of five schools reported that geography had been the worst victim in the competition for teaching time during the first term of the implementation of new curriculum guidance in the non-core subjects (QCA, 1998d).

A reinstatement of geography's place in the curriculum is needed. Geography makes a crucial contribution to the development of children's thinking and to their values. Thorough and detailed planning will show clearly that there are many overlapping and powerful contexts for geographical learning to be developed alongside the core and other subjects of the curriculum. As the world shrinks with faster and easier travel, and instantaneous electronic communication systems, it would be ironic, indeed, if the next generation of children were to grow up devoid of a sense of place.

Further reading

Carter, Roger (ed.) (1998) *Handbook of Primary Geography*. Sheffield: The Geographical Association. A comprehensive recent and very relevant account of all of the facets of primary geography from teaching and learning to managing and planning the geography curriculum.

Scoffham, S. (ed.) (1998) *Primary Sources: Research Findings in Primary Geography*. Sheffield: The Geographical Association. An excellent résumé of research into key aspects of children's geographical thinking and development. Topics range from geographical vocabulary to mapping and environmental awareness themes.

7

History: Making Connections

Caroline Heal

The vicarious experience that is acquired in learning history stimulates imagination and extends the learner's conception of what it is to be human, and therefore of what he or she is and might become.

(Lee, 1984: 13)

Introduction

This chapter argues for the importance of history as a subject in the curriculum for older primary children. The argument is based on a discussion of the nature of history and the special contribution it makes to the development of the knowledge, understanding and skills needed for life in the twenty-first century. Some of the issues and controversy that are inevitably associated with curriculum design in history are explored. Finally, the chapter suggests that in the curriculum for seven- to eleven-year-olds, history's place is in a productive relationship with the other subjects of the curriculum, but that careful consideration must be given to these relationships if the integrity of history as a discipline is to be preserved. However, it is thinking about the curriculum as a whole and the contribution of each subject to a coherent and engaging experience for children that gives some clues to the way forward in shaping a curriculum for the future.

Learning history

To emphasize the importance of history, the eminent historian Arthur Marwick conjured a world in which no one knew any history:

Imagination boggles, because it is only through knowledge of its history that a society can have knowledge of itself. As a man without

memory and self-knowledge is a man adrift, so a society without memory (or more correctly, without recollection) and self-knowledge would
be a society adrift.

(Marwick, 1970: 15)

It is surely a science-fiction horror to imagine such a world of individual and collective amnesia. We each need to know something of
our history to know who we are. This sense of identity is not unitary;
it consists of 'identities', individual and shared. Each of us has a
unique personal identity but this is nested within a range of other
social identities shared with others, for instance, as a member of a
family, of a community, of a cultural group, a nation perhaps, and
(hopefully) of a global community. Many factors will have a bearing
at any one time on the strength of the sense of these overlapping identities, but without a sense of 'history' none of it is possible. This is
just as true for children as they grow as it is for adults and under-
lines the necessity of historical understanding as a vital kind of human
sense-making.

Young children, growing and developing a sense of themselves,
learn first to recognize the familiar sights and sounds of family car-
ers and home. The child's vital sense of personal security depends on
this. Memory is the significant attribute. The immediate past is
remembered and children talk about it with the people around them.
These 'stories' (recollections) of the past are augmented by other stories from a past of which the child is not part; some of these stories
will construct for the child the history of the family. They also begin
to hear stories about the past from other sources and of the wider
community. The range and content of these stories will depend on the
cultures in which the child moves.

As children (and adults) grow older, frameworks develop through
which these narratives of the past are connected to each other in complex ways. It is not, of course, a process that is ever static or complete
either, since one of the intriguing things about interpretations of the
past is that they are just that – *re*constructions from a particular van-
tage point. Moreover, we still know very little about the way mental
frameworks develop in relation to ideas about time and the past. The
contribution of research to our understanding of how ideas about history grow will be discussed later in the chapter.

It is to be expected, therefore, that history has a secure place in the
school curriculum. It is endorsed because it offers induction into a
sense of a shared past. All societies attach a value to the collective
past, however defined, and want the new generation to be inducted
into it.

The impact of the millennium

It is a commonplace to observe that we all learnt and continue to learn history (and other things) from many sources other than through participation in a formal curriculum. Interpretations of the past flood in, solicited and unsolicited. The media offers us many 'constructions' of the past and present, and the critical consumer must distinguish what to accept as fact and what as fiction. We know that young children develop active and critical approaches to what they see, for instance, on television (Buckingham, 1993) but while these skills are developing the potential for misinterpretation can be great.

Alongside this, the 'time' business is booming. There are many indications that our collective interest in the past continues to grow. The volume of commercial publications, the sale of 'historical' books, the numbers of visitors to museums, galleries and historic sites, especially the number of child visitors, are all testimony to this. As the range, variety and ingenuity of interpretations burgeon and exhibitions and displays are made more interactive and child friendly, and as new technologies are applied in ever more creative ways, so younger visitors are drawn in and interests are engaged. The fascination with family genealogy and local history continues to grow. A casual inspection of the television listings shows several programmes every day that reflect and contribute to the interest in history; there is a dedicated television channel and web sites proliferate.

In addition, the turn not just of the century but of the millennium has sharpened this interest. All human societies mark the passing of time, calibrating it in various ways. The Christian calendar has gained a certain universal relevance within the global economy, and the millennium moment seems to sit on the cusp of the past and the future. Time seems to be moving faster, and the millennium threatens to become a media mania that will engulf us all. Merchandising the past is profitable as never before.

It is inevitable that the turn of the millennium will be associated with an explosion in the volume of reviews and commentaries on the past and speculations about the future. Some of these will be serious and scholarly, many will not. Some of the attempts to summarize and to encapsulate will be instructive but many will also simplify and distort. Some will be simply irresponsible. The dangers of 'dumbing down' and reducing the study of history to soap operas in period costume or to comic strip and theme park history are obvious. The advent of the Internet has loosened the constraints on authorship and on the distribution of information and ideas. It remains to be seen what the overall effect of this will be. The historians of the future will, in due course, develop their views.

It is significant in this context to speculate about what young children make of the millennium. Even the youngest of their teachers has a life-span that roots their current sense of themselves in the 1980s and 1990s. In a few years time, the children's own personal memory span will hardly penetrate back into the twentieth century and by the time they are in their teens the twenty-first century will be well under way and the twentieth century will be history. This is the stuff of popular journalism to be sure, but the incantations of 'past' and 'future' are powerful magic and it is hard to imagine that there is anyone, child or adult, whose perceptions of time passing as the twentieth century turns to the twenty-first are not affected.

History in the school curriculum

History has a secure, though clearly not undisputed, place in the school curriculum. The responsibility of the school is to honour the children's entitlement to a planned curriculum for history which will be more carefully orchestrated than the somewhat haphazard education in history that happens outside the school. In addition, the rationale for the school curriculum for history is broader than a simple induction into a shared past. So what are the principles that have governed the development of the history curriculum in the primary school? Some of these are related to an extended view of what history is.

The word 'history' is used in (at least) two ways. Everyday usage tends to the idea that history and the past are the same thing – as if history were (in some uncomplicated way) everything that happened in the past. However, the other more reflective usage of the idea of history is that it is the 'stories' that we tell ourselves about the past, and this view lays emphasis on history as *reconstruction* and introduces implicitly the idea of the story-teller, and a range of important issues about the process of story construction – issues about where the stories come from, who constructs them, for what purposes – and most importantly, opens up the possibility that they can be evaluated by others on the basis of the claims they make to be truthful in some way. This way of looking at history has two outcomes. Firstly, it makes problematic the choice of the stories to be included, i.e. the selection of content of the history curriculum. Secondly, in seeing history as a process of story construction or 'interpretation', it introduces the importance of the skills and special methods of enquiry of the historian.

The issue of the relationship that should exist between content knowledge and process skills is, of course, a familiar one which affected several subject constituencies as they attempted to thrash out a conceptual framework within which to set requirements for a National Curriculum for England and Wales. At its most absurd, this argument took the form of a tussle between the then Secretary of State for Education and the History Curriculum Working Group about whether the word 'knowledge' should appear in the specification of the attainment targets. In an attempt to explain its thinking on this matter the Working Group carefully distinguished among:

- *knowledge as 'information'*: the basic facts – for example, in history, events, places, dates and names

- *knowledge as 'understanding'*: the facts studied in relation to other facts and evidence about them, and placed in an explanatory framework which enables their significance to be perceived (and)

- *knowledge as 'content'*: the subject matter of study – for example, in history, a period or theme. (DES, 1990: 7)

It steadfastly declined to specify 'information' or 'content' in the attainment target, and instead emphasized 'knowledge as understanding'.

> Without understanding, history is reduced to parrot learning and assessment to a parlour memory game ... In the study of history the essential objective must be the acquisition of knowledge as understanding. It is that understanding which provides the frame of reference within which the items of information, the historical facts, find their place and meaning.
>
> (DES, 1990: 7)

The selection of content

The issue here is that the selection of content is never a neutral enterprise, and choices reflect the priorities of those with the power to choose. The act of selection prioritizes some content over some other.

So should the history curriculum for England, say, reflect British history, European history or 'world' history; 'English' history or the history of the constituencies of the United Kingdom? What emphasis should be put on local or regional or national histories? Should a 'patch' approach be adopted that looks at periods in history, or an approach favouring 'themes', such as 'houses and homes' or 'writing and printing' through which a much longer time period can be studied? If it is to be periods, which should be chosen; if themes, which are most significant? What weight should be attached to the argument that the legacy of Ancient Greece for western Europe is so great that it cannot be omitted? How should the histories of the different cultural groups that make up the population of our schools be reflected?

The compromise reached specified a series of study-units to reflect a balance of local (to the pupils in each school), British, European and non-European history. It was also suggested that a balance between political, economic, technological and scientific, social and religious, and cultural and aesthetic dimensions (the PESC formula, DES 1990: 16) should be maintained in the treatments of the topics chosen.

Furthermore, in tackling the question of the selection of content, the Working Group identified the general characteristics that the study of history should aim to develop, following the work of Her Majesty's Inspectorate (DES, 1985a: 2–4). In identifying a sense of chronology and time, an appreciation of continuity and change, and an understanding of cause and effect in human affairs they placed the strongest emphasis on the 'second order' concepts that define the essential nature of historical knowledge.

History's concern with the temporal dimension puts 'chronology' at the heart of things. Understanding the sequence of events is a forerunner to understanding the nature of the links between events and possible 'explanations' for them. It is this historical explanation that is one of the more difficult challenges that young children must attempt. Identifying continuity – noticing what stays the same – is more difficult than noticing change, and change itself may be slow and gradual or sudden and dramatic. Understanding the nature of cause and effect is perhaps the greatest challenge of all. In particular, young children have difficulty in distinguishing between 'intentions' and 'causes', often believing that things happen because people want them to. In addition, they sometimes over-generalize what they are learning about the nature of evidence and seem to believe that the causes of events can be excavated from under the ground like archaeological remains! An ability to achieve in any of these respects may depend on the particular substantive historical material with which the child is engaging. All this makes the assessment of progression in learning in history a most elusive enterprise.

The skills and methods of history

The most pronounced shift in recent years has been a reformulation of the study of history to include an introduction to the process skills of history and this has given central place to the importance of interrogating 'evidence' in supporting historical claims. This approach was embodied in the influential Schools Council History Project (1976), later renamed The Schools History Project, which has been referred to as 'the most significant and beneficial influence on the learning of history and the raising of its standards to emerge this century' (Slater, 1989: 2).

However, this shift has not been unopposed and the vigorous debates which intensified during the 1980s and 1990s received a great deal of public exposure, coming to a head during the preparation of the specifications for the National Curriculum for History (DES, 1989b; 1990) and through its subsequent revisions (DFE, 1995b). The contentious issues were several and the arguments extremely heated, especially in the form in which they appeared in pamphleteering from supporters of the New Right (Deuchar, 1989) and in the national press. Stephen Ball has described the construction of a 'discourse of derision' (1990) during this period, as high-profile opponents of the 'new history' challenged and condemned the consolidation of change in the new national frameworks. Robert Phillips has charted the course of these debates in his book *History Teaching, Nationhood and the State* (1998) which should be essential reading for anyone wishing to gain a perspective on this period of conflict over the teaching of history.

The challenge of the design of the school curriculum for history raises many issues. A model of the curriculum that does no more than outline the historical 'content' – the 'stories' to which young learners must be exposed – has come to be seen as flawed. The present emphasis is on developing in children the ability to engage in historical enquiry, to apply reasoning processes to historical questions and to understand and emulate the research skills of the historian – to think rather than merely to remember.

The development of historical empathy has also been singled out as an important additional skill to be developed by a curriculum for history. The concept of 'empathy' as a goal for children's learning has also been a source of conflict, as some critics have argued that children were being encouraged to believe that they could occupy the shoes of historical figures and 'imagine' what they felt or how they were motivated and that this promoted a comparative disregard for historical evidence as the basis for making historical claims. Others have argued that 'empathy' is a necessary skill, not least because it helps us to appreciate that people who lived at other times and holding to very different ideas and beliefs, nevertheless had reasons for the things they thought and did and it is part of the purpose of the study of history to try to understand those reasons. This 'rational understanding' of people in the past, it is argued, is an important goal of history (Shemilt, 1984: 44).

The development of the National Curriculum for History managed to side-step much of the controversy and took the remarkable step of giving a special prominence to the notion of 'interpretation'. In doing this the History Working Group explicitly sided with those who had voiced concerns that a centrally determined curriculum had the potential to be manipulated for political gain. 'Many people have expressed deep concern that school history will be used as propaganda; that governments of one political hue or another will try to subvert it for the purpose of indoctrination or social engineering' (DES, 1990: 11).

Subsidiary questions, more related to pedagogy, have also exercised curriculum designers. If content can be agreed, are there any developmental considerations that should influence decisions? Are some topics more suitable for younger children? Is the Tudor period more accessible than the Victorian era? Do the arguments for teaching history in chronological order outweigh the argument that starting with yesterday and working backwards is more compatible with what we know about how young children learn? Teachers have been able to discuss these issues and develop approaches in the light of their local circumstances.

The contribution of research

Rather than over-specifying very detailed content, the history curriculum emphasizes the series of second-order concepts such as chronology, change and continuity, and cause and effect as the principal concepts that identify history as a subject.

It is instructive to note that not much is known about the development of children's ideas in relation to these second-order concepts. Inferences have been drawn from much of the early research into children's understanding that suggested that concepts of history and time were very difficult for young children to grasp, but Hoodless points out that we must bring the historian's awareness of 'context' to the interpretation of this. Research since the 1970s presents a much more optimistic view of children's capabilities, and in any case both our aims and our methods in teaching history have been transformed since that time (Hoodless, 1996: 10).

Much research into the development of children's understanding of history has focused on isolated skills such as the ability to sequence objects or pictures, or familiarity with particular substantive concepts such as 'monarchy', 'kinship' or 'revolution'. The search for criteria against which to identify progression in children's learning in history has been a challenging one. The most ambitious research to date which has a focus on these second-order concepts is the CHATA project (Concepts of History and Teaching Approaches at Key Stages 2 and 3) which is investigating, in its first phase, the progression in children's ideas about the nature of historical enquiry and their ability to mount an historical explanation, between the ages of seven and fourteen. This builds on previous work by the same researchers which suggests that it is possible to detect a development in, for instance, children's ability to make sense of people's actions in the past (Lee, Dickenson and Ashby, 1996).

Some children, for instance, when confronting human actions in the past simply deny that such things are amenable to explanation; this is an undeveloped response. Other children offer explanations, but do so by reconceptualizing actions entirely in their own terms and often dismiss actions with which they cannot identify as stupid or morally inferior. Another stage is when explanations for action are evinced by reference to generalized stereotypes; people are presumed to have done things because of their social position or role. The next stage is one at which children begin to grasp that they need to think about the context and circumstances of the particular individuals whose actions they are trying to explain. Finally, as development towards more sophisticated historical understanding progresses, children begin to understand that the ways in which people in the past saw the world were different from our own ways of seeing. Individual actions need to be interpreted, not only by taking account of individual circumstances, but also by interpreting them within the context of the beliefs, values, customs and habits of the time. This is a comparatively sophisticated level of understanding.

These are difficult moves for young children to make but in this and in other areas of the research there is evidence that some younger children are further along the developmental continuum than some older children. This is a tentative model on which the CHATA project is attempting to build. It clearly has implications for the teaching of history in the primary school, and confirms the importance of continued research into the nature of 'progression' in children's understanding.

The future for the curriculum for history

The decade since the National Curriculum was established has seen many and substantial gains in the quality of history teaching and learning. The developments in history teaching to a large extent mirror the developments in geography (see Chapter 6). Reports from Her Majesty's Inspectorate prior to 1989 catalogued a dismal picture (DES, 1989c) but over the past ten years substantial improvement has been achieved (OFSTED, 1998b). History teaching in primary schools has benefited from teachers' enthusiasm for it and from the energetic support that has come from interaction with, in particular, museums and galleries and with publishers working to support the history curriculum.

As is the case so often, we are now presented simultaneously with a constraint and an opportunity. Recent government modifications to the statutory requirements for six foundation subjects are having an impact on history teaching which is very negative. Yet the prospect presented by a future of possible revision of the National Curriculum suggests exciting opportunities beyond the year 2000.

The final part of this chapter explores some of the issues that arise when history is considered as part of a whole curriculum for older primary children. The emphasis in recent years in the United Kingdom has been to turn away from models of the curriculum that invoke ideas of synthesis or integration of subjects on the grounds that the basis for these models is flawed (Alexander, 1988: 61). Recent emphasis has been on the articulation of clear learning intentions at every stage of the curriculum planning process and the intentions are drawn, in the main, from separate 'subject' specifications. This is underpinned by a renewed interest in delineating what is essential to each subject.

However, at the same time, interest is developing in exploring the purposeful relationships between subjects (Murphy *et al.*, 1995) and the similarities and differences in aspects of knowledge, procedures and skills. This is a new and positive move that may hold the key to restructuring a curriculum for older primary children that combines attention to the importance of attainment in the basic skills but also offers them the prospect of a rich and coherent educational experience.

This endeavour is supported by the current debates about the nature and necessity of command of 'subject knowledge' in the professional repertoire of teachers and by a better understanding of the complicated and subtle relationship between this 'subject' knowledge and the associated pedagogic knowledge (Shulman, 1987). As attention is focused on the level of teachers' subject knowledge in each area of the curriculum required to be taught and as teachers review the quality of their subject knowledge in preparation for teaching a new topic, so it becomes more possible to make really informed judgements about when and whether cross-curriculum links can *authentically* be made.

In the present circumstances, when the curriculum remains overloaded, it is vitally important to distinguish between occasions where the gains from bringing subjects together are worthwhile but only minor, and occasions where the gains are major and the subject connections to be made are fundamental and most productive for children's learning. Other instances where the learning intentions are actually in conflict with each other must obviously be recognized and avoided.

We should not be satisfied with superficial connections between subjects; for instance, finding ways to use historical material in the Literacy Hour or getting children to make art work related to the past. Something much more fundamental is required that is rooted in the particular contributions connections between subjects can make towards a deepening understanding of the human condition. All the subject disciplines have developed in an attempt to mount coherent explanations of the world. Children can be introduced to the way that they do this, not just implicitly by being introduced to the subjects themselves but by being encouraged to explore the links explicitly. Bruner (1966) argues persuasively that the central and defining ideas within a subject can be encountered meaningfully by young learners if the material is made accessible through the skill of the teacher.

There are special opportunities in history teaching and learning to encounter the history of *big ideas* and these should be maximized for the older children in the primary school. The story of the changes in accepted ideas about the nature of the universe, for instance, makes connections between history and the development of science in a way that reflects humankind's changing view of itself – its cosmology. A study of the development of writing and printing over time (now, sadly, excised from the National Curriculum) opens up the prospect of the study of the development of human communication systems which offers rich possibilities for developing vital knowledge about language.

We need new models of curriculum that are not examples of subject parochialism, that 'see' curriculum development in broader terms. Robin Alexander (1997) has called for the curriculum revisions for the year 2000 to reflect the courage to contemplate a radical revision that goes back to asking fundamental questions about what an educated citizen of the twenty-first century should know, understand and be able to do. His model echoes with references to the 'cross-curriculum themes' (NCC, 1990). I want to endorse this model but add to it the idea that it is the attempt to theorize the links between subjects that can enrich it. After all, why shouldn't children be asked to think about the nature of knowledge itself? Such an entitlement is in the spirit of the new emphasis on getting children to think about their own learning. If we are asking children to think about learning and building up their metacognitive skills, then an aspect of this is to encourage them to think about knowledge and how it changes. History is especially powerful in enabling them to do this. Curriculum subjects are becoming insulated from each other in ways that are not helpful in stimulating debate.

History and an education for politically literate young citizens

Finally, we should use our history teaching to encourage young people to develop opinions about issues of the day and to understand the possibilities for participation in communities of all sizes, in the knowledge that individual actions have an impact however small and that taken together they can make a difference. This may not be a central aim of the history curriculum but it has that possibility. History is about how individuals and groups make decisions and take action in ways that influence events. It is about (in part) the nature of power. It can introduce the concepts of production and manufacture and distribution of goods and services, profit and loss, employment and unemployment, the beginnings of the study of economics. In this way it links together education for economic awareness and for citizenship. It is history that has the potential to support these endeavours – a particular and unifying possibility.

Further reading

Claire, H. (1996) *Reclaiming our Pasts: Equality and Diversity in the Primary History Curriculum*. Stoke-on-Trent: Trentham Books Ltd. Hilary Claire has written an outstanding book to support primary teachers in developing an inclusive curriculum for history. Accessible and scholarly, this thought-provoking and practical book discusses the possibilities for teaching history across the primary school, raising general issues, supporting the development of history subject knowledge and describing teaching approaches and resource materials.

Dickinson, A., Ashby, R. and Lee, P. (1997) 'Just another emperor': understanding action in the past, *International Journal of Educational Research*, Vol. 27, No. 3, pp, 233–44. This article describes some of the research findings from project CHATA (Concepts of History and Teaching Approaches at Key Stages 2 and 3), a large-scale ESRC-funded research project based at the Institute of Education, University of London, which seeks to investigate the development of children's ideas about historical explanation and the processes of historical enquiry.

Phillips, R. (1998) *History Teaching, Nationhood and the State: A Study in Educational Politics*. London: Cassell. This is a fascinating book which examines the politics of the 'great history debate' from its origins in the 1960s and 1970s to the great explosion of interest that accompanied the development of a National Curriculum for History. Phillips concentrates his analysis on the issue of nationality as the 'most dynamic and contested concept of the period' (p. 7).

8

Design and Technology: Creative Problem-Solving

Rob Johnsey

We all act as designers and technologists in our personal lives. The ability to design and use technical knowledge is a universal attribute of people everywhere, as characteristic of human society as the use of language.

(Baynes, 1992: 19)

Introduction

We are all problem-solvers from the day we are born. Pre-school children use the skills of design and technology in solving their own everyday problems and this process continues into adult life. Those who enjoy creative cookery, designing a new garden or constructing a scale model from matchsticks are all involved in design and technology. Design and technology is about understanding and improving the made world and an important function of the primary school curriculum is to ensure that pupils become better and better at doing just that.

Design and technology is one of the most important and exciting subjects to be taught in the primary school. As a new subject it evolved fairly erratically during the first half of the 1990s, but it has gradually gained a confident rationale for its inclusion in the curriculum for the new millennium. A range of primary school subjects has, in the past, encompassed the elements which are essential to design and technology. Art, craft and design, home economics, the use of construction kits and communication skills have always featured strongly and in the 1980s some schools began to adopt a problem-solving approach towards subjects such as science and mathematics. Today through design and technology these elements are drawn together into a coherent whole which is greater than the sum of its parts.

Society as a whole tends to misunderstand the essence of design and technology. Often the media reports the work of 'scientists' when it more accurately reflects the achievements of those who *use* science, mathematics and art, craft and design ideas in solving problems. These are in fact the technologists, engineers, inventors and crafts people who create new solutions to solve practical problems encountered by a wide range of people.

What is design and technology?

Design and technology is a newly developing subject and most readers will not have studied it when, as pupils, they attended primary school. Most will, therefore, lack the firm understanding which a long history of curriculum experience and development brings. We need to spend some time in clarifying our thoughts about the distinctive characteristics of the subject before we can consider how it might best be taught.

The current view of design and technology incorporates a number of key features:

- *Design and technology is about improving things for people.* Design and technology is a pursuit 'that results in improvement (for someone) in the made world' (Kimbell *et al.*, 1991: 3).

- *Design and technology is about designing and making high-quality products.* 'At the heart of design and technology is the activity of designing and making, which involves the creative process that combines the intellectual with practical skills through purposeful practical activities' (DATA, 1997: 7).

- *Design and technology is about the application of skills and knowledge.* 'Design and technology offers opportunities for children to develop their capability to create high-quality products through combining their designing and making skills with knowledge and understanding' (QCA, 1998a: 5).

- *Design and technology should prepare pupils for citizenship.* 'Design and technology offers opportunities for children to explore values and attitudes to the made world and how we live and work within it' (QCA, 1998a: 5).

- *Learning in design and technology will involve children in a range of activities.* Children will carry out 'design-and-make' assignments;

focused tasks which support the assignment and evaluative tasks in which other people's designs and solutions are examined.

Design and technology, then, is much more than a simple craft lesson in which pupils are able to become proficient in their model-making skills. The subject involves a particular style of creative thinking and reasoning alongside a need to empathize with the needs of others. It provides a vocabulary of practical ideas and experiences which will enable the pupil to face a wide range of challenges within the made world. Pupils will learn transferable strategies for evaluating products which they will encounter as both consumers and manufacturers. They will need to develop a variety of ways of communicating their ideas graphically, orally and in the written form. Furthermore, in developing their knowledge and understanding to support their designing and making, they will be reinforcing skills and knowledge learnt elsewhere.

Teaching design and technology in the primary school requires a great deal of thought and careful planning. The educational benefits, however, are well worth it and are often reflected in the enthusiastic response gained from children as they set about their designing and making tasks.

Design and technology and the primary school

Design and technology has a number of major attributes which it can offer the primary curriculum. The subject is about solving problems and satisfying the needs of people, and so it will provide an essential skill for life. People who can solve practical problems with confidence as well as appreciate why and how others have done so, will be more suited to living in an increasingly technological society. Furthermore, the creative and expressive nature of the subject will develop a part of each child's intellect which may not otherwise be stretched. Children who have previously not enjoyed success in school may display an unexpected talent for design and technology.

The subject can be used as a highly effective vehicle for learning in other curriculum areas. Children will be expected to combine the skills and knowledge they have gained across the curriculum with their designing and making skills to solve practical problems. The primary school, with its relatively flexible modes of curriculum delivery and integrated learning approaches, is the ideal place for developing and supporting learning in the subject.

Learning in design and technology

In coming to appreciate the complexity of design and technology, it is helpful to think in terms of three areas of understanding within the subject. These are:

- procedural skills
- knowledge and understanding
- practical capability.

Learning how best to go about designing and making a product to solve a problem lies at the heart of the subject. The skills that are used and, just as importantly, the way in which these are employed could be described as the *procedural skills* of design and technology. These are often described as the designing and making skills. While these are listed in the National Curriculum documents (DE/Welsh Office, 1995), very little is said about how these skills might be interwoven to achieve an end. While we know that pupils should generate ideas for a product, evaluate their ideas as they proceed and plan ahead, it becomes a much harder task to teach children how best to combine these skills in an effective way.

Knowledge and understanding in a subject is something with which teachers are much more familiar. All National Curriculum subjects have an associated body of skills and concepts listed under this heading. In design and technology these areas are well defined and draw heavily on areas associated with science. Design and technology, however, is unique in the fact that it must draw upon knowledge and understanding from other subjects of the curriculum (especially science, maths, art and information and communications technology (ICT)) to achieve its purposes.

The concept of *practical capability* is one which is unique to design and technology. It is concerned with how pupils use materials and tools to create products, but also how the practical problems that often arise during construction are overcome. Those who are capable, in a practical sense, will have gained the confidence to tackle new problems and will have built up a vocabulary of transferable practical ideas to help them do this. Some practical capability will be required in carrying out a science investigation or creating a piece of work in art but it is in design and technology that this skill becomes an essential ingredient. Teachers need to have practical capability in the classroom. If, for instance, a child seeks help because the wheels on a vehicle keep falling off then the teacher must have some grasp of the issues involved in order to guide the child towards a solution.

Learning procedures in design and technology

If teachers are to encourage children to become better and better at designing and making then they need to know more about what this involves. The question we must ask is, 'When someone is solving problems by designing and making, what skills and techniques do they use and how are these skills combined into a procedure?' There have been many views on this *process of design* or *problem-solving process*, often suggesting that there is a single way in which to proceed. Indeed the structure of this design process often dictated the way in which the subject was taught in schools. It was common for half-termly projects to be arranged to follow the steps in this process. It was a powerful and convenient message for teachers. Teach children to solve problems by following 'the process' and they will then be able to transfer this skill to any other situation. Simplified flow diagrams were often produced to describe the process.

Unfortunately, there were flaws in this approach because, of course, no two practical problems are exactly the same. When the context changes the methods for finding a solution may also change. A much more flexible view was needed in order to describe what is involved in any design-and-make task and to provide guidance in how to teach procedural skills. The Assessment of Performance Unit (APU) were charged with devising assessment methods for design and technology in both primary and secondary education and reported in 1991 (Kimbell *et al.*, 1991). Teachers will know that if you have to assess children's achievement in a subject, it is fundamental to understand the nature of that subject. The APU devised a new image of what it means to design and make something (Figure 8.1).

The group suggested that when confronted with a problem the first thing that happens is that you get some vague idea about how to solve it. This is often followed by doing something about this idea 'outside the head'. This might be a comment you make to a friend, a small sketch, or fiddling with some construction materials. This in turn will give you more ideas which are less vague and again this leads to more action outside the head. This process continues until you have completed the task, your ideas becoming more and more refined as you proceed. This is a useful and more flexible image to have in mind when teaching pupils. It is, however, a theoretical image based on hypothetical situations.

Since the APU report there have been a number of studies which focused on the observation of children as they carried out design-and-make assignments in classroom settings (Hennessy and McCormick,

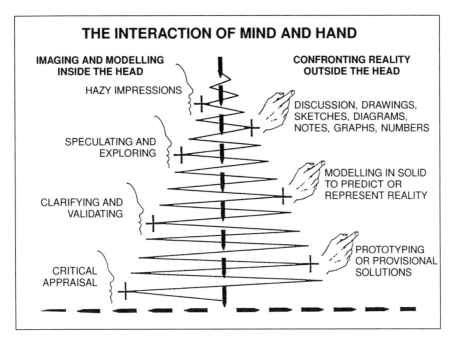

Fig. 8.1 The Assessment of Performance Unit model for the process of design. *Source:* Kimbell *et al.*, 1991.

1994; Johnsey, 1995; Kimbell, 1994; McCormick *et al.*, 1996). The author can provide a number of graphic images of individual children as they carry out a simple design and make task with a partner.

The graph in Figure 8.2 provides a snapshot of a complete task lasting about an hour and is similar to a number of others made from observations of primary-aged children. It describes one child as she made a jack-in-the-box toy for a friend. The separate procedural skills are listed on the vertical axis and the bold horizontal lines indicate when these skills were being displayed on a video recording of the task. The list of procedural skills was developed from a wide range of publications in which they are described together with the results of classroom observations. They are:

- identifying needs, opportunities and potential for design-related tasks

- investigating and exploring the design context

- clarifying the implications of the design task

- specifying criteria for judging the outcome of the design task

- carrying out research into the problem and its solution

The Curriculum for 7–11 year olds

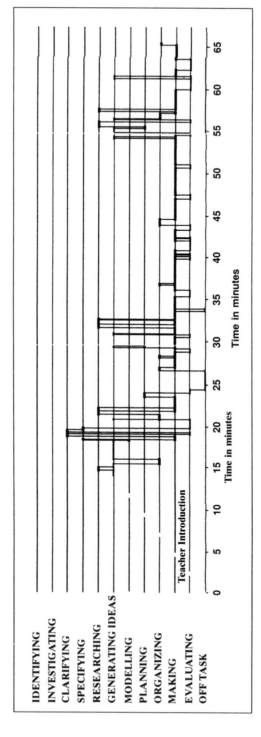

Fig. 8.2 The procedural skills used by one child during a single design-and-make task

- generating ideas for a product which will provide a solution

- modelling ideas – in discussions, as drawings, as mock-ups, etc.

- planning the making of a product

- organizing resources

- making the product

- evaluating various aspects of the process and the product as work proceeds.

The lessons learnt from these observations are that designing and making is a messy business which cannot be adequately described in terms of sequential stages. Each response to a task is different and depends on the context within which the response is made. While the list of procedural skills was found to be appropriate to all the tasks, the order and duration of their use varied from task to task. However, the following patterns were identified:

- Making was clearly a dominant activity but alongside this was the evaluating skill, frequently used to check that the making was proceeding well.

- Many of the skills which are described as designing skills were used whenever necessary and not only at the beginning of the task.

- The making activity was often the vehicle for further designing and thus the two types of skill dovetailed throughout the task.

It is concluded from this study that a simplified 'flow diagram' description of designing and making does not fit reality and therefore an alternative view is required. A model is proposed (Johnsey, 1998) which is considered to be of greater use to teachers who ask 'How should we teach children to become better and better in the procedures of design and technology?'

The design and technology tool box

If we can imagine encouraging children to build a tool box of skills which they are able to use in different ways, depending on the contexts within which they are working, then this can replace the idea of teaching a fixed method. If we also teach children the best ways to combine the use of these tools to suit the situations they find themselves in, then they will have a flexible way of approaching quite different problems. Part of the tool box might look like Figure 8.3.

Fig. 8.3 Part of the toolbox for design and technology

Each section of the box represents a procedural skill or design-and-make skill. The teacher's job is to help children add to the skills that they already possess in each section, and then to provide experiences in which they learn the best ways to combine these skills to solve a problem. For instance, a teacher may teach a child a new way of modelling ideas. This may involve learning how to create card 'mock-ups' before making the resolved idea; for example, a pop-up greeting card. This 'tool' may then be of benefit in future situations; for instance, when the child wants to try out ideas in paper for a decorative fabric hat.

If we imagine a child moving from one section of the 'tool box' to another, selecting the most appropriate tool for the particular problem, perhaps revisiting a section when necessary and moving in an order that is considered to be appropriate, then we begin to understand how problems can be solved in a creative way by different individuals in diverse situations. The teacher's role in the process also becomes clearer.

The teacher should help the child add to the collection of 'tools' in a progressive way, and provide experiences in which the child learns to combine the 'tools' in the most appropriate ways in relation to the nature and context of the design task.

This idea is further developed in the section on the planning of suitable design and technology activities.

The procedural skills

Teachers need to be able to identify the design and technology procedural skills and to know how and when to teach these to children. The following skills may be observed at various times during a design-and-make task, will not necessarily occur in any fixed order and may be revisited many times.

Identifying the potential for a design activity and clarifying the meaning and implications of the design task

Pupils who are identifying the potential for a design activity will be observing and exploring a context in which design tasks might arise. At the same time they will be actively involved in suggesting problems which might be solved, the needs which might be met or the opportunities for designing and making.

Specifying the requirements and purpose of the outcome

Pupils who are specifying the requirements of the product they will make will be creating the criteria by which they, or others, might judge how successful they have been. The specification will be a statement, recorded or otherwise, of the objectives for the task. Specifying what should be achieved in a design-and-make task is closely related to the way it is evaluated at all stages during its construction. If a clear set of purposes is established for a designed product then evaluation involves establishing whether those purposes have been achieved or not.

Evaluating

Pupils will be evaluating when they make assessments and checks and/or carry out tests on their work and their procedures during the task and when it is finished. The evaluation may be subjective or objective or a combination of both. They may ask the opinion of others, or rely solely on their own judgement. Pupils can best evaluate their finished product by referring to the design specifications which they developed earlier. Each criterion can be evaluated in turn and a decision made as to whether the criteria have been met.

Carrying out design-related research into the problem and its solution

Pupils carrying out design-related research will be gathering information and developing skills which might support the design task. Research can take place at any time after a design task has been defined but it will most likely be carried out in the early stages. The research might include focused tasks or evaluative tasks which involve learning how to use a particular tool, carrying out a consumer survey, obtaining advice from an expert or evaluating products made by others. The concept of design-related research could be seen as a vital link with areas of knowledge and understanding across the primary curriculum and thus could be exploited for cross-curricular links.

Generating and communicating ideas for outcomes

At some point in the design process pupils will need to consider what they might make in order to satisfy the design task. They will be generating ideas for outcomes. There are a number of ways in which these ideas might be communicated, one of which is the design drawing.

Modelling and communicating design ideas

Children will be modelling their ideas if they form some representation of the product they might make and can manipulate this so as to explore and develop its potential. This 'representation' can take many forms, such as hand gestures to show the form of something, a discussion about what something might be like, a drawing or painting or the forming of the raw materials available into temporary arrangements.

Planning

Children (and adults) often plan what to do as they proceed rather than at the beginning of a task. Sometimes this is appropriate but at other times a forward plan can be of benefit. Plans might include the order in which to do things, who does what in a co-operative activity or how to allocate the time available to various tasks.

Making

Pupils will be making when they are involved in using tools, materials and components to produce an outcome. Skills such as drawing or marking, cutting and joining will be used in making. The act of making might include the modification and improvement of a product through the process of its construction.

Knowledge and understanding

There are some areas of knowledge and understanding that design and technology has claimed as its own, but inevitably children will draw upon a much wider range of ideas from across the curriculum as they design and make products.

In design and technology children should:

- develop a technological literacy by learning the 'how and why' of designed and made products

- learn about a range of tools, materials and components and consider the properties which make them suitable for making certain products

- learn about structures and objects which employ structural principles and how these ideas might be used in construction

- learn about control technology in which products are controlled by the use of mechanisms, the use of electrical circuits, or both

- learn about issues of health and safety and the correct use of vocabulary

- use the knowledge and understanding they gain from other areas of the curriculum, especially science, mathematics, art and ICT.

Gaining technological literacy

Children will benefit from learning how others have solved problems in the past, both from their point of view as designers and makers and as consumers of technological products and their effects. Where children can learn about the designs of others in order to enhance their own work this will provide added incentive to do so. For example, a child who is intending to design and make a new school bag, using textiles, will be interested in how other bags have been designed and produced in the past.

Materials and components

Most children will be familiar with using materials such as paper, card and plastics at home. In school they will gain further experience in using materials such as wood strips, sheet plastic, food ingredients and textiles. Components such as construction kit pieces, batteries and bulbs will be used during construction but will probably be reclaimed after the project has been completed.

Tools such as pencils, rulers and scissors will already be familiar to most children, whereas more specialized tools like a junior hacksaw, a sharp cutting knife or a needle and thread will be introduced when appropriate for the task. It will be the teacher's job to teach the safe use of all tools as part of the children's design-related research phase.

Children will learn intuitively about the properties of some of the materials of construction as they use these to make products. However, in some instances the teacher may organize a more formal investigation into the properties of materials, perhaps as part of a related science investigation. In science children may learn that some materials such as aluminium foil conduct electricity, and this may be of use when children design electrical switches. In design and technology the teacher may demonstrate how corrugated card has a kind of 'grain' (as wood does) which gives it more strength in one direction, and how this should be considered when constructing a model.

Much can be learned about the properties of materials when evaluating and investigating products made by others. Children might consider the relative weight, strength and waterproof properties of the components of an umbrella. They may explore the different materials used in a torch and how each is related to its particular purpose.

Structures and structural principles

Most people's understanding of structure is that it is to do with large constructions such as bridges, towers and buildings, and the way these stand up. This is the way the word is used in everyday language, but this is not, in fact, appropriate for primary school design and technology. Structures are, in fact, all around us in the simple products we use; from the humble ball-point pen to the furniture we sit on and work at. The hole-punch employs structural principles to achieve its task and these very same principles can be used by primary school children in the products they make. Children need to learn the structural principles from the world that surrounds them in order to be able to construct strong and stable products for themselves. All primary school teachers are familiar with the child who has worked hard to make a model using classroom materials such as card and glue, only to find that it has a number of points of weakness which result in its collapse. A knowledge of structural principles will enhance a child's practical capability, that is, the ability to solve small-scale constructional problems as they arise.

There are some key questions about structures which teachers should be familiar with if they are to support their pupils' making activities. These are:

- What does strength mean?
- How can products be made stronger?
- How can products be made more stable?

When we use the word 'strength' we often mean different things at different times. An object can be strong if:

- it will not bend, i.e. it is rigid
- it will not break, fracture, tear, come apart or snap
- it will not stretch or deform
- it will not wear away.

A strong model vehicle chassis is designed not to bend or come apart. A strong fabric purse will not wear away or tear. A strong plastic carrier bag will not stretch out of shape. It is important when discussing strength with children to be clear about what kind of strength we mean.

Designed products can be made stronger in four basic ways:

- the material used can be changed to something which is inherently stronger (steel is stronger than the same amount of wood)

- more of the same material can be added (a thicker plank will support a person who walks over it)

- the existing material can be shaped to provide strength (corrugated card is stronger than the equivalent three flat sheets of paper)

- the components of a structure can be arranged in 'strong shapes' (the struts in an electricity pylon are arranged in triangles to provide rigidity to the overall structure).

The stability of a product is another key feature which may or may not depend on its strength. A product is stable if, after being disturbed, it returns to its original position. A tall stool is more easily knocked over and is less stable than a shorter one. A motorway sign is made more stable in a strong wind by adding heavy sandbags to its legs. A human being will achieve the same effect on a rocking ship by spreading legs apart and lowering the body. The boat itself may have a ballasted keel which enables the boat to return to an upright postion in heavy seas. Products which ought to be rigid but in fact deform and then spring back into shape could also be described as unstable.

Children can make their models more stable by employing some or all of the methods described above. Providing a wider base for a tall product will give it more stability. Equally, lowering the centre of gravity of the product, perhaps by increasing the weight of the base, will achieve the same effect. Building rigidity into a product will also increase stability.

Control technology using mechanisms and electrical circuits

Control technology involves ensuring the products that children make, do what is required of them. Thus a puppet which is controlled by strings or a motor-driven toy will use some of the basic principles of control technology. In the primary school, products can be controlled by using mechanisms or electrical circuits or both.

A simple pop-up greetings card uses mechanisms such as sliders and levers to achieve its effect. Wheels and axles are the simple mechanisms used when making model vehicles. A jack-in-the-box may pop up by using pneumatics or a pull-along toy may employ cams for its wheels. Strings and rods can be used to pull or push parts of a model, while belts and pulleys can be used to drive a turning part on a toy. Gears from a construction kit may be used to speed up or slow down motion, especially if an electric motor is used.

Simple mechanisms are all around us and children can learn a lot from studying those in the home, in the school and in some instances in industry. A simple can-opener has a lever mechanism which enables it to grip the side of the can. It also employs a handle and toothed wheel which runs around the rim and cuts off the lid. These mechanisms have to be proportioned and positioned to achieve the control required. The bicycle is a wonderful visual aid which can be brought into the classroom to explore control technology. Levers are used to control the steering, the gear changes and the brakes. The pedal system provides an example of a crank and the chain and sprockets behave similarly to a belt and pulley system for controlling the speed of rotation of the wheel. Often there are control cables running between the brake levers and brake pads and the lights on the bicycle may be controlled by batteries and a switch or a dynamo. In many instances, one kind of movement is transformed into a different kind as when the up-and-down movement of the legs is changed into a rotation of the chainwheel.

In the primary school, children will be using batteries, bulbs, motors and buzzers to make circuits which are controlled by switches. Children can design and make the kind of switch they want using aluminium foil, paper fasteners or drawing pins and wires. Switches may range from those operated by hand to those which connect when stepped upon or tilted, and will often involve the use of simple mechanisms such as levers. Children will combine their knowledge of control by mechanisms and electrical circuits when they design and make an electric-powered vehicle or a moving fairground ride powered by a motor and a belt-and-pulley system.

The use of information and communications technology (ICT)

ICT is often, but not always, a useful tool to be used by children as they design and make products. The two subjects share the same title word, 'technology', and were originally described in the same National Curriculum document. Furthermore in some countries the phrase *technology* will refer only to ICT and not include designing and making. This may have given rise to some confusion in the past.

ICT is a sophisticated electronic tool which should be used to service learning and achievement in other curriculum subjects. It is so sophisticated that its intricacies often need to be taught directly to children, and it therefore has taken on the status of a curriculum subject. However, ICT should be no more associated with design and technology than it is with all other subjects.

There are a number of ICT applications which are particularly helpful to design and technology. In the primary school, art and graphics software can support children as they communicate their ideas and also graphic printouts may be used as part of the finished product. Word processors and databases may be used to execute and analyse consumer questionnaires. Sensing equipment may be used as a part of a science investigation which would support a design task especially in evaluating the effectiveness of selected products. Computer control technology can be used to drive the models children make, using simple motors. Buzzers, bulbs and sensors can be used to trigger an action in these models. Information which may be of value in the design task can be gained via a CD-ROM or by using the Internet. Computer-aided design and manufacture can be used in primary schools at a fairly simple level to achieve significant learning outcomes.

Practical capability

Practical capability is closely related to the skill of making. Teachers can help children to gain a repertoire of strategies for solving problems by providing a wide range of practical experiences. The following is a list of areas in which capability can be gained:

- basic construction – marking, cutting and shaping, joining and fixing materials and components

- making things stand up in a stable way

- enabling parts of a product to turn

- making hinges, pivots and fulcrums

- creating strong frameworks – shell frames, strut frames, sheet frames

- employing finishing techniques

- making wheeled vehicles

- harnessing sources of energy for driving models

- using textiles in construction

- controlling movement.

Within each area there are manipulative skills and 'tricks of the trade' to be learnt that can be employed when the right moment arrives. The list outlined above is not exhaustive but can provide a useful checklist for schools that have developed their own schemes of work for design and technology. This would ensure that children receive a balance of practical capability skills while in the primary school.

The complete 'tool box'

If we now take the tool box analogy further, we must include a part of the box for knowledge and understanding and one for practical capability. The complete tool box is presented in Figure 8.4. Each of the three layers will be divided into a number of sections. The child who achieves capability in design and technology will have a wide range of 'tools' at her disposal and know how to combine these to achieve a successful result.

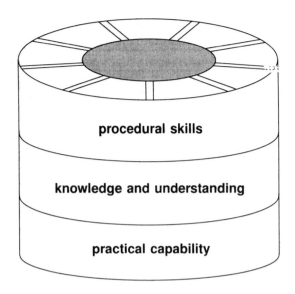

Fig. 8.4 The complete toolbox for design and technology

Values and attitudes in design and technology

This chapter, so far, has demonstrated that there is more to design and technology than making a product.

> Products are developed in response to needs, desires or opportunities. Decisions that influence design, production processes or marketing are made by balancing technical, economic, aesthetic, environmental and moral criteria. These value judgements are also influenced by personal, social and cultural priorities.
>
> (DfEE, 1995b)

Design and technology provides opportunities to make decisions and personal choices. These choices will be influenced by the person or persons for whom the product is made (even if this turns out to be the actual designer). Products made in the classroom may have an effect on the environment as well as the consumer, and this becomes a factor which may have an effect on the decision-making. The value judgements that children make as they design and make enable them to develop a greater awareness of the world around them and the people who live in it. These judgements are not solely part of the design and technology curriculum but form part of the general education of all children. Education for citizenship and spiritual, moral, social and cultural education should be the concern of all schools.

In design and technology children can be encouraged to:

- consider the needs of others in designing and making a product

- consider the impact on society in general of the product that will be made

- consider the effect on the environment of using the product, making the product or disposing of the product

- take into account the feelings and beliefs of themselves as designers and makers.

Children can further the knowledge gained in the above activities by considering what went on in the minds of other designers as they made their own products. It may be in a history lesson, for instance, that children can use and reinforce their understanding of designing and making by examining historical artefacts. Children's knowledge of what it means to be a designer would be put to good use in a science lesson in which an invention such as the first flying machine was being considered. The advantage of examining products made in the past is that their impact on people and the environment can also be explored in retrospect. This will provide children with an insight into how their own products may have unexpected effects in the future.

Conclusion

There is no doubt that design and technology in the primary school is an exciting subject. Many children react very positively to the creative and practical nature of the work. At the same time, the subject can stretch them intellectually if it is planned well. Excitement, too, is felt by the teachers who have embraced this evolving subject. Part of its attraction is knowing that we are all at the forefront of its development. The issue of technological literacy has yet to be fully explored as is the contribution the subject can make to citizenship and a child's moral, spiritual and aesthetic understanding. Some areas of knowledge and understanding such as structures and the use of ICT are still waiting to be developed more fully so that these are taught appropriately.

In many ways primary teachers have been given a difficult task with little support. The practical nature of the subject requires special consideration when resourcing a school and organizing the work in the classroom. Furthermore, the procedural nature of much of the work means that teachers have found difficulty in grasping the essence of the subject in the same way that they struggle sometimes with science investigative work.

The support for teachers is growing in the form of high-quality publications and a strong national association (the Design and Technology Association, DATA). Unfortunately, the most effective forms of support – in-service training, advisory teachers working in the classroom and compulsory initial teacher training in the subject – are being removed or reduced in many instances. This is happening just when major initiatives such as an exemplar National Scheme of Work has been published (QCA, 1998a) and we gain a revised National Curriculum for the new millennium.

Nevertheless, the view ahead is a positive one. England and Wales are being acknowledged as world leaders in primary design and technology and a growing body of educational research is beginning to inform practice in schools. The future for the subject, however, lies in the classroom where, in many instances, teachers are taking the subject forward with relish. These teachers intuitively know how much their children are benefiting, when they witness the pleasure and commitment that the children display in their work as they become involved in creating their own solutions to the problems in the world around them.

Further reading

Design and Technology Association (1996) *The Design and Technology Primary Co-ordinator's File*. Wellesbourne: DATA. Contains sections on all aspects of a design and technology co-ordinator's role as well as background information on the knowledge and understanding required to teach the subject.

Design and Technology Association (1998) *Primary School-Based INSET Manual for Design and Technology Volumes I and II*. Wellesbourne: DATA. Written for those who provide in-service training in the subject; contains useful sections on all aspects of the subject especially background knowledge for teachers on structures and control technology.

Design and Technology Association (1999) *DATA Helpsheets for the National Exemplar Scheme of Work*. Wellesbourne: DATA. These provide support for schools who use Units of Work from the National Exemplar Schemes of Work for design and technology.

Kimbell, R., Stables,K. and Green, R. (1996) *Understanding Practice in Design and Technology*. Buckingham: Open University Press. A useful discussion of current issues affecting design and technology.

School Curriculum and Assessment Authority (1995) *Key Stages 1 and 2 Design and Technology – The New Requirements*. London: SCAA. This contains some very down-to-earth advice and suggestions which have remained useful and relevant throughout the many curriculum changes of the past decade.

9

Information and Communications Technology: A Learning Revolution?

Sarah Martyn

Many of us have argued that IT can be more than a workhorse, it has the potential to change our patterns of thinking and our ways of knowing.

(Underwood, 1994: 8)

Introduction

This chapter recognizes the impact of information and communications technology (ICT) on the world beyond the classroom and considers this in relationship to the promotion of learning in the primary school, with particular reference to children between seven and eleven years of age. As one of the most powerful tools ever invented, ICT offers huge potential to enhance children's learning. It has the power to motivate children, to assist them with many labour-intensive aspects of learning and to encourage the development of thinking in a variety of mind-changing ways.

The demands that the use of ICT in the classroom make on primary teachers' subject knowledge will be addressed. This discussion will embrace a consideration of the level needed of information technology (IT) (technical competence and confidence), which is the crucial prerequisite for teachers to be able to exploit ICT, in order to stimulate, to challenge and to extend the horizons of their pupils.

What is information and communications technology?

Information and communications technology refers to the purposeful use of technological tools to support pupils' learning across a range of subjects. It is distinct from (but reliant upon) information technology, which involves the development of technical skills and understanding across a range of electronic equipment and computer applications. The development of pupils' IT capability provides the foundation upon which effective use of ICT can be built. This sequence of skill acquisition and competence has relevance, also, for primary teachers and their capabilities, and this aspect will be discussed later in the chapter. The National Curriculum for Information Technology (DfEE, 1995a) provides a framework for the development of IT skills.

Why use ICT in the primary classroom?

The world beyond the classroom, and particularly in the place of work, has been irreversibly changed by information and communications technology. It is likely that every occupation in the future will require capability with many aspects of ICT. Commentators have argued that, in order to maximize opportunities for living productive and fulfilling lives, children must be provided with both effective tuition in the use of ICT from an early age (DfEE, 1997b) and the opportunity to appreciate its potential.

As adults, we can only guess at what that world will be like in the next century when today's primary pupils will be earning their livings (or not!) in the economists' predicted 30–40–30 ratio of wealth versus despair, with only 30% of the population in the affluent category (Kress, 1997). Secure employment for the whole of an individual's working life is unlikely to be an option in the future. Children may have to face retraining several times during their adult lives. The concept of a 'learning society', where citizens are free to access further education and training through the use of ICT, is currently intriguing academics, educationalists and policy-makers. (DfEE, 1997a; Wragg, 1997).

The government is actively promoting an 'online' society, one in which people can engage in 'life-long learning' and 'distance learning'. This further strengthens the argument that the current school curriculum *must* promote the development of the skills, knowledge and understanding required to enable pupils to make appropriate, self-motivated use of these powerful resources to support their current and future learning.

Issues regarding equality of opportunity have also been highlighted as a further reason for the use of ICT in the classroom. Pupils without access to ICT at home, particularly computer-based applications, risk being seriously disadvantaged in their attempts to secure employment if schools fail in their responsibility to provide opportunities for them to acquire IT skills and relevant experience in the use of technological tools. On both pragmatic and moral grounds, the future employment prospects of pupils provide valid and important arguments for the inclusion of ICT in every primary classroom.

The main focus of this chapter is the accumulating research evidence (Crook, 1994; Light, 1993; Underwood and Underwood, 1990; Underwood and Brown, 1997) which suggests that there is tremendous potential for ICT to support and enhance teaching and learning in the classroom. Clearly, if tools exist that are of benefit to pupils' learning, teachers have a responsibility to ensure that they are effectively and enthusiastically incorporated and utilized within their teaching.

ICT and teaching and learning in the primary classroom

Teachers now have access to, and are familiar with, some or all of the following 'high and low' technological tools:

- radio
- television: terrestrial, satellite and digital
- tape recorders
- CD players
- video players
- calculators
- cameras – analogue, digital and video
- computers
- scanners
- fax machines
- the world wide web
- the Internet
- email
- video-conferencing.

Each of these tools can be used by primary teachers to enhance their teaching and to support the learning of their pupils in various ways.

Technology to motivate engagement with learning

Children at the end of the twentieth century are habituated to high levels of stimulation. They are visually aware, steeped in a culture of rapidly moving images and sound, a synaesthesia of sensory experience. Many pre-school children are technologically adept with videos, tape recorders and computer games. The primary school needs to capitalize on this technically sophisticated cultural background, and to embrace it in order to be in sympathy with the child's perception of the world and means of responding to it. The stimulating presentation of ideas and information is not just desirable, it is *essential* if we are to engage today's child in the learning needed for the world of tomorrow.

Television, videos, radio and tape recorders are long-established vehicles for learning within primary classrooms. Whilst effective in certain situations, such technology nonetheless restricts the presentation of content to those ways chosen by the programme directors. Newer technologies, such as CD-ROMs are able to communicate information in more versatile ways, and importantly, give children and teachers greater control over its use.

The open-ended, content-free applications allow imaginative, creative work to be carried out, with children in charge of the outcome and with high levels of stimulation generated by the different presentational components. Modelling and control applications allow the exploration of a number of different avenues through permitting children to conduct their own questioning in order to satisfy curiosity, in addition to building on what is already known. Pupils' realize, particularly in programming, that their mistakes, if critically discussed, can be useful in order to get closer to a solution to a problem. The empowerment these programs offer learners is immensely motivating through their ability to be in control and to work towards a desired outcome. Applications that engage pupils include:

Electronic stories

The publication of high-quality, interactive electronic stories, although still in its infancy, promises to provide reading material with the potential to motivate even the most reluctant reader. The interactive nature of its content, the inclusion of animation and the possibilities created by the addition of audio elements, engages and sustains attention.

Games

One of the strengths of the format for adventure games, according to McFarlane (1997), is the ability to engage children's interest and commitment through repeated involvement with a 'compelling fictional world'. It is the meaningful contexts of computer games and simulations that helps to arouse curiosity and to motivate, in addition to their fast-moving, appealing presentation.

Information retrieval

Applications involving children in independent and successful information retrieval for a given purpose are positively reinforcing in supporting learning.

ICT to support a variety of individual learning styles

Gardner (1993) proposes a theory of preferred learning styles. Individuals, he claims, are a rich amalgamation of different intellectual aptitudes and competences, each person possessing a variety of strengths and dispositions. All are important, and he does not suggest that the separate intelligences should be seen as hierarchical. The various dispositions are merely different and require, in Gardner's view, to be developed appropriately.

> There is persuasive evidence for the existence of several relatively autonomous human intellectual competences or 'frames of mind'. The exact nature of each intellectual frame has not so far been satisfactorily established, nor has the precise number been fixed. But the conviction is that there exists at least some intelligences, and that these are relatively independent of one another.
>
> (Gardner, 1993, cited in Scottish Consultative Council on the curriculum, 1996: 5)

He concludes that, given intelligence is not a unitary concept, that it is multi-faceted in nature, ideas and information presented via a single mode or approach are likely to facilitate understanding for some, but not all, pupils. Providing diverse experiences for pupils through a range of different presentational styles increases the possibility of developing understanding via a preferred learning route or style, and might also improve aptitude to learn through other channels for all children.

Multimedia software of quality presents ideas and information through the simultaneous use of a range of different media. Consider, for example, the benefits of following up a practical science activity on forces with exploration of multimedia software that reinforces the concepts through a combination of images, audio, video extracts, animations, question and answer opportunities and chances to engage in the modelling of investigations into forces on screen.

The use of ICT to release thinking capacity
Word processing

Information and communications technology as a tool offers the opportunity to allow pupils to experience the thought-enhancing effect of written language. Jeni Riley (see Chapter 1) cites Donaldson (1993) regarding the potential to develop thinking achieved through the translation of 'inner speech' into permanent text. A written text invites an individual to consider, to develop and to perfect thoughts. This use of the cultural tool of written language to order systematically and to expand thought can be hugely facilitated with a text-processing application on a computer.

The major benefits of ICT in assisting pupils with their writing, particularly those in the later years of primary school, cannot be underestimated. On achievement of mastery of the appropriate technical skills of word processing and typing (even to a very basic level), text-processing applications can ease the laborious, physical or manual aspects of drafting and redrafting. The child is thus free to concentrate on the rigorous, exacting task of composition. Composing can be undertaken detached from concerns about other elements of writing, such as spelling and punctuation. Teacher-supported use of text-processing packages can be of significant value to children who have the ideas but who get disheartened because they are still struggling with the mechanics of writing.

A second draft can be achieved through painless amendment. Spelling and punctuation should be handled in the penultimate draft of the text production, relegating transcriptional skills to their rightful place in the creative process. A built-in thesaurus provides an opportunity to extend vocabulary and to improve further the quality of written work. Less able children are liberated from the continuous spoken word to written word translation problems through the appropriate use of computer word banks, and those with handwriting difficulties can escape (on occasions) from the production of unappealing, poorly written, final drafts.

At another level of computer sophistication, multimedia authoring allows pupils to combine text, graphics, audio, video, animation and music to produce impressive on-screen electronic books. For a child to produce work of high technical quality can be motivating and confidence boosting.

Data-handling packages

Making sense of information gathered through the course of investigative work is an important aspect of learning in the later years of primary school. ICT allows children to short-circuit the painstaking task of re-presenting the data generated through science, mathematics, history or geography investigations, making it possible to order, analyse, see patterns and trends in and make comparisons between aspects of the data they have collected. This use of ICT is valuable and it mirrors authentic employment of ICT in the workplace. Prior to using a database, a branching database or a spreadsheet application, however, pupils need to have experienced (and understood) all elements of the processes through more traditional methods, in order to appreciate what the computer is going to accomplish on their behalf. Children can only appreciate the advantages of using a data-handling package if they have first experienced the whole sequence of processes involved. Obviously, for learning to occur, the child must be able to interpret, with insight, her own data.

The further manipulation of stored information and data

The capacity to store data on computers in a variety of formats allows older primary pupils to save their information and so have easy access to their work for further exploration, analysis and amendment. Often learning objectives for such tasks are focused on the identification of patterns in data, but the time taken by children to make graphs or tables of data, by hand, can leave little opportunity (or enthusiasm) to explore and analyse the data fully.

Access

Every primary classroom has the potential to offer pupils and teachers access to a vaste store of resources through ICT. This is particularly valuable for those older children whose reading skills are well developed. It is, literally, the equivalent of having the opportunity to use the most up-to-date educational library. Alongside the wealth of information stored now on CD-ROMs, the Internet and world wide web provide ways of obtaining materials from what is effectively an enormous world resource bank, accessible at the click of a mouse, to which more and more material relevant for primary teaching is constantly being added.

Developing thinking and positive attitudes to learning

The last twenty years have seen huge changes in the use of computers in schools. Over this period of time a range of computer applications have been marketed with various claims of their benefit to children's learning, based on different interpretations of what constitutes effective learning.

Originally, 'drill and practice' programs were created specifically to practise basic literacy and numeracy skills or to develop factual knowledge. These applications, designed with a transmission model of learning, envisage the computer as the teacher providing information for the pupil to access. Feedback informs the child on her progress and she works through repetitive exercises until she achieves the learning objective. Whilst these programs can be effective within a limited scope, the value of using such expensive equipment as simply a rote-learning mechanism has been questioned. As McFarlane states, 'Pro-computer educationalists in the UK have always been unhappy with their use for drill and practice exercises . . . this seems a somewhat trivial use of a scarce resource' (1997: 9). Integrated Learning Systems (ILS) are a more sophisticated version of the 'drill and practice' application, which also places the computer in a teaching role, albeit in a more responsive and differentiated way. With this type of software, the intention is that the child learns progressively through engagement with a particular program, to develop systematically the skills and/or knowledge required with some 'scaffolding' support from the computer (Underwood and Brown, 1997). The computer is programmed to assess individual pupils' responses and then provide an appropriate next step. This use, with good reason, is criticized for the limited responses a computer can make to children's input and the ways in which that input is necessarily restricted by both the format of the program and the nature of the tasks with which the children are asked to engage.

Nonetheless, claims have been made that the use of ICT in the primary classroom can enhance learning. Perhaps the difficulty is with the terms 'enhance' and 'learning', and clarification is needed before exploring what evidence there is for such a claim. The fundamental question is – what is it that we want children to learn?

Criticism has been raised about the benefits of teaching facts through information transmission programs in a world where information is now so readily available, stored in a variety of forms in books, on CD-ROM, video and on the Internet, and accessible via fax machine, tele-conferencing and email. Perhaps pupils' time can be more profitably spent in developing skills that would enable them to:

- find, extract and use relevant information from the wide range of sources available

- reflect on data and explore its meaning

- apply what they have learnt to a range of meaningful and productive tasks.

With ever-increasing access to a wide range of information sources, pupils will need to develop critical evaluation skills of both the information and content.

Promoting thinking

Learning is about providing opportunities for pupils to develop ways of thinking that go beyond the recall of facts. ICT is heralded as having great potential as a tool to assist in this cognitive development (Underwood and Underwood, 1990; Wragg, 1997). Research (Independent ICT in Schools Commission, 1997; Whitebread, 1997) indicates that collaborative ICT-based problem-solving tasks involving decision-making adventure games and modelling applications can promote higher-order thinking, through providing exciting, relevant and meaningful opportunities to:

- discuss and debate
- raise questions
- listen to others' points of view and evaluate them
- analyse data
- rationalize decisions
- hypothesize
- predict
- modify ideas.

Wegerif and Scrimshaw (1997) indicate that the use of ICT in context-free problem-solving activities has an important role to play in developing productive classroom talk. It is through the interrogation of challenging situations in which pupils ask 'what would happen if . . . ?' and explore alternative approaches to a given situation, that the intellectual mechanisms mentioned above have been found to be generated. Context-free applications, such as word processing and data-handling packages, also promote opportunities to develop higher-order thinking by allowing children to explore, experiment and be producers, rather than mere consumers. Underwood and Underwood (1990) found that being in control of direction and decision-making within a task, rather than being 'taught' by the computer, had a significant impact on the development of:

- logically sequenced thoughts
- clearly articulated understanding
- developing connections between ideas.

Enhanced learning could be said to have occurred if children have developed ways of thinking that enable them to undertake successive tasks more easily and with greater understanding. Working with programming languages (such as LOGO, designed by Papert, 1981), other modelling and control applications, text processing and creating multimedia publications can all provoke examination and reflection by pupils on their own thought processes. Thinking skills developed during work on such ICT applications have been found to be transferable to more general abstract problem-solving situations in other areas of children's learning.

The interactivity of ICT to promote learning

In recent years, computer software has become increasingly interactive. Programs are now designed to react to a user's input, permitting choice about ways and forms in which ideas and information are communicated and the order in which they are accessed. When interrogating a CD-ROM with this potential, a pupil can make choices about ways in which to explore a chosen line of enquiry. A CD-ROM's presentation of ideas and information can be halted and subjected to re-examination. Links within the text can be taken up, leading to greater clarification and connections being made with other subjects. Children are able to be selective, to build on what they already know and seek enlightenment on what they don't know. The process involves judgements based on understanding, modifications being made in the light of experience. Meaning and purpose drive the thinking and learning.

Learning about distant locations through the use of ICT

As children progress through the primary school, they become increasingly able to cope with thinking, the context of which is distanced from their immediate environment and the 'here and now' of their lives. Recent developments in communications technology have opened up new avenues for achieving this important intellectual task, by offering ways for pupils to explore ideas about the world beyond their local environment. Through web sites and the use of email, pupils can engage in meaningful 'virtual' contact with children living in distant locations. Email facilitates exchanges of information that can make possible comparison of lifestyle, culture and experience and motivation is maintained because of the speed at which responses can be received. Options exist for pupils to become involved in discussion groups to explore and exchange ideas about topics being studied with children in schools around the world. They can pose questions to experts via the world wide web. In the near future, video-conferencing could become a regular opportunity for face-to-face interaction with people from far-off locations. Such links allow pupils to witness important events taking place across the globe as they happen. Horizons will be literally and metaphorically enlarged.

Through simulation software, ICT can give pupils the chance to experience 'virtually' situations that they would not otherwise be able to. They are able, for example, to take a journey inside the human body, take a guided tour of a location in India or explore Ancient Egypt. This powerful capacity of ICT assists the development of geographical concepts such as an understanding of distance and place, the teaching of which previously posed a major challenge in the primary classroom.

Primary teachers and the effective use of ICT?

What is the route and what are the means for children to have their eyes opened to the potential of ICT? What are the current impediments that prevent this happening in every primary classroom?

Developing confidence and competence

It would seem that many primary teachers lack both the confidence and competence in their own grasp of IT and the subsequent use of ICT in the classroom. In 1997, in one-third of primary schools teachers of seven- to eleven-year-olds were considered less than satisfactory in their delivery of the IT National Curriculum (Independent ICT in Schools Commission, 1997). This was due to many teachers' poor IT capability, and the lack of awareness of the huge potential of ICT, as both a support for their teaching and a tool for their pupils' learning. Many teachers lack confidence and competence in the computer-based technologies, and especially the more recently developed ones, such as email and the Internet. A large number of primary staff have little or no training, nor sufficient experience of working with electronic equipment and applications. This inexperience has also been coupled with the lack of a perceived need for ICT. This perception has been compounded by the senior management in primary schools very often not prioritizing ICT as an essential area for development.

One way of addressing this problem is for teachers to be allocated specific time when they can explore and experiment with computer-based technologies and develop an understanding of their benefits as tools to assist their own work. There is a need for every member of a school staff to be computer literate for their own professional purposes. Introducing primary teachers to ways in which ICT can assist them with planning, resourcing, administrative work as well as in their professional development is crucial. One effective way to encourage teachers' personal use of ICT is through an introduction to the Internet and its many advantages.

Teachers can use ICT to:

- keep class information on a database for easy searching and sorting

- create lesson plans and record-keeping pro formas

- create resources using desktop publishing

- develop subject knowledge using CD-ROMs and material from the Internet

- share ideas with other teachers via bulletin boards on the Internet

- enter on-line discussion with other teachers regarding questions related to their work

- make multimedia books for work with groups of pupils during literacy sessions

- use email to communicate with other teachers, colleagues and parents.

Only when the educational workforce is comfortable with IT and able to employ ICT daily in carrying out a range of professional duties will the true value of ICT in the classroom be realized. The small-scale but very successful 'computer and loan scheme' enabling each primary teacher to have access to a lap-top for personal use is to be extended.

The mismatch between the perceived potential of ICT for primary schools and concerns about the effectiveness of the use of technological tools in the classroom has prompted the government's interest in, and increased funding for, improvements. A significant commitment has recently been made to teachers' professional development in ICT. Initiatives (DfEE, 1997a) are under way to upgrade all teachers' skills and levels of competence by the year 2002. To ensure that those entering the profession are well equipped to teach ICT, the Teacher Training Agency has issued the *Initial Teacher Training National Curriculum for the use of Information and Communications Technology in Subject Teaching* (DfEE, 1998b), which sets out stringent standards that must be met by primary teachers in training in order to achieve Qualified Teacher Status. These standards apply to their teaching of ICT in the core subjects and the curriculum areas in which students specialize.

The National Grid for Learning (DfEE, 1997a) has been introduced to enable teachers to make successful use of all available resources. This is just one initiative aimed at 'unlocking the potential' of computers for teachers. Unprecedented opportunities exist for schools to update resources, both material and human, through the provision of new equipment and extra staff training in order to extend and evaluate their curriculum and so place ICT as an integral part of teaching and learning. Skills specific to one type of technology are often transferable to other modes, so once achieved, teachers can make rapid progress, but regular guidance and support from more experienced colleagues will be required, especially in the early days of exploration and experimentation.

Selecting ICT applications

The IT National Curriculum (DfEE, 1995) identifies three broad areas in which IT skills should be developed in the later years of the primary school. Pupils need to explore opportunities to:

- communicate information
- handle information
- use ICT to model and control.

Teachers, therefore, are required to select a range of applications that will enable pupils to develop skills within these areas, whilst using the various applications as tools to support learning across the curriculum. As a starting point, schemes of work should be examined to identify learning objectives across the curriculum that could be supported by ICT. If none seem to exist, the curriculum then needs to be adapted with the use of ICT held clearly in mind.

The key issue, if learning of quality is to occur, is that pupils must be given opportunities to experience the benefits of the judicious use of ICT as a tool – understanding that there are tasks that can be achieved more successfully with ICT, but also recognizing that there are situations where alternative and traditional methods remain more appropriate. Consideration should continue to be given to the levels of pupils' IT capabilities. IT skills develop through usage, opportunity and purpose and must be built on progressively throughout the primary years. They are more likely to be internalized when being used as a means to achieving a relevant goal. The recently published IT scheme of work (DfEE, 1998a) provides a useful framework for developing progression in IT skills and understanding. Activities within the scheme are linked to work in specific subjects.

Resourcing issues

It is the case that much hardware and software in primary schools is out of date. However, with only one PC and a small range of up-to-date software many useful and relevant tasks can be undertaken, especially in small groups. Every pupil in the later years of primary school requires access to, at the very least, the following types of computer-based software, if she is to explore the multi-purposeful use of ICT:

- a text-processing package
- a graphics package
- a data-handling package
- a piece of modelling software
- an adventure game appropriate for the age of the class
- CD-ROMs that support the year group focus
- a multimedia authoring package
- simulation software.

Management and organization of teaching with ICT

It would seem that one of the reasons why 'drill and practice' and ILS were readily accepted by teachers over the last few years, despite there being applications with more far-reaching consequences for learning, is the ease with which they could be incorporated into existing classroom practice. These applications involve pupils in self-sustaining work, thereby leaving teachers free to concentrate on work elsewhere in the classroom. The adoption of computers for open-ended tasks requires direct teacher intervention and therefore much more consideration of the organization of sessions involving them.

Pupils need regular opportunities to experience ICT tools across the range as suggested above. This will involve teachers in making decisions about the most appropriate ways of grouping pupils to meet learning objectives. Experiences should provide for work in pairs and in groups, plus individual exploration and whole-class introduction and discussion. The classroom organization of computer-based ICT work obviously depends on how many computers are available and how many children are being required to work on them. Clearly, the development of computer suites in schools will provide increased access for pupils, but because of the physical dislocation from the learning in the classroom, IT skills alone can be the sole or even main focus of the suites' use. This is a missed opportunity. In addition, in teacher-led collaborative work around a computer, the focus should be on the thinking and any discussion needed to utilize the application, rather than development of keyboard skills. Thus, in an attempt to avoid the separation of IT and ICT, keyboard skills should be developed wherever possible in individual sessions (for instance, in creative writing times), alongside regular teaching input to groups or the whole class.

Conclusion

People have always had to adjust to a changing world. However, the changes that the present generation is now encountering are more far-reaching than ever before. Information and communications technology has already made a dramatic impact; it has altered the ways in which our lives are lived, how we relate to people, to ideas and to the environment.

ICT is not simply a fast-track way of achieving things we can already do, nor are we merely using electronic equipment to organize and reorganize existing information and familiar experiences. ICT enables us to do things that until now we did not know existed to be done. We are able to understand the world in ways we did not think possible through the simultaneous processing of information and images. This capacity poses a challenge to the way we deal with time and space. ICT can change the ways in which we perceive the world and also the ways in which we think about it.

Children live in this world now. They are not just consumers of commercially generated material, they are able to interact with and to take control over the production of the material. We are on the brink of a learning revolution. On this Professor Gunther Kress says:

> We are, it seems, entering a new age of the image, a new age of hieroglyphics; and our school system is not prepared for this at all. Children live in the new world of communication, and on the whole seem to

find little problem with it . . . [It] is essential for humans to understand the world . . . We may want to foster rather than suppress this activity. In the new communicational and economic world, it may well be that all of these [skills] will be essential requirements for culturally, socially, economically, *humanly* productive and fulfilling lives.

(1997: xvii–xviii)

No case has to be made for the inclusion of information and communications technology in the curriculum for older children in the primary school. ICT is self-evidently there, in the prominent position accorded it, due to the full recognition of its power and the negative consequences for individuals and our society if it is not used creatively and with fluency. However, insufficient material resources and under-trained teachers hinder the maximum use of ICT in primary schools. Too many teachers lack sufficient understanding, skills or enthusiasm for the effective employment of ICT in their own lives and classrooms. Too many classrooms are still denied the appropriate technological equipment.

This *cannot* be allowed to continue. Much has been and is being done at national and local levels to improve this state of affairs. Members of the teaching profession neglect the urgency of the situation at their peril, if pupils are not to be relegated to an electronic and digital underclass.

Acknowledgement

Sarah Martyn is grateful to Jeni Riley for support in the production of this chapter.

10

Art: Visual Thinking

Roy Prentice

The sources of artistic action emanate not only from the dream and the vision, nor from the desire to move the senses, nor from the effort to capture the moment and make it magical; artists are also moved by the social character of the society and world in which they live.

(Eisner, 1972: 12)

Introduction

The starting point for this chapter is an acknowledgement that learning in art develops a particular way of demonstrating intelligence. It is argued that to engage in art activity of quality is to participate in an intellectually demanding, rigorous and disciplined form of valued human endeavour, to which, from an early age, everyone should have access. The chapter's main aim is to help teachers clarify their ideas about the purpose, nature and content of a coherent and relevant education in art, for children between the ages of seven and eleven, at the beginning of the twenty-first century. Throughout the chapter, unless otherwise stated, the term 'art' should be interpreted as art, craft and design, and references to artists should also embrace craftspeople and designers.

The wider context

The arts, unlike any other group of subjects in the curriculum, are repeatedly required to justify their existence. Those educators involved in the arts are fully aware of the importance attached to their skills of advocacy. It is recognized that in order to strengthen the position of art in primary schools it is necessary to change the way that the arts in education are perceived by a large number of politicians, policy-makers, parents, administrators, headteachers and teachers. Repeated attempts to achieve a higher profile for the arts, nationally, within the *mainstream* education debate have in recent years fallen short. Progress has been hampered by a cycle of confusions and contradictions that cloud understandings of key issues.

In spite of the sustained efforts of those committed to the development of art in primary education and the introduction, in 1992, of a National Curriculum for Art, the quality of and provision for art in primary schools remains disappointingly uneven. Whilst in some schools and individual classrooms art continues to flourish, it is apparent that it has been relegated to the margins of the curriculum in many schools and thus to the edges of children's lives. These twin concerns – 'unevenness' and 'marginalization' – have been prominent recurring themes in the art education debate over the past thirty years. During this period, whatever the political, social, educational and economic climate of the day, successive arguments in support of art in primary schools were considered by those presenting them to be 'timely'. The present chapter is no exception. The discussion that follows brings more sharply into focus three factors, the combined impact of which will determine the nature and position of art in primary schools beyond the year 2000.

Firstly, from September 1998 the government provided an opportunity, for headteachers who so choose, to 'slim down' the art curriculum available to children between seven and eleven years of age. Art continues to be a compulsory subject of the National Curriculum but it is now the responsibility of each school to decide the level of detail to be taught. Clearly, the growing pressures on headteachers to significantly raise standards of literacy and numeracy are likely to further erode time formerly available for art. This contentious shift in policy was criticized by a key member of the government's School Standards Taskforce, Lord Puttnam (1998). He drew attention to 'the danger of allowing arts education to be marginalized, unnecessarily sacrificed at the altar of numeracy and literacy targets.' The timing of this action was particularly unfortunate. To devalue art in this way during the period in which the National Curriculum as a whole is under review for the year 2000 gives serious cause for concern about the subject's future.

Secondly, a National Curriculum for all courses of initial primary teacher education, based on new and very strictly applied criteria, was also introduced in September 1998 (DfEE, 1998e). These criteria provide the basis on which such courses are funded and inspected and predictably the majority of time is allocated to the teaching of literacy, numeracy, science and information communications technology. For intending teachers of seven- to eleven-year-olds, opportunities to acquire the basic skills and understanding required to teach art have been reduced in many courses and in some removed completely. A recent survey commissioned by the Royal Society of Arts (Rogers, 1998) reveals the seriousness of this situation. By narrowing the educational experience of student teachers it is feared that a cycle of lack of confidence will be perpetuated as far as the teaching of art is concerned.

Thirdly, there is growing awareness within the field that change is needed to ensure art education not only meets the complex demands of the twenty-first century but fosters and channels the creative energy and vision of the children who as adults will shape it. Current orthodoxies are criticized for clinging to a nineteenth-century tradition (Hughes, 1998) and further challenged by those who propose an alternative approach to art education informed by postmodern ideas (Swift and Steers, 1998).

It is essential that the complex interrelationship between these three factors is taken fully into account in any reconceptualization of art in the primary curriculum. In order to reaffirm its value, much more is required than the revisiting of an argument that advocates a return to a (mythical) golden age of art education, however passionately expressed. Writing thirty years ago (Field, 1970: 47) makes the point that, 'Ideas in art education change, develop, become modified, in response to pressure and needs from inside and outside.' Changes in art education at primary school level that have taken place over the past three decades are a reflection of mainly superficial concerns rather than an indication of fundamental shifts in purpose, content and pedagogy.

While the Plowden Report (CACE, 1967: 247) heralded art as 'a form of communication and a means of expression of feelings which ought to permeate the whole curriculum and the whole life of the school', in reality this was rarely achieved. Eleven years later the extent to which reality fell depressingly short of Plowden's aspiration was revealed in a survey undertaken by HMI, *Primary Education in England* (DES, 1978). Wider fears that the arts in education, as a whole, had dropped off the agenda during the period of political positioning, plotting and planning that preceded the introduction of a National Curriculum prompted the influential report, *The Arts in Schools* (Gulbenkian Foundation, 1982). Notwithstanding the 'pockets' in which the arts continue to thrive, largely as a result of committed, inspirational teachers, headteachers and advisers, 'the problems facing the effective provision of arts education in schools ... have been unresolved for at least the last quarter of this century' (Rogers, 1998: 47).

Influences that affect art teaching

As far as the teaching of art is concerned, a number of confusions and contradictions that inhibit its effectiveness can be identified in relation to purpose, content and pedagogy. Sometimes the rationale that underpins the art curriculum lacks clarity. Increasingly art is justified in terms of its instrumental function for the contribution it is claimed it can make to children's learning in higher-status academic subjects, rather than for its intrinsic value. Research evidence shows that such claims rest on somewhat flimsy foundations (Eisner, 1998; NFER, 1998). Further misunderstandings apply to the nature of art, its different forms and functions in different cultures and at different times and the range of processes and procedures involved in making and responding to art. A narrow view of art based exclusively on a western European tradition of painting often informs teaching that overemphasizes the acquisition of practical skills. However, it is not uncommon for such an approach to coexist with ideas about ability in art as having more to do with innate talent and giftedness than with effective teaching. The misapplication of ill-defined concepts that include self-expression, freedom, creativity, imagination, originality and child-art have over the years led many teachers to adopt a non-interventionist attitude towards art activity. Thus it is possible to observe such an approach in one classroom and a highly prescriptive approach in another in the same school.

At the macro level glaring contradictions exist between the government's education policy as it applies to primary schools and teacher education and its highly publicized promotion of a more creative society ('Cool Britannia'). In a newspaper article entitled 'Schools to teach creativity' (*Independent*, 1998a), the Secretary of State for Education declared that, 'children should learn to be creative and artistic in schools.' The article went on to report his establishment of a national advisory committee on creativity. It is ironic that the announcement of this initiative was made three weeks after the government's decision to allow a narrowing of the primary curriculum to place more emphasis on English and mathematics.

The large contribution to the economy made by the so-called 'creative industries', embracing music, film, architecture, advertising and design businesses, is widely recognized. It is estimated that this sector generates an annual turnover of £50 billion and employs around one million people (Smith, 1998). The business world acknowledges the need to employ creative individuals and 'the creative professions will be the fastest growing source of new jobs between now and 2006' (*Independent*, 1998b). As part of its drive to strengthen the economy through developments in this field, the government set up a Creative Industries Task Force with a membership that spans the worlds of politicians, civil servants and arts and design professionals. Sadly there is a dislocation between the ideas explored at this level and the vision of the future they support, and an understanding of the kind of school curriculum through which such a vision is most likely to be realized.

The basis on which the discussion continues relies on an acceptance that 'art is a learning activity' (Field, 1973: 157) and that it is vital to maintain a dynamic relationship between art and art education. Only then is it possible to argue from a position of intellectual integrity with confidence and conviction for art to be taken seriously in the curriculum *for its own sake*; for the particular contribution it makes as another way of knowing – a way of knowing through which a different mode of demonstrating intelligence is developed based on the articulation of a visual language. In this way art can be seen to communicate through a symbol system that is different from, but of equal importance to, the symbol systems of other subjects into which children are initiated. It is in support of this argument that the concept of multiple intelligences (Gardner, 1993) has been warmly received by art educators although in practice Gardner's work seems to have had little impact on schools in the UK.

Learning in art

As Field (1970: 4) makes clear, 'By education in art I mean primarily an understanding of art as a mode of organising experience.' However, art is not merely a non-verbal means through which to communicate ideas that already exist; it is a powerful way of generating and exploring new ideas and feelings, of giving them visual form and in the process making personally significant meaning. It is the way in which this meaning-making comes about through engagement in practical work and through informed personal responses to diverse works of art that is central to learning in art. Regular opportunities for children to learn in this way are essential if they are to develop a wide repertoire of human intelligence. This point is reaffirmed by Gentle who says:

Art is profoundly important for the full growth of the individual because it deals with ideas, feelings and experiences visually and develops a language of visual, tactile and spatial responses which create and sustain images. To develop an intelligence about visual matters is not a haphazard affair any more than it is with other languages. Experiences of looking, and interpreting, analysing and solving problems, visualising and finding appropriate forms and images for our feelings and ideas are all capable of refinement and enrichment through teaching.

(Gentle, 1985: 96)

Some fundamental issues embedded in Gentle's comments deserve to be highlighted here as they provide an excellent starting point for teachers to share with colleagues their ideas about the teaching of art. Firstly, there is an acceptance that art has the power to change people. Through their active engagement in art experiences of quality children develop their potential in ways that they would otherwise be denied. The concept of lived-through experience is central to learning in art. Each individual's understanding is created and re-created through a creative process of construction and reconstruction of events. Secondly, learning of this experiential kind involves the whole person, it embraces in a holistic way thinking and feeling, perceiving and doing. Thirdly, it is recognized that both makers and consumers of art need to be initiated into a framework within which the language of art operates as a means of communication and expression. Fourthly, there is a clear expectation that art can and should be taught, and taught well, in every primary school and that for teaching to be effective a positive form of teacher intervention is necessary. This form of teacher expectation is restated as a characteristic of 'good teaching in primary schools', when in art 'pupils receive focused support from the teacher' (OFSTED, 1998e: 7).

Key features of an art curriculum

Through their engagement in a structured programme of broad-based and imaginatively resourced art activities, children acquire, develop, extend and have opportunities to apply a range of skills, knowledge and understanding. In order to help teachers gain a better grasp of what this means in practice, so that they feel better equipped to provide 'focused support' for pupils, four fundamental but interdependent features of an art curriculum are addressed. They are: investigating, making, responding and reflecting.

Investigating

Art makes available to children a richness of opportunity to investigate ideas and feelings in relation to an external world of things seen and an internal world of things imagined. An intelligent use of the procedures and processes of art enables visual, tactile and spatial qualities to be explored and interrogated in different ways to understand them better. Thus the investigative function of art can be regarded as a kind of research with an accompanying range of methodologies.

At the heart of the matter is visual perception. It is recognized that strategies need to be adopted in order to teach children how (rather than what) to see. A major challenge for teachers of seven- to eleven-year-olds is to find ways of focusing their attention and sustaining their active involvement in looking for increasingly long periods of time. This requires concentrated effort over time.

Many children of this age are already familiar with a visual culture dominated by instantly gratifying, rapidly changing, simultaneously available images through television programmes and advertisements, popular music videos, CD-ROM, computer games and the Internet. Not only are they avid consumers of such material, they are often accomplished producers and manipulators of sophisticated, electronically generated moving images and sound. The key point for teachers is to acknowledge the coexistence of these alternative ways in which children experience the world and understand the ways in which they help to shape their developing perceptual skills.

The use of art as an investigative tool requires an ability to think in terms of visual, tactile and spatial qualities. A project based on a visit to a garden, for example, could begin with an investigation into the nature of the tactile qualities of the different surfaces it contains. In order to collect and record evidence, rubbings and simple prints from inked-up surfaces could be made, along with a series of photographs to show how dramatic contrasts between light and dark areas 'reveal' depth, and make surface details, irregular patina and regular patterns 'come alive'. Impressions could be made of fragments of cast-iron railings, twisted tree roots and sections of a statue using small slabs of clay or plasticine to follow the forms.

As confidence and competence is gained in relation to ways of seeing and focusing attention, investigating and recording skills, children should be encouraged to select from a wider field those aspects of their work they find most interesting and wish to develop. As the work becomes more complex, further personal research is necessary in order to make informed judgements about what to do next.

Connections are made with the working methodologies, intentions and preliminary studies of other artists and this locates children's creative efforts in a wider historical, social and cultural context. Throughout this process the focused support of the teacher relies heavily on the role of spoken language to sharpen skills of visual analysis, interpretation and recording by posing questions and challenging predictable ways of seeing.

Sketchbooks are central to the development of enquiry in art. When they are used intelligently evidence of knowledge and understanding is revealed through personal responses to experience, traces of thought processes, insights into decision-making, and experiments carried out over a period of time. Thus as a means of collecting information, recording observations, exploring and developing ideas, sketchbooks might contain drawings, colour studies, photographs, illustrative material, fragments of materials, computer-generated data and imagery and words. Above all, a sketchbook of this quality becomes a valued and highly personal resource for learning. It is a reaffirmation that rigorous research is an essential dimension of creative work in art and that it can take a variety of forms. Time and effort need to be invested in preparatory work if the content of later work is to have substance. As Gilbert (1998: 265) says, 'Sketchbook research provides a cognitive bridge to the independent ground of knowing how to develop in art alone.'

Making

When children's creative work in art is rooted in personal experience and informed and enriched by a critical understanding of works of art, making becomes more meaningful for the maker.

Intention: The starting points for practical work need to be carefully planned, well structured and sharply focused, with clearly identified learning intentions. It is necessary to invest time and energy in preparatory work in order to generate and record ideas of sufficient substance to motivate pupils and withstand development over an extended period of time. For making to be successful it needs to be firmly rooted in well-informed ideas, the full potential of which becomes clearer to the maker through the process of making; supported and strengthened through discussions with other makers and teachers. It is important for teachers to empathize with children's emerging ideas in order that they can help them pose appropriate questions about the content of their work and the issues involved, to encourage alternative interpretations and directions, as well as questions related to choice of media and technical concerns.

Visual language: In order to communicate intentions effectively through the making of art it is necessary to use a visual language. As with any other language, children need to understand how its components work in combination. They need to be taught how to use it in increasingly complex ways and for a variety of purposes that might include ways of analysing and recording things observed and expressing feelings about things imagined or remembered. Opportunities for children to explore different modes of visual communication enrich their understandings of what it means to be visually literate. Teachers can help children to see how the natural and made world is organized and 'operates' in terms of line, shape, pattern, colour, tone, texture and form. In order to become fluent and flexible users of this symbol system it is essential to experiment with it before using it to realize a particular intention. It is equally important for children to gain insight into the specific ways that artists, craftspeople and designers think in terms of visual language. They should be helped to appreciate the different styles, conventions and code systems through which visual communication occurs and to acquire a critical vocabulary through which, in groups, they can discuss similarities and differences.

Media: Opportunities should exist for children between seven and eleven years of age to work with a range of processes to create images and artefacts for different purposes. For ten- and eleven-year-olds there is much to be gained by concentrating on a more limited range of materials and processes in order to foster work of greater depth. Building upon earlier forms of experiential learning, in particular exploratory play, experimentation should be encouraged in order to become familiar with the qualities and properties of materials; particularly with those not previously encountered. However, it is essential that children are taught how to gain increasing control over a chosen medium in order that it can be used to transform ideas and feelings into images and forms. Too often the (mindless) manipulation of materials is seen as the purpose of making and when this happens their creative potential as expressive media is denied. Between a chosen medium and a maker there evolves a special kind of intimacy. Eisner (1998: 14) captures this relationship well using 'metaphors such as "getting a feel" for the process and "getting in touch"'. He goes on to say:

Both metaphors, getting in touch and getting a feel, relate to bodily processes. Both convey a sense of 'getting into it' . . . Both convey a sense of knowing that is not reducible to words, certainly not the literal use of words, hence metaphor.

(Ibid.)

There develops between the maker and the work-in-progress a conversation-like exchange. At one moment the maker is engaged in the manipulation of visual images, tools and materials while at the next the role of critic is adopted. Certain conditions must be created by the teacher if children are to develop 'dialogues' with their work-in-progress through which it grows and changes as medium impacts on idea. Uncertainties have to be lived with if situations are to remain open for sufficiently long periods of time to encourage explorations of alternative approaches, interpretations, ways of solving visual or technical problems that could not have been envisaged at the outset. Risks need to be taken.

It is commonplace for discussions about appropriate media to which children should be introduced to include references to drawing, painting, printmaking, sculpture and textiles. Indeed it is in such traditionally defined terms that the National Curriculum for Art (DfE, 1995a) promotes practical work. Whilst it is important for children to acquire a range of skills through which media associated with these areas can be handled with confidence and purpose, it is also important to extend the concept of appropriateness as far as materials for creative work in art are concerned. Many contemporary artists work in ways that do not fit the neatly defined categories of painting, sculpture and so on, to which the National Curriculum for Art refers. Increasingly artists are exploring ideas and issues through inventive combinations of materials using an eclectic approach to old and new technologies. Collections of found objects, ephemera, constructions using industrial components, videos, photographs, projected light and sound are used in combination with what might be regarded as more traditional materials for art-making. Very often work is created out of humble or discarded materials that are not widely associated with art. In a description of her approach to work inspired by the Freud Museum in London, Susan Hillier says:

My starting points were artless, worthless artefacts and materials – rubbish, discards, fragments, trivia and reproductions – which seemed to carry an aura of memory and to hint at meaning something, something that made me want to work with them and on them.

(Hillier, 1995: Afterword)

Installations, created environments, often require the active participation of the 'viewer' without whom the work would be incomplete,
devoid of meaning. The computer artist Simon Biggs writes his own
software for his multimedia work. One piece, *Halo*, was described as
follows in the computing section of a national newspaper, under the
heading 'Painting by digits':

> As you move around the darkened space, three bodies swirl across the
> screens that surround you in a strange aerial dance; they fly up, fall
> down and sometimes cluster together.
>
> (*Guardian*, 1998)

Contemporary artists break boundaries; they push forward the
frontiers of art. They use materials in ways that challenge ideas about
the 'appropriateness' of media for art.

Responding

The development of children's responses to art, both to their own creative efforts and to other artists' work, has been a somewhat neglected
aspect of the art curriculum in many primary schools. This is unsur-
prising. In the limited time available for art the emphasis has traditionally been given to practical work. In addition, appropriate visual
resources of quality are often lacking and most primary teachers feel
they have insufficient knowledge of art to foster children's responses
to it. Certainly responding to art entails more than an expression of
likes and dislikes and to foster informed responses a number of teaching strategies can be employed. About the development of critical
skills, Buchanan says:

> Enhancing pupils' ability to be critical requires not only enough time
> to be allocated to evaluative activity in which judgements are made,
> discussed and modified, but also the creation of a suitably supportive
> learning environment in which the expression of personal feelings,
> points of view, tentative judgements and emotional responses is
> socially acceptable and safe. This is equally true in the museum and
> gallery as in the more familiar environment of the classroom.
>
> (Buchanan, 1995: 42)

Various frameworks have been proposed to help teachers structure
ways in which children's personal responses to a wide range of work
can be nurtured. Taylor (1986) identifies 'process, form, content and
mood' as the four 'fundamental areas' to be addressed. Using Taylor's
framework it is possible for children to respond to the processes and
methods used to make a piece of work, its formal elements (visual

language), its subject matter (content) and the atmosphere the work evokes.

In order to guide teachers in their questioning and planning of activities, a three-tiered structure is suggested by Buchanan (1995: 43). The first level is concerned with information. Children are invited to share 'what is known about the artist or the work'. This might include information about when, where and how the work was made 'deduced from visual clues'. The second level, description, 'requires close observation, analysis and the precise use of language' and 'allows pupils to classify, compare and draw parallels between different types of information'. By the third level, interpretation, pupils are expected to engage in discussions in order to articulate reasons for things being as they are. For purposes of lesson planning, it is suggested that teachers categorize these tiers as 'knowing, decoding and exploring'. This sequence moves responses from those of a factual nature, towards a recognition of the way the visual language operates and beyond to those that reveal personal feelings.

For Dyson (1989: 129) the most powerful teaching tools to illicit pupils' responses are frameworks within which comparisons can be made and classification systems adopted or invented. He states that, 'to seek similarities and differences in related images is an effective means of compelling (pupils) to look and to think'. Whatever the approach adopted, the role of language, particularly the rich use of analogy and metaphor, to focus children's looking, to prompt response and sustain attention is central. However, unless over a period of time the work to which children are required to respond represents a broad-based experience of art, craft and design, responses will, unavoidably, be limited. The fundamental question is on what basis are works of art selected to promote children's learning in art? Very often the answer relates more to the availability of reproductions of familiar images (paintings by Monet and Van Gogh), with which teachers feel comfortable, than any educational criteria. When this occurs two problems are apparent. Firstly, responses to popular impressionist and post-impressionist painters tend to involve the making of uncritical and ill-informed copies of the works that fail to reveal any understanding of the artists' intentions or the historical, social and cultural contexts in which they were created. Thus such responses are reduced to a level of visual cliché. Secondly, the choice of artwork to which children are exposed often reinforces a very narrow view of art, of those who make art, its function and its appearance. After all, in a recent survey carried out by Mori for the BBC television programme *Close Up*, the nineteenth-century landscape painter, John Constable, emerged as Britain's favourite artist! (*Independent*, 1998c.)

In order that children are able to see more clearly and directly the *relevance* of artists' work, it is argued that more emphasis should be placed on contemporary work or the work of the recent past. This view is strongly held by Burgess and Holman who say:

> The inclusion of contemporary artists and their work in education is often seen as synonymous with loss of heritage and traditional values, and even the art of the last 30 years has, in many schools, been barely acknowledged, or has been seen as too problematic to be dealt with ... If teachers continue to rely exclusively on monographs about safe, well-documented painters, they will be discounting not only many black artists and female artists, but equally important histories of craft, design and popular culture.
>
> (Burgess and Holman, 1993)

By helping children to make connections between their responses to the working methodologies and content of work by living artists, and their own making, they are better able to make sense of their own lives. A vital contribution that art should make to primary education is the celebration of present reality. Art experiences are direct, all-engaging of the individual, now. In this sense art reaffirms the intrinsic value of the primary stage of education in which childhood experiences are valued for their own sake. The relevance of the responses that pupils are able to make to the work of contemporary artists is well documented by a teacher of seven- and eight-year-olds in a multicultural, inner city school. She says:

> Art can play a very important role in the promotion of cultural understanding and awareness. For art to be meaningful and relevant to children it must not only give them some understanding of the power and vitality of historic works of art; it must also encourage children to see art in terms of its relevance in a particular time and place. If we concentrate solely on presenting children with options to respond to the works of Monet, Van Gogh and Turner, for instance, we are attaching value judgements to these works and implying that there is a hierarchy of art to which we should adhere. One of the most successful art projects I have taught was based on the young black artist Jean Michel Basquiat. The reason for its success was that the children identified completely with the project because Basquiat was part of *their* culture; it opened up discussions about issues in *their* lives – drugs, graffiti, fashion, music. It made them feel that they too could be 'artists', that it was not just the prerogative of the few.
>
> (Hughes, 1999: 32)

Relevance was the basis of the Crafts Council exhibition *Decadence?*, the aim of which was to 'establish a collaborative dialogue about our creative climate at the end of the twentieth century' (Schoeser, 1999: 3). In the notes for teachers that accompanied the exhibition, a number of key questions were posed to which children were invited to respond. They included, 'What are the ultimate luxuries of today?' and, 'Is there evidence of a "live for today, forget tomorrow" attitude?' Children were helped to get to grips with the work exhibited by posing questions rather than receiving answers. The themes explored included the duality of private and public life today, the power of icons (both religious and from popular culture) and the inclusion of the spectator, through reflections, in the appearance of the work. Children were further challenged by being asked, what constitutes a luxury material?

Perhaps the most controversial area of design education in which children are required to make their views known is architecture: 'the art form to which we are continually exposed' (Rogers, 1997: 68). Art education should ensure that children are equipped to participate in this controversial debate. Ultimately it will be the decision-making capacity of present-day seven- to eleven-year-olds that will decide the quality of the built environment in the twenty-first century.

Reflecting

For learning in art to have personal significance for the learner more than an ability to make responses to experience is required. Ways of reflecting on responses need to be developed. As Salmon says:

> In place of top-down knowledge, pupils must construct things for themselves. And what is learned must go beyond merely doing things; the learner must come to reflect on that practical experience, to articulate something of what it means.
>
> (Salmon, 1995: 22)

Effective reflective behaviour involves individuals in qualitatively different relationships with their own work and their responses to the work of others. Previous action is subject to scrutiny by being revisited, viewed 'afresh', in a contemplative mode. The evidence of sense impressions and intuitive responses is an important dimension of this process. It is therefore necessary for teachers to acknowledge the value of insights into experience that can be gained through ways of human functioning other than linear, logical, rational patterns of behaviour (Claxton, 1997).

Provision should be made for children to acquire and apply reflective skills at different stages in the development of their work. The deeper insights gained, in turn, inform and shape ideas as the work progresses. Individually, in small groups and as a whole class pupils can be helped to understand how ideas emerge, grow and change in the act of making. Of fundamental importance is their ability to recognize that alternative ways of seeing, of handling media and responding to works are possible, indeed desirable, and that they change over time. Language has a central role to play in this process as Buchanan points out:

> High quality dialogue, prompted and supported by the teacher, is pivotal in the process of analysis, reflection, comparison and evaluation. Over time and with practice pupils develop confidence in expressing ideas and emotions, their views and judgements become more incisive and their critical vocabulary becomes more extensive.
>
> (Buchanan, 1995: 46)

Through language the implicit becomes explicit. Ideas can be shared with others (but first with oneself) and through verbal articulation they are modified further. 'Conceptual clarity emerges through experiential learning and an ability to reflect upon it; it can hardly precede it' (Prentice, 1995: 16).

Extending the scope

In order to increase the coherence and relevance of the art activities in which seven- to eleven-year-olds participate, it is proposed that the *scope* of the art curriculum should be *extended*. This should not be interpreted to mean the mere addition of new components to what already exists. The National Society for Education in Art and Design (NSEAD, 1999) argues for, 'a general rethinking of objectives prompted by close consideration of postmodern ideas' as a basis for 'curriculum reconstruction'. At the heart of such a reconstructed curriculum for art would be an emphasis on 'difference, plurality and independence of mind' (Swift and Steers, 1998: 3).

It is suggested here that primary school teachers can be best supported in their attempts to develop their art teaching by alerting them to ways in which they can extend the scope of art experiences in relation to *issues, media* and *context*.

Issues

Once the key features of art, as a way of knowing, are understood, it is a relatively easy next step for teachers to appreciate the potential of the processes and procedures of art for the exploration of important issues. In particular, the range of personal concerns with which children are emotionally involved can be used as subject matter. Projects might promote various modes of enquiry into personal identity, family relationships, the immediate locality and distant places, ecological and environmental problems, along with issues of gender, race and culture.

Media

Changes in the ways that pupils create images and artefacts are largely determined by the choice of materials and tools available, their accessibility, attitudes towards materials and their uses, and the products of previous making activity. There is a need to review the criteria used to make decisions about what two- and three-dimensional materials should be made available in the first place. The ways in which individuals are introduced to materials also influences how they use them. By combining and recombining a range of materials long-held ideas about compatibility and incompatibility are challenged. Through the inventive juxtapositioning of different ways of giving form to ideas and feelings children develop new ways of seeing the world and of harnessing the creative potential of old and new technologies.

Context

An extended context should embrace a wider range of opportunities for children to locate at the centre of their creative work in art current interests, concerns, likes and dislikes, passions and problems. It should also help them to position their work in a wider cultural landscape and to develop the necessary critical skills through which it can be interrogated. More use should be made of contemporary artists, through residencies and placements plus museum and gallery education departments to assist and accelerate this process. An important outcome of projects that bring into partnerships teachers, children, artists and arts agencies is that they reveal a wider context of adult participation in, and commitment to, the arts as an essential part of life-long learning and for some a means of earning a living.

Teachers' subject knowledge

The ideas presented in this chapter are likely to have a wider impact in classrooms only when ways of developing primary teachers' subject knowledge in art is properly addressed in initial teacher education courses and through a systematic approach to subject-specific professional development. Given that a large number of teachers have never experienced art as a meaningful dimension of their own lives, it is hardly surprising that they lack the confidence and understanding required to initiate children into art experiences of quality. Central to this issue is the contentious debate about the organization and funding of primary schools, at the heart of which lie cherished beliefs about the very nature of primary schools staffed by generalist teachers. The arguments for and against different organizational structures that might include subject co-ordinators, semi-specialists or specialists, are well recorded (Alexander, Rose and Woodhead, 1992; Alexander, 1998). Whilst in relation to the teaching of art specifically, the continuation of a generalist approach is favoured by Holt (1997: 84–95), it is asserted by Swift and Steers that, 'There is a need for specialist art teachers at Key Stage Two' (1998: 8).

The view adopted here is that a redefinition of the role of subject leader, to include direct teaching alongside less confident and less knowledgeable colleagues, would go a long way towards the implementation of a more rigorous art curriculum throughout a school. Too often the role of subject leader is restricted to 'servicing' the teaching of the subject by generalist teachers. Traditionally it has been assumed that subject leaders would not play an interventionist role in colleagues' classrooms. Curiously, many headteachers seem to value enthusiasm and personal qualities more highly than subject expertise 'that is grounded in a deeper adult-level understanding of the subject' (Alexander, 1998: 31).

It is now widely recognized that successful teachers demonstrate an ability to transform their knowledge of subject content into teaching material. They use appropriate representations of content to match the particular needs, interests and abilities of learners. Effective teaching of this order relies on what has been referred to as professional understanding: a complex combination of knowledge of subject matter and knowledge of pedagogy (Shulman, 1986).

Whilst all teachers who teach art use representations through which subject content is transformed into teaching material, it is possible to identify qualitative differences in the representations chosen by teachers who function from a strong subject knowledge base in art. Predictably, such teachers reveal a deeper understanding rooted in concepts, underlying principles, major themes and styles. As a result they are able to adopt a more flexible pedagogical style that is 'open to children's ideas, contributions, questions and comments' (Aubrey, 1994: 5). Imaginative connections are more likely to be explored between topics and such teaching is less likely to perpetuate stereotyped ideas about art and its appearance. This ability to transform subject matter, through carefully selected representations, using metaphor, analogy, illustration and demonstration displays the depth of understanding from which a knowledgeable teacher of art can generate alternatives.

It is towards an achievement of this level of functioning that teachers with responsibility for art in primary schools must aspire. One positive step within postgraduate courses of initial teacher education would be to focus in greater depth on the teaching of art with those students who intend to become subject leaders. In this way the key expectations of a co-ordinating and leadership role is embedded during initial training. A second positive step would be to redesign undergraduate courses of initial teacher education in such a way that a reciprocal relationship exists between personal experience of art and developing understanding about art education. From courses of initial teacher education of these kinds, networks of curriculum projects and further professional development opportunities could be made available through partnerships involving schools, universities, arts agencies, professional artists, museums and galleries and the 'creative industries'.

The larger vision to which an extension of the scope of art education contributes might be thought of in terms similar to Bruner's 'new breed of developmental theory':

> It will be motivated by the question of how to create a new generation that can prevent the world from dissolving into chaos and destroying itself; I think its central technical concern will be how to create in the young an appreciation of the fact that many worlds are possible, that meaning and reality are created and not discovered, that negotiation is the art of constructing new meanings by which individuals can regulate their relations with each other.
>
> (Bruner, 1986: 149)

Bruner of all people would recognize the potency of art in education as a means of constructing and sharing new meanings.

Further reading

Robinson, Gillian (ed.) (1995) *Sketch-books: Explore and Store*. London: Hodder & Stoughton. The educational value of sketchbooks is made clear through examples of sound practice located in a philosophical framework. This book emphasizes the importance of sketchbooks as a tool for research.

Prentice, Roy (ed.) (1995) *Teaching Art and Design: Addressing Issues, Identifying*

Directions. London: Cassell. Each chapter explores a contemporary issue in art and design education in such a way that the ideas explored are equally relevant to subject leaders for art in primary schools and secondary art specialists.

11

Mathematics: All in the Mind?

Tim Rowland

Far from mathematics being all around us, I offer the alternative tenet that mathematics is only inside us.

(Pimm, 1986: 51)

Introduction

In writing a single chapter on primary school mathematics, there is little point in attempting to be comprehensive, but every incentive to be topical. I shall discuss the teaching of numeracy – unchallenged as *the* current issue in primary mathematics education in Britain – from a broadly post-war perspective. The National Numeracy Strategy (DfEE, 1999), in accepting and promoting the pedagogy of the National Numeracy Project (NNP, 1998) and its particular curricular emphases, is forcing primary teachers towards a radical shift in their classroom practice. The most highly publicized aspect of this shift is the move away from individual instruction towards whole-class inter-active teaching. Whilst I welcome that move, I believe that the most significant aspect of it is not instructional group size, but the empha-sis on the teacher's instructional (as opposed to managerial) role. I also believe that the most important change in train is in approaches to calculation, with a new emphasis on mental methods. Far from being a 'new idea', this is a very late response to recommendations going back some twenty years. Research can enable teachers to sys-tematize and support the teaching of mental calculation.

This chapter also re-asserts the potential of affordable ICT (the cal-culator) in the teaching of mathematics.

Background

Hooray for New Math, It's so simple, So very simple, That only a child can do it!

(Lehrer, 1965)

Mathematics education in the UK is currently experiencing its second major upheaval since the Second World War. Although it might feel like the fifth in the ten years since the introduction of the National Curriculum in England and Wales, general trends have moved in two broad directions. A cynic might say that the pendulum is returning to the position from where it started in the 1950s.

In the immediate post-war years, the 1944 Education Act offered the prospect of free education for the nation's children (to age fifteen at least) and selection at eleven to determine the most appropriate type of secondary school for each child. The eleven-plus test for mathematics was in arithmetic. Small wonder, then, that primary school mathematics consisted of training in arithmetic, principally in the efficient execution of algorithms for the 'four rules'. Although little changed until the mid-to-late 1960s, there is evidence of a mood for change at least ten years earlier. A long-forgotten but quite remarkable report of the Mathematical Association conveys attitudes and aspirations which would be perfectly in keeping with 'progressive' ideas some thirty years later:

> The emphasis in the primary school is on unity of experience and fullness of life rather than on 'subjects'. The basic principles of learning are the same whether we are concentrating on poetry or arithmetic.
>
> (Mathematical Association, 1956: 4)

The clearest pre-Plowden sign of a widespread shift towards a different approach to primary mathematics – broad, 'practical' and child-centred – is to be found in *Curriculum Bulletin No. 1* (Schools Council, 1965). To some extent, this was a response to developments in secondary schools set in train by the Schools Mathematics Project (SMP). The *Bulletin* set out to show how 'important branches of mathematics [sets, data handling and mathematical modelling] now being introduced into secondary schools have their roots in the work of the primary schools' (ibid.: 4), I am not alone in thinking that this may have been mistaken; the recent retreat from probability, for example, in the primary school mathematics curriculum reflects a reappraisal of the view that every Key Stage 3 topic should be encountered by five-year-olds.

Just as significant as the *Bulletin*'s argument for enhanced mathematical content is its advocacy of a different approach to teaching and learning in primary mathematics, summed up in the word 'discovery', which, interestingly, is justified in terms of efficiency and performance.

> though discovery methods take longer in the initial stages . . . far less practice is required to attain and maintain efficiency in computation when children have been enabled to make their own discoveries. There is an increasing volume of evidence to suggest that where selection tests (in mechanical arithmetic) are still in use the proportion of children obtaining grammar school places has shown a steady increase in those schools where a different approach to mathematics has been introduced.
>
> (Ibid.: xvi)

Theoretical justification for 'discovery learning' is attempted in a chapter quaintly entitled 'Research in children's method of learning'. The chapter reviews Piaget's conservation experiments and his stage theory, summarizing the pedagogic inferences of psychologists such as Lunzer and Dienes. In the end, the link with discovery is somewhat forced, and the chapter concludes:

> With discovery methods in mind and encouraged by Piaget's experiments, let us create a dynamic definition . . . 'Mathematics is the discovery of relationships'.
>
> (Ibid.: 9)

Incidentally, it is ironic that the Platonic assumptions of ontological reality underpinning 'discovery' are at odds with Piaget's subsequent epistemological position (Piaget, 1970: 57–8).

The emphasis on discovery was unfortunate inasmuch as it was taken to imply that the teacher's contribution to children's learning was best restricted to providing the right sort of ('rich') classroom environment, as though instruction were unimportant.

The inevitable backlash to such practices – which always focuses in the minds of the public on children who can't do column arithmetic and don't know their 'tables' – can be seen in the *Black Papers* of the late 1970s (Cox and Boyson, 1977). This in turn led to the establishment of a Committee of Inquiry into the teaching of mathematics in schools. Its published findings are the Cockcroft Report (DES, 1982a). The tone of the report is measured and prosaic, in contrast to the evangelical ardour of *Curriculum Bulletin No. 1* nearly twenty years earlier. Although silent on the subject of 'discovery', as such, the Cockcroft Report (DES, 1982a: 70–80) nails its colours to the mast of rationality in the name of 'understanding'.

There are certainly some things in mathematics which need to be learned by heart but we do not believe that it should ever be necessary in the teaching of mathematics to commit things to memory without at the same time seeking to develop proper understanding of the mathematics to which they relate ... such an approach is unlikely to meet with long term success.

(Ibid.: 70)

As well as rejecting 'mere' rote learning of facts, the report rejects rote training of algorithmic skills in the name of 'standards':

There is evidence that the public focussing of attention on standards in schools which has occurred in recent years has created pressure in some quarters for a 'back to basics' movement. This has encouraged some primary teachers [and others] to restrict their teaching largely to the attainment of computational skills. ... The results of a 'back to basic' approach ... are most unlikely to be those which its proponents wish to see, and we can in no way support or recommend an approach of this kind.

(Ibid.: 80)

In devaluing recall and algorithmic learning, the report promoted conceptual learning and the development of problem-solving skills and strategies.

Despite the appointment of large numbers of mathematics advisory teachers – 'Cockcroft missionaries' – to local authorities, the influence on primary practice was barely discernible, especially when compared with that of a trend that was already having – and continues to have – a major effect on children's learning experiences. Teachers' difficulty in engaging with the puzzling additional content of 'New Maths' – sets, graphs, geometry and the like – fifteen years earlier had been superficially resolved by enterprising publishers, with the explosion of commercial mathematics schemes into primary classrooms in the 1970s and 1980s. This is a story in itself, but the consequence was effectively supportive of those teachers who were reluctant actually to *teach* mathematics. With few exceptions, commercial schemes are designed so that the pupils' books *address the child directly* and assume the role of teacher (Gray, 1991). The pupils' task is to engage with the book in isolation. The task of teaching is effectively delegated to the books – as if the book were a surrogate teacher (Rowland, 1991).

By 1993, some three-fifths of teachers of seven- to eleven-year-olds used a commercial scheme for more than half of the mathematics work with their pupils (Millett and Johnson, 1996: 57). Millett and Johnson point out that this dependence on mathematics textbooks for *explanation* as well as for exercises is a world-wide phenomenon (Merseth, 1993; Robitaille and Garden, 1989), and reason that

> Pressure to use a commercial scheme as the mainstay of their mathematics ... may stem from feelings of inadequacy about mathematics which afflict many primary teachers in particular. ... In arguing for a more measured approach to scheme use, however, it should be noted that it may be the case that some teachers have little confidence in their mathematical or pedagogical content knowledge, and hence a scheme would be of benefit to them and their pupils.
>
> (Millett and Johnson, 1996: 72)

Millett and Johnson seem to be saying that it is easier to change the textbook than to change the teacher, which is doubtless true on a large-scale basis. Nevertheless, the National Numeracy Strategy (DfEE, 1999) is apparently braced to bite the bullet.

Turning the tide

There are clear signs that the tide is turning, and it is possible to identify some of the factors that have brought about this reversal. Surprisingly, perhaps, the introduction of a National Curriculum from 1989 does not appear to be one of them. If anything, it increased the range of mathematics topics that teachers were required to 'cover' with their pupils and diminished their sense that they could cope. This offered a field day for the publishers of schemes, who flooded the market with materials, 'guaranteed' to meet the requirements of the new curriculum.

The relatively poor performance of English (and Scottish) pupils in number items in international comparative tests (Harris, Keys and Fernandes, 1997; Lapointe, Mead and Askew, 1992) has undoubtedly touched national pride, and the sense of hurt has been inflamed by some sections of the press. The ranking is admittedly surprising, given that children in Britain typically begin compulsory schooling one or two years earlier than their more successful peers in the Netherlands, Germany, Japan and Singapore. The possible causes are numerous and complex (Alexander, 1997; Brown, 1996; 1998) and it is clearly unwise to leap to simplistic conclusions. Nevertheless, there is a definite sense that all is not well.

The last five years have also seen the willingness of the newly empowered inspection service, OFSTED, to be outspoken in criticism of what its inspectors judge to be poor practice and low standards in arithmetic in schools. OFSTED has reported that:

standards of achievement in number ... in Key Stage 2 ... are less satisfactory mainly because the rate of progress is too slow and misconceptions are not addressed. Too many pupils are unable to recall important number facts or to compute with sufficient speed and accuracy.

(OFSTED, 1995b: 6)

Furthermore, too many teachers, especially at Key Stage 2, lack an understanding of the way pupils learn, or do not learn, mathematics so are not aware how to help them overcome their mistakes.

(Ibid.: 9)

Another important influence was the publication of a comparative study of primary school mathematics textbooks in Britain, Germany and Switzerland (Bierhoff, 1996) for the National Institute of Economic and Social Research. The evidence presented by Bierhoff appears to support her claim that the teaching of elementary arithmetic in Britain (as presented in school textbooks) is a rather hit-and-miss affair, both unscientific and unsystematic when compared with practice in countries such as Germany and Switzerland, where the teaching of arithmetical procedures is paramount. The greater breadth of curriculum which characterizes English primary mathematics results in frequent changes of topic in the textbooks, with poor attention to progression and consolidation. Crucially, the English textbooks encourage teachers to introduce vertical algorithms for calculation prematurely, where the continental books aim first to consolidate mental fluency and recall of key number facts. The apparent superiority of German or Swiss textbooks does not, however, necessarily point to the wisdom of their being adopted in Britain, since they are designed for a much more homogeneous teaching grouping than is typically found in our primary schools (Brown, 1998: 39–40).

Mental arithmetic

With hindsight, one can see that an aspect of the Cockcroft Report which was neglected, with the most serious consequences, was its unequivocal advocacy of mental methods and plea for mental arithmetic as a 'first resort' for calculation. That is not to say that nobody took any notice. The report reflected concerns which had already been expressed by Plunkett (1979), for example, and the mathematics professional associations responded enthusiastically, although the splash they created at the centre made few waves in school classrooms. The literature generated by such enthusiasts as Smith (1989b) and the

Mathematical Association (1992) demonstrated the ingenuity and variety of children's mental methods. What was lacking was any *systematization* of the pedagogy of mental arithmetic. At best, fluency in mental arithmetic was perceived as the aggregation of a somewhat hit-and-miss collection of 'tricks'. For example, to add 9 to 34 it is relatively inefficient to count on 9 from 24; a good 'trick' is to add 10 and then subtract 1, which can be done by reference to the first and second digits of 24. It is interesting to reflect that, for this shortcut to be meaningful, the child needs some prior knowledge which certainly cannot be taken for granted, e.g. the effect of adding 10 to a two-digit number, and the ability to identify the number preceding any given number.

Only very recently, under the impetus of the National Numeracy Strategy (NNS) (DfEE, 1999), have we seen an attempt to identify clearly what might be described as the knowledge and key number skills needed to underpin these and other such 'tricks'.

This is best illustrated by a simple example.

Think about how you could work out the sum of 7 and 8.

Your first reaction may be that you 'know' that 7+8=15. This, in itself, illustrates that isolated number-facts can and do become committed to memory as 'known facts'. Our task is to step back and reflect on the possible strategies that *could* be used to evaluate the sum if we had not already learned it 'by heart', and what prior known facts would be required to apply these strategies (see Table 11.1). These strategies can be analysed as follows:

Table11.1 Possible strategies to find the sum of 7 and 8

1.	Count out 7 cubes and then 8 cubes. Combine the two sets and count all the cubes
2.	Start from 7 and count on 8 more ('8, 9, 10, . . ., 15') using fingers to keep track of the count
3.	Start from 8 and count on 7 more ('9, 10, 11 . . ., 15') using fingers to keep track of the count.
4.	Double 7 and then add 1.
5.	Double 8 and then subtract 1.
6.	To 7, first add 3 (taken from the 8) to make 10. Then add the remaining 5 to make 15.
7.	To 8, first add 2 (taken from the 7) to make 10. Then add the remaining 5 to make 15.
8.	Partition 8 into 5+3 and 7 into 5+2. Add the 5s to give 10. Add 3 and 2 to give 5. Finally add 5 to 10.
9.	To 7, add 10, then subtract 2.
10.	To 8, add 10, then subtract 3.

Counting methods

The first three methods are known respectively as 'count all', 'count on' and 'count on from the larger'. These methods are elementary and commonplace in primary classrooms. To use them effectively, a child must be able to count in two different respects: to select two sets of objects of a given size, and to enumerate the combined set. Methods 1 to 3 are essentially algorithmic, i.e. they do not entail strategic choices and will work for all numbers (albeit laboriously and with potential for error if both numbers exceed 10). The first strategy is hardly a mental method, although it involves no writing. It could be called an 'enactive' method – one that achieves the calculation by manipulating materials or apparatus of some kind (like an abacus or Dienes material). Whilst the second and third approaches might be classified as mental methods, they require no strategic reflection on the properties and characteristics of the numbers to be added (such as – are they close? is one of them close to a multiple of ten?). Admittedly, the third method requires the child to select the larger of the two numbers, and to appreciate that addition is commutative, i.e. $a+b=b+a$.

Using doubles and near-doubles

Strategies 4 and 5 require prior knowledge of (at least some) doubles and the ability to adjust up or down from the double. The associative property of addition is used implicitly, i.e. $7+(7+1)=(7+7)+1$.

Bridging through 10

Strategies 6 and 7 exploit place value structure and notation, recognizing decade boundaries (multiples of 10) as secure and convenient markers for navigation along the sequence of whole numbers. They require knowledge of addition bonds to 10 (1+9, 2+8, etc.) and the ability to partition the second addend accordingly. The associative property of addition is again used implicitly, i.e. $8+(2+5) = (8+2)+5$.

Using flexible partition

Strategy 8 partitions both addends, then combines the constituent parts so as to exploit place-value structure. The associative and commutative properties are used extensively, albeit implicitly, i.e. $8+7 = (5+3)+(5+2) = [(5+3)+5]+2 = [5+(3+5)]+2 = [5+(5+3)]+2 = [(5+5)+3]+2 = [10+3]+2 = 10+[3+2] = 10+5 = 15$.

Adding 10 (with 'compensation')

Strategies 9 and 10 require prior knowledge of the effect of adding 10, of number bonds to 10 (such as 7+3=10), along with awareness that subtraction 'undoes' addition (so that 10–3=7).

Each of these approaches, then, requires prior knowledge of some items within a range of: .

- number facts – such as bonds to 10, to be memorized and available by instant recall when required

- facts about number structure – such as the place-value system and awareness of commutativity

- strategic options – such as near-doubles.

There is a chicken-and-egg relationship between this factual knowledge and these strategic options. Option 5 (above) for 7+8 is unlikely to appeal or even to occur to the child who has not yet committed 8+8 to memory. Even at the most basic level, the 'count all' strategy is unavailable to the child who cannot recite the counting numbers in the standard order (see Gelman and Gallistel, 1978, on the sub-skills that underpin counting).

The facts and strategies associated with the approaches to 7+8 listed above can be summarized as in Table 11.2.

The systematization of the pedagogy of mental arithmetic amounts to identifying those key facts and strategies which underpin a child's developing competence in such mental calculations (Askew, 1997). The sophistication and complexity of these facts and strategies is likely to increase during the later years of primary schooling and embrace multiplicative as well as additive arithmetic structures, larger numbers, decimals and so on.

The acquisition of some of these facts and strategies seems to occur informally or spontaneously for some children, but by no means for all. In the earliest stages of schooling, if not before, children are sure to be taught 'count all' as the most basic aggregation model of addition (Haylock, 1995: 21). Most progress in the early primary years to 'count on' and even 'count from the larger', although many children persist in using these basic strategies well into their later primary years (Gray, 1997) rather than adopting more compressed strategies such as numbers 4 to 8 in Table 11.1. In effect, for many children, the more creative 'tricks' for mental arithmetic will *not* be acquired by chance. The strategies in question need to be explicitly drawn to their attention – they need to be taught – and the prior number facts need

Table 11.2 Analysis of the prior knowledge needed to implement the addition strategies in Table 11.1

	Number facts	Structure facts	Strategy
1.	standard number word sequence (SNWS		count all (aggregation))
2.	SNWS		count on (augmentation)
3.	SNWS	commutativity	count on (augmentation)
4.	required double	one more (place value), associativity	near-doubles
5.	required double	one less (place value) associativity, commutativity	near-doubles
6.	bonds to 10	place value	bridge through ten
7.	(partitions of n<10)	associativity	
8.	partitions of 5<n<10	place value, commutativity, associativity	flexible partition
9.	bonds to 10	inverse relation of	add 10 (with
10.		addition and subtraction, commutativity, associativity	compensation)

to be rehearsed so that they are instantly available to them. Threlfall (1998) points out that it is not at all obvious how the range of possible strategies are best to be taught so as to enhance the likelihood that children really will make inventive and efficient strategic choices when faced with genuine number challenges, as opposed to those they meet in a controlled classroom situation.

The range of strategies to be learned between the ages of seven and eleven is more extensive than that listed above, even for addition. To add 35 and 17, for example, there are additional possibilities (see Table 11.3). In fact, the second of these is a version of bridging through 10, and the third involves partition of each addend into its conventional place-value components. Such strategies are explicitly listed in the Summary of Objectives for each year in the NNP *Framework* (1998), with increasing range and sophistication from year to year.

Many of these ideas are codified in Dutch research undertaken in the 1980s and 1990s. The Dutch 'didactic' research in arithmetic

Table 11.3 Some strategies for adding 35 and 17

1. adding 10 to 35 (45) and then 7 to 45
2. adding 5 to 35 (40) and then 12 to 40
3. adding the 'tens' (40) and 'units' (12) separately, and finally adding 12 to 40

associates a label such as 'N10' with strategies which have been identified as significant in empowering children in mental calculation (see Table 11.4). The assignment of these codes or labels is, I believe, much more than a piece of teacher-jargon; it serves to sharpen teachers' awareness of a fragment of their professional knowledge.

The pedagogy of primary school mathematics in the Netherlands has derived principally from the Realistic Mathematics Education (RME) Project (Streefland, 1991). Unlike post-1960s practice in the UK, continental educators make little or no use of tactile, structured materials such as Dienes' base ten blocks (Bierhoff, 1996: 20). The RME approach is first to embed arithmetic in meaningful problem situations, identifying and fostering the informal mental strategies that children bring to their solution. The subsequent task is enabling them to develop and to use these and other strategies consciously and efficiently. Such strategies are included in Table 11.4. Three outcomes from the Dutch research (summarized in Beishuitzen and Anghileri, 1998) merit special attention:

1. Prioritizing mental mathematics for most of the primary years, delaying the introduction of standard written algorithms for column arithmetic until after Grade 3 (Year 4).

   The Dutch RME argument should be well understood: *priority for mental arithmetic means postponement of written procedures,* and not the combination of both as we see in many British textbooks and suggestions today.

   (Ibid.: 522, emphasis added)

Ironically, the arguments for 'postponement of written procedures' were well-rehearsed in England some twenty years ago (Plunkett,

Table 11.4 Dutch didactic research: labels for some mental arithmetic strategies to add 35 and 17

N10	jumping in tens, e.g. 35, 45, 52
N10c	N10 with compensation, e.g. 35, 45, 55, 52
A10	rapid resort to decade marker, e.g. 35, 40, 50, 52
1010	dealing with tens and units separately, e.g. (30+40)+(5+7)

1979), but with little or no observable effect in classrooms, whereas the practice is commonplace in continental Europe (Bierhoff, 1996: 22ff.).

2. Identification of 'jumping in tens' (N10) such as 26, 36, 46, . . . (and backwards) as an important key skill which is *not* spontaneously acquired by most children, and is a commonplace learning barrier.
3. Introduction of the 'empty number line' (ENL) as a pedagogic tool to record and support mental strategies.

This third point needs further elaboration. Many of the informal strategies adopted by children for addition and subtraction within 100 can be effectively represented on a number line. Three examples (Figures 11.1, 11.2 and 11.3) suffice to illustrate the point (see also Beishuitzen, 1997).

34 + 27 (N10)

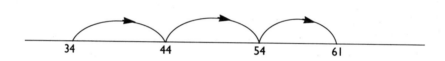

Fig. 11.1   Example 1: 34+27 (N10).

48 + 23 (A10)

Fig. 11.2   Example 2: 48+23 (A10 – bridge through 10, jump 20, add 1).

Whilst the number line with markings (like a tape measure) is a well-established support for calculation (Haylock, 1995: 22), the novel feature of the ENL is precisely its emptiness – no decade markings are made initially. The child then takes responsibility for showing on the line those (and only those) numbers that have significance in the mental calculation in question.

The crucial purpose of the ENL is to assist metacognition rather

83–28 (N10C)

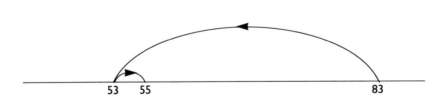

Fig. 11.3   Example 3: 83–28 (N10C – back 30, forwards 2).

than to aid actual calculation. This point needs to be emphasized because it is likely to be misunderstood in the British context. The conventional (British) number line is offered to the child as a calculating device as such. To add 12 to 27, for example, the child identifies the marker for 27 on the pre-divided icon, and advances 12 steps forwards (usually in ones) to 39. In effect, it replaces mental calculation. By contrast, the child uses the empty number line to record the stages of her *mental* calculation strategy, marking by choice those stages on the line that reflect the preference for N10, bridging through ten, and the subtle range of alternatives relating to such strategies – such as jumps of 20, compensation (Figure 11.3) and so on.

The identification of key facts and skills for mental calculation, and the use of the ENL as a means of recording and reflecting upon them, offers a practical framework for the systematization of the teaching of elementary arithmetic. This framework need not be a straitjacket for primary school teachers. It is important that teachers feel a sense of ownership and success as they work with it in the classroom, marvelling at and building on children's ingenuity.

Calculators

Over the last twenty years, there has been a great deal of interest in the potential of the four-function calculator, and much speculation about how it might force a rethink of the curriculum for mathematics in the primary school. Despite specific reference to calculators in the National Curriculum Programmes of Study for Key Stages 1 and 2, it is fair to suggest that this apparently modest technological revolution has not yet come.

When a calculation needs to be performed, it can be done in one or more of three basically different ways; mentally, with pencil and paper or with a calculator. The third of these options has been available for a mere blink of time in the long history of arithmetic. Electronic reckoning differs from the other means of calculation in a number of respects. For example, complex calculations such as 276×467 are in principle no more 'difficult' to execute than trivial ones such as 2×3. There is a very real and obvious sense in which responsibility for the technical details of the actual calculation are delegated and entrusted to the 'black box' machine, which accepts our input and responds with an output.

It is therefore hardly surprising that the use of such machines should commonly be viewed as inconsistent with the rational training of young minds. The suspicion that using a calculator is 'cheating' is deeply ingrained in the public perception; it surfaced, for example, in the response of Kenneth Baker (the then Secretary of State for Education) to the *Interim Report of the Working Party on Mathematics in the National Curriculum* (DES, 1987). In the event, the 'educationalists' had their way; indeed, the National Curriculum Council (1989) published the following advice to teachers implementing the then-new National Curriculum:

> The attainment targets and programmes of study in mathematics demonstrate a recognition that calculators provide a powerful and versatile tool for pupils to use in both the development of their understanding of number and for doing calculations ... and should be available to pupils for use at all four key stages.
>
> (1989: E5)

In its third incarnation, the National Curriculum Programme of Study for Mathematics (DFE, 1995c) still requires that 'pupils should be given opportunities to ... use calculators both as a means to explore numbers and as a tool for calculating with realistic data.' Nevertheless, simmering political anxiety about the neglect of mental calculation in schools surfaced in an unexpected way in October 1997. In a letter (to which reference is made in DfEE, 1998`d, para. 58) to the Qualifications and Curriculum Authority (QCA), Estelle Morris (then Under-Secretary of State for Education), wrote:

> I shall now be grateful, therefore, if the Authority can ... develop guidance for teachers ... at Key Stages 1 and 2. In addition to emphasising the importance of mental arithmetic, the guidance should also discourage as far as possible the use of calculators in Key Stage 1 and 2 mathematics.

The Numeracy Task Force offered its considered verdict on calculators in its final report:

> The Task Force believes that calculators are best used in primary schools in the later years of Key Stage 2. ... Used well, however, calculators can be an effective tool for learning about numbers and the number system, such as place value, precision, and fractions and decimals.
>
> (DfEE, 1998f: para. 113)

The 'spin' given to this measured paragraph in the instant DfEE press release was as follows:

> The national numeracy strategy will see pupils in every primary school benefiting from ... a ban on the use of calculators by children up to the age of eight and restricted use throughout the remainder of primary school.
>
> (DfEE press release 353/98: 8 July 1998)

There was a prophetic pessimism in my observation that, 'Prejudice both for and against calculators is surprisingly strong: moreover recent events have suggested that any rational basis for curriculum change is less powerful a force than strong political will' (Rowland, 1994: 6).

A clue to the source of the prevalent 'political will' can be found in the autobiography of the Secretary of State for Education and Employment, who writes:

> What a pity it is that recent research has shown that children's lack of numeracy can be put down to the fact that calculators have taken over from the use of their brains. Yes, I am a fundamentalist when it comes to education.
>
> (Blunkett, 1995: 48)

The book is not intended to be a contribution to education research, and no reference is given. The recent ministerial interventions constitute a significant marker in the history of the demonization of the four-function calculator, since – as I shall show – there is *no* evidence to suggest that any decline in mental arithmetic facility can be attributed to classroom use of calculators. It is extremely difficult to square such an official paranoia about cheap, low-technology calculators with the evangelical zeal with which the British government currently promotes the use of expensive, high-powered computers in schools, and the belief that teachers can be enabled to use them well (DfEE, 1997a).

The debate about the place of calculators in primary schools has been confused by the failure to distinguish between two fundamentally different purposes for using them.

1. The calculator as a *computational* tool – so that human cognitive effort and time is freed to concentrate on *strategic* aspects of problem solving.

Examples:

Find two numbers whose sum is 30 and whose product is 221.
Design a cube whose volume is half a litre.

There is no dispute with the view that children should learn to make intelligent choices of method of calculation, and that mental methods are invariably preferable when small, whole numbers are in play.

2. The calculator as a *pedagogical* tool – to enable enquiry, directing or structuring mathematical thinking:

Examples:

[Y1/2 – age 6]   What happens when 10 is added to any whole number?
[Y3 – age 7–8]   What happens when you count backwards from 5?
[Y5 – age 9–10] What happens when 1, 2, 3, 4, . . . are divided by 10? By 5? By 4?

Of course, discussion of findings with a teacher (of the kind commended in DfEE, 1998b: para. 113) is essential to meaningful interpretation of the calculator output, connecting the experience to existing knowledge. Under such conditions, the child's learning is a form of active sense-making.

The fear that children who regularly use calculators fail to develop and use mental methods for calculation is not supported by the evidence. (Paradoxically, this may be true for children who use calculators *in*frequently – see Rousham and Rowland, 1996, for the related concept of 'threshold'.) OFSTED's review of research reported that 'calculators can improve both performance and attitude. Open access to calculators does not lead to dependence, and can improve pupils' numeracy' (Askew and Wiliam, 1995).

In one study (Groves, 1994) a sample of nine- to ten-year-old 'project children' (habitual calculator users) were interviewed about their approach to twenty-four computational items. Their responses were compared with those of a matched sample of non-project pupils. The performance of the project group was significantly better than that of the control group.

Example: 62750+50 (presented on a card)
Facility rates: control 56%, project 89%.

Whereas 22% of the control group resorted to using a calculator for this item, only 16% of the project children did so – after three years of free access to calculators at school!

Recent evidence brought to light by Pike (1998) seems to refute the popular myth of the pervasive and malignant influence of the calculator in the primary classroom:

> Last summer's special key stage 2 calculator test paper should have been a gift to a techno-dependent generation. But to the amazement of examiners, most 11-year-olds ignored the technological option and resorted to pencil and paper. Early reports of how children tackled the tests will baffle ministers who have accorded the machines near demon status. They claim that the technology undermines pupils' mental arithmetic and have asked the Qualifications and Curriculum Authority for advice on how to limit their use. Yet, according to the QCA's own (unpublished) research from 1996, *calculators are hardly used in the primary classroom*.
>
> (Pike, 1998: 1)

Arguably, the problem is not excessive use of calculators, but that they are not used enough. Without regular access to this very affordable form of ICT, children in most schools appear not to be developing sufficient familiarity with their use to cross a threshold where novelty gives way to self-directed and purposeful exploration and experimentation with numbers, as well as sensible choices of calculating methods (Rousham and Rowland, 1996: 69).

Conclusion

The resurgence of mental mathematics in the primary school is to be welcomed. The National Numeracy Strategy will attract its fair share of complaint and criticism, yet its promotion of mental arithmetic just might achieve the emphasis advocated by the Cockcroft Report, albeit nearly twenty years late.

One misconception to be avoided is the identification of mental mathematics with mental arithmetic 'tests' reminiscent of the 1950s. The Schools Curriculum and Assessment Authority (SCAA) did not help in this regard, piloting a short, sharp mental arithmetic test in the 1997 KS2 (age 11) Standard Assessment, condemned by the Dutch educator Beishuitzen (1997) for emphasizing mental recall at the expense of mental strategies. The Secretary of State's description of the new mental tests as 'tough' (DfEE Press Release 463, 1998) in an attempt to explain away the drop in KS2 Standard Assessment scores between 1997 and 1998, does nothing to promote the idea that mental mathematics is natural and enjoyable, building on children's natural propensities and idiosyncratic methods to develop a fluent and meaningful repertoire of calculation strategies. The need to promote strategic thinking as well as good recall is at the root of another dilemma: giving pupils the space and time to think through strategies for mental calculation does not sit comfortably with the current official promotion of a 'brisk pace' in mathematics lessons. By age 10, children should be expected to know instantly that 7×8 equals 56 (although when asked the same product on a radio interview in February 1998, Stephen Byers, then Minister of Education, claimed it was 54). They should also be encouraged to compute 49×8 mentally, or 13×13, but this kind of mental arithmetic needs time and concentration.

The fact that the rehabilitation of mental arithmetic is being implemented with such a sense of national anxiety will not help the many teachers who will need a good deal of incentive, encouragement and support to change their teaching styles and modify their understanding of how children learn about numbers and how to calculate with them.

Further reading

Thompson, I. (ed.) (1997) *Teaching and Learning Early Number*. Milton Keynes: Open University. This is an important book, offering clear proposals for an alternative approach to teaching early number based on counting, mental calculation and teaching styles that exploit and develop children's interest and creativity. Along with some relevant and readable research reports, the book includes plenty of clear suggestions for practical action in the classroom.

Plunkett, S. (1979) Decomposition and all that rot, *Mathematics in School*, Vol. 8, no. 3, pp. 2–7. This inspiring article must be one of the most cited and reprinted in mathematics education. The title refers to meaningless rote learning (or failure to learn) of the standard subtraction algorithm. Written in the infancy of the affordable electronic calculator, it offers a common-sense, compelling argument for their acceptance and use, along with mental methods for calculation.

12

Science: Learning to Explain how the World Works

Dorothy Watt

Science depends on questions. It is the way in which human knowledge is taken forward. Should scientists ever stop asking questions then the consequences are unimaginable; progress and understanding of the world would remain static.

(Feasey, 1998: 156)

Introduction

Science in primary schools has undergone a huge revolution since 1989 when it became a core subject within the National Curriculum. Before then, only enthusiastic teachers and schools addressed this subject in any serious way, whereas now every teacher is required to provide children with their entitlement to a science curriculum. Fortunately, over the same period of time there has been an increase in the amount of research into primary science, meaning that we are now in a better position than ever before to describe effective practice based on what we know about how children learn and how teachers teach successfully. In this chapter, I will consider what science in the later years of primary schooling can contribute to children's overall education and how this learning can be facilitated.

The importance of science

Science, as a discipline, is the source of explanations about how and why things happen in the world around us. While these explanations may appear to be a set of 'right answers' which will never change, they are actually based on the accumulated evidence we have to date, and as such may change as we learn more. It is therefore more helpful to see science not as a set of facts to be learnt but as a series of explanations which the community of scientists currently considers to be the best. Some of these explanations, such as the earth being roughly spherical, have been around for a long time and are now considered pretty uncontroversial, particularly as we now have photographic evidence from satellites to support that viewpoint. Others, such as ideas about global warming, are gradually becoming more accepted as more evidence is accumulated to support this explanation for climatic change.

So what does the nature of science have to do with science education? An understanding of what science is like, how it is a constant search for explanations based on evidence, is very important for both teachers and children because it affects how individuals view those scientific ideas they interact with. It is important for children's all-round development that they are made aware of the changing nature of science and its dependence on evidence. In that way, they will better be able to make decisions about the media's presentation of science which tends to be sensationalist and such that each small piece of new evidence is presented as the definitive right answer. It is not only the media which make wild and exaggerated claims for science but also the advertising and marketing industries. In fact, a poor level of scientific literacy pervades the population and this perpetuates the problem – the journalists often do not properly understand the claims any research is making, and this lack of comprehension is what leads to some of the distortion which is presented.

The fact that an understanding of science enables us to appraise scientific information in a more enlightened way is only one reason why science is important for children. Thomas and Durant (1987, cited in Millar, 1996) propose several others:

- that our society can be more democratic if we are all able to enter into informed debate about such issues as energy and transport

- that our country's economic wealth will benefit from having qualified, trained scientists

- that science is the major achievement of our culture and should be both seen and celebrated as such.

Obviously, these lofty aspirations are ones which would need to permeate children's whole educational career, but because these are concerned with a way of looking at the world, it is important that such notions are introduced early in each child's life so that messages about science can consistently be given.

In order that this generation of children grow up to be more scientifically literate than earlier ones, it is important that science is part of a broad curriculum which enables children to learn the necessary skills to acquire and evaluate scientific evidence. Some children will go on to be scientists but the majority will not, and it is an understanding of what science is about, an understanding of some of the 'big ideas' which scientists talk about and an ability to think critically, to acquire and interpret evidence, which will stand all children in good stead.

Working towards society's science ideas: developing conceptual understanding

Contexts and experiences

Having considered what science is about, we need now to focus on how we can help children begin to understand some of the science ideas which are generally accepted and which are considered to be appropriate for children aged seven to eleven to be learning. The notion of appropriateness is introduced at the beginning of this section as science explanations are often very abstract and sometimes they are difficult to understand. Developing an *understanding* in some areas – for example, forces – is going to be beyond the reach of children and in such circumstances we need to think about how we can prepare children to understand the ideas later on. I am not suggesting that we provide a watered-down version of a curriculum designed for older children, rather that a careful selection of experiences for young children will provide them with a firm and coherent foundation on which to build. This preparation would involve providing experiences from which children would be able to make relevant observations across a wide range of related contexts.

Having identified related contexts for children to explore, what we need to consider is how children can be helped to make scientific sense of their observations, and this we can do by encouraging them to find patterns in their observations of phenomena. For example, staying with the context of forces, children can very appropriately make observations related to objects which are stationary and which can be made to move, that is, balanced and unbalanced forces. There are many examples in everyday life of two equal pushes or two equal pulls acting against each other and balancing. Children can explore what happens when the two pushes or pulls become unequal. If children can begin to identify a pattern across different contexts of what will happen and start to hypothesize about why this might be, then they will gain very useful experiences relating to what makes objects in our world move in the way they do. These experiences can then be likened to the same ideas in a completely different context; for example, a consideration of the skeleton and how muscles control our movement, a situation in which the same scientific principles apply. Being able to see those similarities will give children a much clearer appreciation of the power of some of the 'big ideas' in science to explain what goes on in our world.

These 'big ideas' in science, or what a recent report into the future of science teaching calls 'explanatory stories' (Millar and Osborne, 1998: 13), relate to the overarching concepts which link together pieces of knowledge so these can be seen in relation to each other and be used to help explain events across a range of different contexts. Having such a broad understanding has the advantage over lots of separate, unlinked pieces of knowledge that it can be applied to new situations and should still explain the phenomenon – hence the importance of children working with an idea in a wide range of contexts so they can see how the explanation is generalizable from one situation to another. The National Curriculum for older primary pupils (DFE, 1995e) currently veers towards ensuring children learn isolated facts about science which can be integrated at a later stage of their education. One problem with this approach is that it does not assist children in forming a wider view, that is, understanding how different ideas can link together to form a coherent picture. While the approach outlined above is not at odds with the content of the current National Curriculum for Science, it requires an understanding of what science is really about. This is necessary to ensure that statements in the Programme of Study are not used as learning objectives for particular lessons in which the ideas are taught out of context as a set of facts to be learnt. 'Pupils should be taught that forces act in particular directions' (DFE, 1995e: 12) is a good example of a phrase which could be quickly learnt but which requires substantial experience in order to understand what it means.

Beyond the observable

From the age of seven or eight, children are moving out of the phase of education in which their learning experiences need to be based on their immediate surroundings in a very concrete way. In fact, for their scientific development, the ability to begin to handle more abstract notions is very important. We cannot, for example, see plants growing, sound travelling or water evaporating so to be able to explain these phenomena we need to take a leap into the 'invisible'. Our observations can help us to detect patterns, such as that sounds get quieter the further away we are from them, but without an understanding that air is composed of molecules and is a substance that vibrations travel through, it is not possible even to begin to conceive of a mechanism by which sound gets from one place to another. On a similar molecular level, in order to explain a process such as dissolving it is necessary to adopt the model that all matter is composed of molecules, some of which are further apart than others. By means of drama, children can be helped to 'see' how a solid such as sugar can dissolve in a liquid such as water, and how heating or cooling the water will affect the rate at which this process happens.

'Hands-on' and 'minds-on' experiences

So how can we give children these types of experiences to develop their conceptual understanding without just giving them facts to learn? There can be no substitute for children experiencing things for themselves, where the topic lends itself to such work, but the experience itself is only a starting point which needs to be followed by questions – from both children and teacher – and discussion in order to set it in that all-important broader context. Discussion, too, will facilitate the introduction and use of an essential science vocabulary, a topic I will return to in a later section.

It can be tempting to spend most of the available curriculum time engaged in practical work so that children do activities which will demonstrate particular principles, but there are a lot of scientific explanations which cannot be worked out through experiment alone. It is therefore very important that children are given opportunities to engage in 'minds-on' science activity as well as 'hands-on' activity. By 'minds-on' activity I mean giving children opportunities to imagine what would happen in a given scenario; to explain to each other how they think something works; to listen to teachers explaining science using analogies. These two activities should be seen as complementary and need to be used flexibly. The study of human bodies and of the earth in space are examples of topics in which opportunities for first-hand observation and investigation are limited, while much practical work is possible in relation to changes in materials before observations would need to give way to explanations of the 'invisible'.

The important thing to bear in mind is that models, such as molecules, provide ways of explaining phenomena we cannot see, and because of this definition it is possible to use models as the basis for predictions to test how well the model does actually explain something. For example, if sound really does need air (or another substance) to travel through, we should be able to stop sound travelling by removing the air. Not an easy prediction to test in a primary classroom, but there are good quality video tapes available to demonstrate what happens to the sound from a ringing alarm clock when all the air is removed from around it. So, models are not things to be accepted and learnt by rote, they should feed into practical science work and be useful for increasing our explanatory power.

Learning to think and act scientifically: developing procedural understanding

In order to think scientifically we need to engage in using the processes, shown in Table 12.1, which are associated with science: observing, predicting, hypothesizing, raising questions, interpreting, evaluating and communicating. These processes are necessary if we are to be active thinkers and explainers because these provide the critical capacity to make sense of and use information. None of these processes is specific to science, but without these it is not possible to be scientific because we need to be able to evaluate the evidence we collect either for or against particular scientific views. Some or all of these processes are used in any scientific activity, along with practical skills such as measuring, selecting and using equipment and presenting data.

There is some contention as to whether children need to be taught these processes or whether they just require opportunities to develop their proficiency in using them during science work. In either case, it

Table 12.1 The scientific processes

Observing	Taking in information using one or more of our senses
Predicting	Using previous experience to decide what will happen
Hypothesizing	Using previous experience and/or scientific knowledge to explain why something happens
Raising questions	Asking what will happen in a particular situation in such a way that it can be tested scientifically
Interpreting	Identifying trends and patterns in results
Evaluating	Using results to draw conclusions
Communicating	Presenting how the question was investigated scientifically, and how the results and their interpretation suggest a particular hypothesis

is important that attention is paid to identifying where children's use of science processes can be encouraged explicitly. Practical skills, on the other hand, do need to be taught *in the context of science*. Research has shown that children's abilities to make measurements and to construct and interpret graphs in mathematics rarely generalize to science without this support (Goldsworthy, 1998).

I have suggested in the previous section that children should engage in both 'minds-on' and 'hands-on' science activity. 'Minds-on' activities will involve children in using their mental processes to think through a scenario in relation to developing understanding. 'Hands-on' activities can take a range of forms, and Table 12.2 defines the types of practical activity which are likely to occur in primary science and suggests the purposes for which each is best suited. Each of the four types has a distinct value and it is important to be clear which is being used at different times because the possible learning outcomes for children are significantly different. Where our intentions are first and foremost to develop understanding, illustrative activities will

Table 12.2   Types and purposes of practical activity in primary science

---

Basic skills: To develop skills such as:
- selecting or using equipment
- displaying data, such as in graphs
- basic measuring techniques.

Observations: To use some or all of the senses for a variety of purposes, such as:
- describing, sorting and classifying, noting similarities and differences
- identifying important features of events or objects using knowledge and understanding
- providing starting points for investigations, encouraging the formulation of questions, predictions or hypotheses.

Illustrations: To give children first-hand experience of a concept in a structured way, providing detailed instructions of:
- what to do
- what apparatus to use
- what to measure
- how many measurements to take
- in what order to carry out tasks.

Investigations: To apply, and possibly develop, children's understanding of concepts and procedures in a way which enables children to make their own decisions.

(Adapted from NCC, 1993b: 13–15)

be particularly beneficial. Such activities are quite closed and tend to consist of a 'recipe' of instructions to follow which should ensure that a particular science principle is demonstrated. Where we want children to learn the basic skills necessary to collect data in a reliable way then it makes sense to make that the focus of the activity, ensuring there is little new conceptual information involved so that children can concentrate on increasing their skill proficiency. Observation is so fundamental to collecting evidence and developing understanding that it has several distinct purposes in practical activities. The ability to identify similarities and differences is necessary for the sorting and classifying which underpins the identification of patterns in any data and thus informs our mental frameworks for making sense of the world. Having found the patterns, children can begin to wonder what might happen at, for example, a higher temperature, or with a smaller weight, or with a brighter light. Using patterns in this way leads children to predict the likely outcome and hypothesize about *why* that pattern might be there, what a possible explanation might be. Here, then, are observations leading to investigations during which data will be collected to test out the ability of a hypothesis to explain the findings. Through such investigations children are involved in making decisions at various levels: about the equipment to use; the measurements to take and the best means of presenting the data. Whether these decisions are taken individually, in small groups or as a class, and with or without teacher support, will depend on the children's previous experience and on the particular context. Children of the age of seven should be capable of beginning to make these decisions with support, the amount of support decreasing as they become more experienced.

From this brief discussion of practical work, it should be clear that it is through investigations that children will develop the procedural understanding of science which will help them to understand the nature of science and how it depends on reliably collected and evaluated evidence. We should not, however, expect children to reinvent the wheel by rediscovering accepted scientific principles through investigation. It is an understanding of the *procedures* which can lead to the gathering of evidence and the testing of hypotheses with which children need to become familiar.

Having said that, there is no one particular approach which we can say is the one professional scientists use in order to develop their understanding: sometimes they start with a hypothesis to test, but more often they are engaged in routine data collection to see what happens to a particular organism or substance in a particular setting over a period of time. Occasionally there is a huge leap forward in understanding and this is often the result of a flash of inspiration which provides the spur to collect data to see if their hunch is correct. Rarely is there an investigation set up to explore a scientific idea, the type of experience often given to children in order to help them learn to be scientific. Some important aspects of procedural understanding to which we should give children access are objectivity, fair testing and replicability. Each of these concepts is hard for children to understand and it is only towards the age of eleven that children will be beginning to work with notions of replicability and be able to make independent decisions about fair testing.

Objectivity

For evidence to be scientific it is important that we engage in these processes as objectively as possible, taking care to consider different possible interpretations. However, while doing this we have to acknowledge that we must interpret any observations we make from our own particular point of view because we see the world through our own eyes and interpret everything in a way which makes sense to us. For example, if we see a bare tree in winter, our theory will tell us that it is likely to be a deciduous tree that has shed its leaves because it is winter. If, on the other hand, we see the same tree bare in the summer, that same theory would tell us the tree should now have leaves, and only then would the absence of these lead to an alternative interpretation, that the tree is likely to be dead. It may have already been dead during the winter, but we interpreted our observations using a theory which precluded that as an explanation for us.

Fair testing

There is the notion of a fair test which ensures (as far as possible) that only one variable is changed at a time. So, in order to determine what effect the height of a ramp has on how far a toy car moves before it stops, we would need to vary the height of the ramp (the independent variable) while keeping everything else the same – the car, the ramp, the surface at the bottom of the ramp, the prevailing wind conditions (the control variables) – and measure the distance travelled along the flat surface (the dependent variable). By the age of seven or eight, children should be developing these ideas related to fair testing, recognizing when a test is fair or not, and they should become increasingly adept at devising their own as their age, experience and understanding grow. They also progress in the type of variable they can work with, from discrete variables, things which are separate and have a finite, distinct 'value' such as colour, number (of), days of the week, to continuous variables which are, as their name suggests, able to take continuous values, such as temperature, length and weight. This meaning of 'fair' is precise and different from the everyday definition which children will often invoke of something 'not being fair' (Goldsworthy, 1998), so care is needed to develop this scientific notion with children.

Replicability

In order to ensure that results have not happened by chance, it is necessary to repeat all data collection in exactly the same way so that results can be compared. This notion of replicability increases the chance of data being reliable and thus improves the status of science knowledge.

Identifying starting points and recognizing learning

Much research in recent years, most notably in the UK the Primary SPACE Project (Osborne *et al.*, 1990; Russell and Watt, 1990a), has shown that children bring their own ideas with them to school science. These ideas are often quite unlike the accepted science view and a selection of children's ideas about water evaporating from a transparent fish tank is shown in Figure 12.1. It is possible to see a range of ideas being expressed here, and it is also possible to hypothesize about what experiences these children had of water which could have led to their particular notion being developed. These seem to children to be sensible explanations for the experiences they have had to date.

(a)

(Age 8 years)

"Mrs. Stewart (caretaker) drank it." [Teacher note]

Fig. 12.1 Childrens's ideas about evaporation (from Russell and Watt, 1990a: 27–33)

(b)

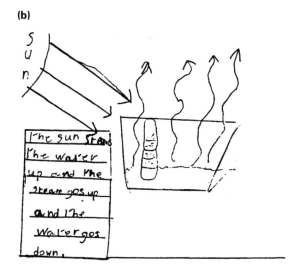

(Age 8 years)

"*The sun steams the water up and the steam goes up and the water goes down.*"

(c)

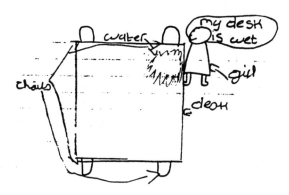

(Age 10 years)

"*I think that the water will lift itself out of the box and land on one of the tables and when we all come back to school the next day somebody will find that their desk has got water on it.*"

Fig. 12.1 Continued

(d)

I think the water has
split up into millions of
micro bibs and floated up
and floating as it floabs out
of the doors or windows when
they are opened.

(Age 10 years)

"I think the water has split up into millions of micro bits and floated up and it floats out of the doors or windows when they are opened."

Fig. 12.1 Continued

It is important to remember that these ideas show how the world can be interpreted through different frameworks from the one that scientists accept, and that it is often the science ideas which are not intuitively sensible rather than the children's!

There is a range of techniques, brought together originally by the SPACE Project and subsequently augmented, which teachers can use to find out about children's current understanding of a certain topic. These are practical and for use with a whole class at the same time because there is no dependence on one-to-one conversation between teacher and child. These techniques include:

- Free writing and drawing in a 'logbook' (Russell and Watt, 1990a) which is useful when the topic being studied involves slow, gradual changes such as growth, evaporation, rusting and rotting. Over a period of time, children's considered thoughts can be gathered.

- Structured drawing and writing in response to a particular question (Russell and Watt, 1990a) means children's thinking can be focused on one area such as evaporation; for example, show where you think the water goes and what makes it go.

- Completing a picture by including relevant, missing aspects (Osborne *et al.*, 1990) – for example, where light is in a room – which can help ensure children are not hampered by any inhibition about their drawing skills and are able to focus on demonstrating their understanding in the particular area of study.

- Concept cartoons (Keogh and Naylor, 1997) which provide a focus for discussion through presenting alternative views on the same scenario.
- Concept maps (Novak and Gowin, 1984) which show how children link different aspects of a scientific topic together.

These techniques can work very successfully once children have been taught the particular skills which are required for each of them. As there need be few language demands if the focus is drawing, it is possible for all children to undertake such work quite independently even where English is an additional language and conceptual expression is poor, or there is a particular learning need linked to reading and writing. While such work is being carried out independently, it is possible to circulate and discuss the activity with individual children to seek clarification or expansion of expression.

While it is easy to find out children's ideas, it can be difficult to know how to engage with these as part of the teaching process. What the ideas represent is the explanation the child is currently using. Harlen (1993) suggests that these ideas should represent the starting point for classroom activity, and that the children should be encouraged to test out their own hypothesis to see whether they can find any evidence to support it. In this way, children are helped to realize that other ideas are better at explaining what is happening than their own. However, by adopting this approach, there is no guarantee that the explanation the child adopts in place of their previous idea will be any nearer the scientific view, or that their investigation was rigorous and their testing fair.

A more productive way of using the children's ideas is to think of the process of finding these out as being an initial formative assessment. In that way, planning can be pitched to bridge the gap between what children have shown they already know and what they still need to learn. For example, if we look at the ideas expressed in Figures 12.1b and 12.1d, the child in Figure 12.1b seems to understand that heat (in the form of the sun) is making the water level sink but there is no evidence that she has considered what the 'steam' is made up of, in terms of water droplets or gas. On the other hand, the child whose work is shown in Figure 12.1d has considered what the water turns into but not what factors make the process happen. The former child could profitably focus on the change of state of water as it evaporates, while the latter could focus on the factors which lead to evaporation, or on the nature of reversible and irreversible changes. By focusing on what the children still need to learn, it is possible to make teaching more focused for individual learners. This need not be as unmanageable as it sounds as, by looking carefully at the science ideas which are and are not shown in the children's drawing or writing, it is possible to group children together so that those with similar learning needs can work together.

Such formative assessment will enable teaching to be focused clearly on the areas in which a child needs experience, ensuring that limited teaching time can be used to its full potential in developing a coherent understanding of the topic being taught. It has the additional benefit of making it clear what evidence of learning it is appropriate to look for during, and as a result of, teaching.

Developing scientific language

One of the advantages of formative assessment is that it provides children with opportunities to demonstrate their understanding without being constrained by their knowledge of scientific terms. However, children do need to be introduced to correct scientific terminology in a way which enables them to attach clearly understood meaning to each item of scientific vocabulary. While it is possible for children to learn the terminology by rote, without an underlying understanding of what they are talking about, their future scientific development is likely to be hampered. The most important thing for children to be able to do with a scientific term is to define it in their own words. Thus, the tempting practice of writing the word and its dictionary meaning on the board for children to copy is probably the least helpful approach to take.

There will be times when it will seem appropriate to introduce a new word at the start of a topic. Time spent brainstorming for synonyms within the children's vocabulary would be time well spent in order to help the children learn the meaning of the word in context. On other occasions it may be more appropriate to introduce the term at the end of a session in which children have been exploring the relevant concept. In these cases, the teacher will already be aware of the alternative words children are using which will be as those identified in formative assessments and through on-going listening to children while they are working. A third scenario is the construction of an activity around vocabulary to make children focus sharply on what they mean when they use particular words. One of the teachers involved in the SPACE Project helped her class of seven-year-olds clarify the difference between 'stretching' and 'growing':

The children appeared to have defined the word 'grow' in terms of 'stretching' – increasing the length of something without adding any more material to it – and they often seemed to use the two terms synonymously, e.g.

'I think when the plant is taking in water it is stretching the plant, stretching it from the seed as high as it can.'

The teacher made a collection of articles which increased in size by either growing or stretching, e.g. Christmas decorations, bubbles, knitting, sticking, treacle toffee, springs, and the children stretched themselves during a movement lesson. The children were able, during discussion, to explain quite clearly that stretching needed help and could not go beyond a limit, that things would break if stretched beyond a certain point or would return to normal if let go. The definition of growth was still unclear; it was thought that knitting might grow, by adding more wool on, but that as it could be unravelled and animal or plant growth was permanent, they might not be the same.

(Russell and Watt, 1990b: 72–3)

It is clear from the above example that the teacher had a very clear understanding of the terminology she was encouraging the children to grapple with and it is essential that this is the case – otherwise a teacher's rote learning will be passed on to the children in similar fashion.

Science explanations

Children are not in a position to be able to 'discover' scientific explanations for themselves through their own practical investigation. They can obtain valuable evidence to support an accepted hypothesis but it is hard for them to do more than this because many explanations rely on 'invisible' phenomena. Thus, for children to progress in their understanding of science, they must be assisted by teaching which helps them move towards being able to give explanations themselves. We have little experience in knowing which types of explanation are effective for primary school children but it certainly is not one to be found in a science textbook which is suitable for older children and adults. It is likely to have the following features:

- it will use everyday language rather than rely on scientific terminology

- it will be set within a familiar context, one which children have been investigating

- it might make use of an analogy, that is, it might liken a phenomenon to something which is familiar to children's everyday lives;
for example, an electrical circuit is like a bicycle chain

- it is one the teacher understands and uses with confidence.

Teachers' understanding of science

There has been much research in recent years into what sort of understanding of science helps teachers to teach it effectively (Grossman,
Wilson and Shulman, 1989; Shulman, 1986). These researchers suggest
there are several different types of subject knowledge which comple-
ment each other in the teaching process. Firstly, there is subject knowledge – a teacher's understanding of the nature of science and their
understanding of scientific procedures and concepts. This alone is not
enough to guarantee that a teacher will be able to convey any of their
understanding: they also need a second type of knowledge, pedagogical content knowledge, which gives an understanding of what children are likely to bring with them to their school science and a
knowledge of how to match activities and explanations to the learning
needs of particular children. Thirdly, there is curricular knowledge
which relates to an understanding of the structures of the curriculum
a teacher is required to teach. How these different types of knowledge
relate to each other is still far from clear, but some light is being shed
on the matter. Bennett and Carré (1993, in Carré and Ovens, 1994) identified that student teachers with a higher level of understanding about
science showed the following characteristics of effective teaching:

- They planned organizational matters in detail and provided appropriate activities for children to make sense of science.

- They used their presentation at the beginning of the lesson to
explain the learning intentions and to offer a clear link with the
practical work to follow.

- They taught flexibly, employing both knowledge-telling and knowl-
edge-transforming methods.

- They were able to come up with ways of explaining concepts to
children.

- They were good listeners, respecting children's prior knowledge
and indicating if their responses were correct or inappropriate. They
were able to challenge children's ideas and beliefs. (Carré and
Ovens, 1994: 8.)

Few studies have explored the effect of good subject knowledge on experienced teachers teaching science, but those that have (Holroyd and Harlen, 1996; Osborne and Simon, 1996) found similar characteristics to Bennett and Carré while at the same time identifying particular features of the practice of teachers with a low level of subject knowledge in science. These characteristics were:

- closing down opportunities for discussion

- teaching only preferred areas of science

- teaching according to activities rather than objectives

- emphasizing the development of processes or skills rather than understanding.

From these perspectives, it certainly seems as if children will receive a far richer science education when they are taught by a teacher who both understands how children think and learn in science and also understands the science they are intending to teach.

The role of the science curriculum leader

It is likely that the science curriculum leader will have some expertise in each of the different types of knowledge identified above: they will understand the science they are teaching; they will know how to convey science ideas clearly to children; they will be aware of children's ideas about science; they will know the requirements of the curriculum and what potential sources of support are available for teachers.

In order that all the teachers in the school can benefit from this expertise, the curriculum leader will be asked to co-ordinate the development of science throughout the school. This co-ordination should ensure there will be continuity in the teaching approaches used and progression in the conceptual and procedural understanding the children are being asked to develop. Aspects of the curriculum leader's role will be:

- co-ordinating the development and updating of the policy for science teaching and learning

- co-ordinating the development and updating of the scheme of work

- ordering, purchasing, organizing and monitoring the use of resources

- advising on appropriate curriculum support materials

- providing staff development and support.

It is beyond the scope of this chapter to consider each of these aspects in detail. However, in the light of the arguments I have presented, there are three main points I would like to emphasize. Firstly, it is important to ensure that both facets of science, the conceptual and the procedural understanding, are included as coherent strands in the scheme of work. Practical work and procedural understanding are not synonymous: opportunities for children to become proficient in collecting evidence to support and develop explanations need to be incorporated deliberately in ways which encourage children to become progressively more rigorous and independent so that, by the age of eleven, they can not only plan, carry out and interpret an investigation but also explain what investigations are for.

Secondly, it is easy for ideas relating to the nature of science to play only a very minor role in science education. By supporting colleagues in their own understanding of how science ideas are developed and become accepted while always being regarded as provisional, such notions should be able to permeate science teaching and inform children's learning.

Thirdly, recent research (Watt, 1997; Watt and Simon, in press) has suggested that where teachers lack confidence in their personal science knowledge, a scheme of work alone may not provide adequate support for planning. What is needed are clear examples of:

- activities which work successfully with children

- questions which are productive to ask as part of formative assessment during each session

- effective explanations to use

- definitions of key vocabulary written in everyday language.

One of the most valuable things the curriculum leader can do to support staff in their science teaching is to annotate the school's scheme of work to include such examples. As a result, teachers who lack confidence in their science knowledge and teaching repertoire will be well supported and able to make their teaching more like that of more experienced science teachers.

Summary

Science forms a very important part of the curriculum of children between the ages of seven and eleven. At these ages they are growing in their awareness of different subjects and are ready to see science as the way we, in our society, explain how the world works.

They will be able to use their practical experiences to help them develop their understanding of important 'big ideas' in science, as well as gaining fully from appropriate explanations to move their thinking from a focus on what is observable to a consideration of more abstract, 'invisible' notions.

Teachers can cue themselves into the children's current level of understanding by using questions to assess children in a formative way, thus establishing what will be appropriate provision for children with their particular learning needs. This cueing will also enable teachers to introduce scientific vocabulary to children in a way which should ensure they have understood the meaning of the term.

In order to teach effectively in this way, teachers need either to have, or to have support in, suitable understanding of the science they are teaching as well as an understanding of the types of activity from which children will learn best. The role of the curriculum leader is crucial in providing this support.

Further reading

Carré, C. and Ovens, C. (1994) *Science 7–11: Developing Primary Teaching Skills.* London: Routledge. This book draws on recent research to present a balanced account of how primary science can be taught effectively to children aged seven to eleven. It is readable and contains many classroom examples.

Sherrington, R. (ed.) (1998) *ASE Guide to Primary Science Education.* London: Stanley Thornes. This book contains chapters which address a wide range of topics, each written in an accessible style by an acknowledged authority in the field. It is the most comprehensive, up-to-date text currently available.

References

Aboud, F. (1988) *Children and Prejudice*. Oxford: Blackwell.

Advisory Group on Education for Citizenship and the Teaching of Democracy in Schools (1998) *Summary of the Final Report of the Advisory Group on Education for Citizenship and the Teaching of Democracy in Schools.* London: The Qualifications and Curriculum Authority.

Alexander, R. (1984, 1988) *Primary Teaching*. London: Cassell. 1st and 2nd edition.

Alexander R. (1992) *Policy and Practice in Primary Education*. London: Routledge.

Alexander, R. (1997a) International comparisons and the quality of primary teaching, in C. Cullingford, (ed.) *The Politics of Primary Education*. Buckingham: Open University Press.

Alexander, R. (1997b) The basics: core or margins? Paper presented at the SCAA Conference on Developing the Primary Curriculum: The Next Steps, London.

Alexander, R. (ed.) (1998) *Time for Change?* Warwick University: Centre for Research in Elementary and Primary Education.

Alexander, R., Rose, J. and Woodhead, C. (1992) *Curriculum Organization and Classroom Practice in Primary Schools: A Discussion Paper*. London: Department of Education and Science.

Almond, L. (1989) The place of physical education in the curriculum, in L. Almond (ed.) *The Place of Physical Education in Schools*. London: Kogan Page. pp. 13–36.

Ames, C. and Archer, J. (1988) Achievement goals in the classroom: students' learning strategies and motivation processes, *Journal of Educational Psychology*, Vol. 80, pp. 260–7.

Armstrong, N. (1990) Children's physical activity patterns: the implications for physical education, in *New Directions in Physical Education (Volume 1)*. Illinois: Human Kinetics. pp. 1–15.

Armstrong, N. and Welsman, A. (1997) *Young People and Physical Activity*. Oxford: Oxford University Press.

Arnold, P. J. (1979) *Meaning in Movement, Sport and Physical Education.* London: Heinemann.

Asher, J. J. (1983) *Learning Another Language Through Actions.* Los Angeles, CA: Sky Oaks.

Askew, M. (1997) Mental methods of computation, *Mathematics Teaching,* Vol. 160, pp. 7–8.

Askew, M. and Wiliam, D. (1995) *Recent Research in Mathematics Education.* London: Her Majesty's Stationery Office.

Aubrey, C. (ed.) (1994) *The Role of Subject Knowledge in the Early Years of Schooling.* London: Falmer.

Bailey, R. P. and Farrow S. (1998) Play, and problem-solving in a new light, *International Journal of Early Years Education,* Vol. 6, no. 1, pp. 265–75.

Bailey, R. P. (1999) Play, health and physical development, in T. David (ed.) *Young Children Learning.* London: Paul Chapman pp. 46–66.

Balchin, W. (1996) Graphicacy and the primary geographer, *Primary Geographer,* no. 24, Geographical Association.

Ball, S. (1990) *Politics and Policy Making in Education: Explorations in Policy Sociology.* London: Routledge.

Bangert-Drowns, R. L. (1993) The word processor as an instructional tool: a meta-analysis of word processing in writing instruction, *Review of Educational Research,* Vol. 63, no. 1, pp. 69–93.

Baynes, K. (1992) *Children Designing.* Loughborough: Loughborough University of Technology.

Beard, R. (1984) *Children's Writing in the Primary School.* Sevenoaks: Hodder & Stoughton Educational.

Beard, R. (1991) Learning to read like a writer, *Educational Review,* Vol. 43, no. 1, pp. 17–24.

Beard, R. (1997) Meeting the needs, *English 4–11,* Vol. 1, no. 1, pp. 11–14.

Beard, R. (1999) *The National Literacy Strategy: Review of Research and Other Related Evidence.* London: Department for Education and Employment.

Beishuitzen, M. (1997) Mental arithmetic: mental recall or mental strategies? *Mathematics Teaching,* Vol. 160, pp. 16–19.

Beishuitzen, M. and Anghileri, J. (1998) Which mental strategies in the early number curriculum? A comparison of British and Dutch views, *British Education Research Journal,* Vol. 24, no. 5, pp. 519–38.

Bereiter, C. and Scardamalia, M. (1987) *The Psychology of Written Composition.* Hillsdale, NJ: Lawrence Erlbaum.

Bierhoff, H. (1996) *Laying the Foundations of Numeracy.* Discussion Paper no. 90. London: National Institute of Economic and Social Research.

Bierton, C., Mitchell, S., Radnor, H. and Ross, M. (1993) *Assessing Achievement in the Arts.* Buckingham: Open University Press.

Birtwistle, G. and Brodie, D. (1991) Children's attitudes towards physical activity and perceptions of physical education, *Health Education Research,* Vol. 6, pp. 465–78.

Bjorkvold, J. R. (1989) *The Muse Within – Creativity and Communication, Song and Play from Childhood Through Maturity.* New York: HarperCollins.

Blacking, John (1995) *Music, Culture and Experience*. Chicago: University of Chicago Press.

Blunkett, D. (1995) *On a Clear Day*. London: Michael O'Mara Books.

Blyth, W. A. L (1984) *Development, Experience and Curriculum in Primary Education*. London: Croom Helm.

Boardman, D. (1990) Graphicacy revisited: mapping abilities and gender differences, *Geography Educational Review*, Vol. 42, no. 1.

Britton, J. (1970) *Language and Learning*. Harmondsworth: Penguin.

Brown, M. (1996) FIMS and SIMS: the first two IEA international mathematics surveys, *Assessment in Education*, Vol. 3, no. 2, pp. 181–200.

Brown, M. (1998) The tyranny of the international horse race, in R. Slee and G. Weiner (eds), *School Effectiveness: for Whom?* London: Falmer. pp. 33–48.

Bruner, J. (1957) Going beyond the information given, in H. Gruber (ed.) *Contemporary Approaches to Cognition*, Cambridge, Mass.: Harvard University Press.

Bruner, J. (1966) *Toward a Theory of Instruction*. Cambridge, Mass: Harvard University Press.

Bruner, J. (1983) *Child's Talk – Learning to Use Language*. Oxford: Oxford University Press.

Bruner, J. (1986) *Actual Minds, Possible Worlds*. Cambridge, Mass: Harvard University Press.

Buchanan, Michael (1995) Making art and critical literacy: a reciprocal approach, in R. Prentice (ed.) *Teaching Art and Design*. London: Cassell.

Buckingham, D. (1993) *Children Talking Television: The Making of Television Literacy*. London: Falmer.

Burgess, L. and Holman, V. (1993) Live studies. *Times Educational Supplement*, 4 June.

Callaghan, M. and Rothery, J. (1988) *Teaching Factual Writing: A Genre-Based Approach*. Sydney: Metropolitan East Disadvantaged Schools Programme.

Carré, C. and Ovens, C. (1994) *Science 7–11: Developing Primary Teaching Skills*, London: Routledge.

Catlin, S. (1998) Children as mapmakers, in S. Scoffham (ed.) *Primary Sources: Research Findings in Primary Geography*. Sheffield: The Geographical Asssociation.

Central Advisory Council for Education (England) (1967) *Children and Their Primary Schools* (the Plowden Report). London: Her Majesty's Stationery Office.

Claxton, Guy (1997) *Hare Brain Tortoise Mind*. London: Fourth Estate.

Clay, G. (1997) Standards in primary physical education: OFSTED 1995–96, *Primary PE Focus*, Autumn, pp. 4–6.

Cochran-Smith, M. (1991) *Learning to Write Differently*. Hove: Ablex.

Coleman, J. A. (1961) *The Adolescent Society*. New York: Free Press.

Commission on Religious Education in Schools (1970) *The Fourth R: The Report of the Commission on Religious Education in Schools*. London: SPCK.

Cope, B. and Kalantzis, M. (eds) (1993) *The Powers of Literacy: A Genre Approach to Teaching Writing*. London: Falmer Press.

Cox, C. B. and Boyson, R. (eds) (1977) *Black Papers 1977*. London: Temple Smith.

Cox, Gordon (1993) *A History of Music Education 1872–1928*. Aldershot: Scholar Press.

Creemers, B. P. M. (1994) *The Effective Classroom*. London: Cassell.

Crook, C. (1994) *Computers and the Collaborative Experience of Learning*. London and New York: Routledge.

Crystal, D. (1990) *The English Language*. Harmondsworth: Penguin.

Cullingford, C. (1990) *The Nature of Learning*. London: Cassell.

Daley, D. (1988) Language development through physical education, *British Journal of Physical Education*, May, pp. 132–3.

Dearden, R. (1971) What is the integrated day? in J. Walton (ed.) *The Integrated Day in Theory and Practice*. London: Ward Lock Educational.

Department for Education (1995a) *Art in the National Curriculum*. London: Her Majesty's Stationery Office.

Department for Education (1995b) *History in the National Curriculum: England*. London: Her Majesty's Stationery Office.

Department for Education (1995c) *Mathematics in The National Curriculum*. London: Her Majesty's Stationery Office.

Department for Education (1995d) *Physical Education in the National Curriculum*. London: Department for Education and Employment.

Department for Education (1995e) *Science in the National Curriculum*. London: Her Majesty's Stationery Office.

Department for Education/Welsh Office (1995) *Design and Technology in the National Curriculum*. London: Her Majesty's Stationery Office.

Department for Education and Employment (1995a) *Information Technology in the National Curriculum*. London: Her Majesty's Stationery Office.

Department for Education and Employment (1995b) *Looking at Values Through Products and Applications* (Conference Proceedings). London: Department for Education and Employment.

Department for Education and Employment (1997a) *Connecting the Learning Society: National Grid For Learning*. London: Department for Education and Employment.

Department for Education and Employment (1997b) *Excellence in Schools*. London: The Stationery Office.

Department for Education and Employment (1998a) *Information Technology: A Scheme of Work for Key Stages 1 and 2*. London: Department for Education and Employment.

Department for Education and Employment (1998b) *Initial Teacher Training National Curriculum for the Use of Information and Communications Technology in Subject Teaching*. London: Department for Education and Employment.

Department for Education and Employment (1998c) *News*. London: Department for Education and Employment.

Department for Education and Employment (1998d) *Numeracy Matters: The Preliminary Report of the Numeracy Task Force*. Crown Copyright.

Department for Education and Employment (1998e) *Teaching: High Status,*

High Standards. Circular Number 4/98.

Department for Education and Employment (1998f) *The Implementation of the National Numeracy Strategy*. Sudbury: Department for Education and Employment.

Department for Education and Employment (1998g) *The National Literacy Strategy: Framework for Teaching*. London: Department for Education and Employment.

Department for Education and Employment (1999) *The National Numeracy Strategy: Framework for Teaching Mathematics from Reception to Year 6*. Sudbury: Department for Education and Employment.

Department for National Heritage (DNH) (1995) *Sport – Raising the Game*. London: Her Majesty's Stationery Office.

Department of Education and Science (1975) *A Language for Life* (The Bullock Report). London: Her Majesty's Stationery Office.

Department of Education and Science (1978) *Primary Education in England*. London: Her Majesty's Stationery Office.

Department of Education and Science. (1982a) *Mathematics Counts*. London: Her Majesty's Stationery Office.

Department of Education and Science (1982b) *National Curriculum for Music*. London: Her Majesty's Stationery Office.

Department of Education and Science (1985a) *History in the Primary and Secondary Years: an HMI View*. London: Her Majesty's Stationery Office.

Department of Education and Science (1985b) *Music From 5–16*. London: Her Majesty's Stationery Office.

Department of Education and Science (1987) *Interim Report of the Mathematics Working Party on Mathematics in the National Curriculum*. London: Her Majesty's Stationery Office.

Department of Education and Science (1988) *Report of the Committee of Inquiry into the Teaching of the English Language* (the Kingman Report). London: Her Majesty's Stationery Office.

Department of Education and Science (1989a) *English for Ages 5 to 11* (the Cox Report). London: Her Majesty's Stationery Office.

Department of Education and Science (1989b) *National Curriculum History Working Group: Interim Report*. London: Her Majesty's Stationery Office

Department of Education and Science (1989c) *The Teaching and Learning of History and Geography. Aspects of Primary Education Series*. London: Her Majesty's Stationery Office.

Department of Education and Science (1990) *National Curriculum History Working Group: Final Report*. London: Her Majesty's Stationery Office.

Department of Education and Science (1991) *Geography in the National Curriculum, Non-statutory Guidance*. London: Her Majesty's Stationery Office.

Design and Technology Association (1997) *DATA's Initial Thoughts on the National Curriculum Review*. Wellesbourne: DATA.

Deuchar, S. (1989) *The New History: A Critique*. York: Campaign for Real Education.

Dewey, J. (1938) *Experience and Education*. New York: Collier-Macmillan.

Donaldson, M. (1978) *Children's Minds*. Glasgow: Fontana/Collins.

Donaldson, M. (1992) *Human Minds: An Exploration*. London: Penguin.

Donaldson, M. (1993) Sense and sensibility: some thoughts on the teaching of literacy, in R. Beard (ed.), *Teaching Literacy: Balancing Perspectives*. London: Hodder & Stoughton.

Durrant, C. and Welch, G. (1995) *Making Sense of Music*. London: Cassell.

Dweck, C. S. (1986) Motivational processes affecting learning, *American Psychologist*, Vol. 41, pp. 1040–8.

Dyson, A. (1989) Art history in schools: a comprehensive strategy, in D. Thistlewood (ed.), *Critical Studies in Art and Design Education*. Harlow: NSEAD/Longman.

Education Reform Act. (1988) Norwich: Her Majesty's Stationery Office.

Edwards, D. and Mercer, N. (1987) *Common Knowledge: The Development of Understanding in the Classroom*. London: Methuen.

Eisner, Elliot (1972) *Educating Artistic Vision*. New York: Macmillan.

Eisner, Elliot (1998) Does experience in the arts boost academic achievement? *Art Education*, Vol. 51, no. 1, pp. 7–15.

Evans, J. and Roberts, G. C. (1987) Physical competence and the development of children's peer relations, *Quest*, Vol. 39, pp. 23–35.

Feasey, R. (1998) Effective questioning in science, in R. Sherrington (ed.), *ASE Guide to Primary Science Education*. London: Stanley Thornes. pp. 156–67.

Fentem, P. H., Bassey, E. J. and Turnbull, N. B. (1988) *The New Case for Exercise*. London: Sports Council/Health Education Authority.

Field, Dick (1970) *Change in Art Education*. London: Routledge & Kegan Paul.

Field, Dick (1973) Art and art education, in D. Field and J. Newick (eds) *The Study of Education and Art*. London: Routledge, Kegan, Paul.

Fisher, R. (1990) *Teaching Children to Think*. Oxford: Blackwell.

Fisher, R. (1995) *Teaching Children to Learn*. Cheltenham: Stanley Thornes.

Fountas, I. C. and Pinnell, G. S. (1996) *Guided Reading: Good First Teaching for All Children*. Portsmouth, NH: Heinemann.

Fox, G. (ed.) (1995) *Celebrating Children's Literature in Education*. London: Hodder & Stoughton.

Friend, C. (1995) Can positive attitudes be developed towards economically developing countries in the primary phase? Unpublished dissertation. Canterbury Christ Church College.

Fullan, M. (1993) *Change Forces: Probing the Depths of Educational Reform*. London: Falmer.

Galloway, D. and Edwards, A. (1991) *Primary School Teaching and Educational Psychology*. London: Longman.

Galton, M., Simon, B. and Croll, P. (1980) *Inside the Primary Classroom*. London: Routledge & Kegan Paul.

Gamble, Tom (1984) Imagination and understanding in the music curriculum, *British Journal of Music Education*, Vol. 1, no. 1, pp. 7–25.

Gardner, H. (1983, 1993) *Frames of Mind: The Theory of Multiple Intelligences*. London: Fontana Press. 1st and 2nd editions.

Gelman, R., and Gallistel, C. R. (1978) *The Child's Understanding of Number.* Cambridge, MA.: Harvard University Press.

Gentle, Keith (1985) *Children and Art Teaching.* London: Croom Helm.

Gilbert, Jean (1998) Legitimizing sketchbooks as a research tool in an academic setting, *Journal of Art and Design Education*, Vol. 17, no. 3, pp. 255–66.

Gildenhuys, C. A. and Orsmond, C. P. (1996) Movement and second language acquisition: the potential and the method, *Sport, Education and Society*, Vol. 1, no. 1, pp. 103–15.

Goelman, D. (1996) *Emotional Intelligence.* London: Bloomsbury.

Goldsworthy, A. (1998) Learning to investigate, in R. Sherrington (ed.) *ASE Guide to Primary Science Education.* London: Stanley Thornes. pp. 63–70.

Gray, E. (1991) The primary mathematics textbook: intermediary of the cycle of change, in D. Pimm and E. Love (eds) *Teaching and Learning School Mathematics.* London: Hodder & Stoughton. pp. 122–36.

Gray, E. (1997) Compressing the counting process: developing a flexible interpretation of symbols, in I. Thompson (ed.) *Teaching and Learning Early Number.* London: Open University Press.

Grossman, P. L., Wilson, S. M. and Shulman, L. S. (1989) Teachers of substance: subject matter knowledge for teaching, in M. C. Reynolds (ed.) *Knowledge Base for the Beginning Teacher.* New York: Pergamon Press. pp. 23–36.

Groves, S. (1994) The effect of calculator use on third and fourth graders' computation and choice of calculating device, in J. P. da Ponte and J. F. Matos (eds) *Proceedings of PME-18.* Vol. 3. Lisbon: University of Lisbon. pp. 33–41.

Guardian (1998) Painting by digits. 5 November.

Gulbenkian Foundation (1982) *The Arts in Schools.* London: Gulbenkian Foundation.

Hall, C. and Coles, M. (1999) *Children's Reading Choices.* London: Routledge.

Hargreaves, L. M. and Hargreaves, D. J. (1997) Children's cognitive development 3–7, in N. Kitson and R. Merry (eds) *Teaching in the Primary School: A Learning Relationship.* London: Routledge.

Harlen, W. (1993) *Teaching and Learning Primary Science.* London: Paul Chapman. 2nd edition.

Harrington, V. (1998) Teaching about distant places, in S. Scoffham (ed.) *Primary Sources: Research Findings in Primary Geography.* Sheffield: The Geographical Association.

Harris, S., Keys, W. and Fernandes, C. (1997) *Third International Mathematics and Science Study: Second National Report Part 1.* Slough: NFER.

Harwood, D. and McShane, J. (1996) Young children's understanding of nested hierarchies of place relationship, *International Research in Geographical and Environmental Education*, Vol. 5, no. 1, pp. 3–29.

Hastings, N. and Schwieso, J. (1995) Tasks and tables: the effects of seating arrangements on task engagement in primary lessons, *Educational Research*, Vol. 37, no. 3, pp. 279–91.

Haylock, D. (1995) *Mathematics Explained for Primary Teachers.* London: Paul

Chapman.

Hayward, K. M. (1993) *Life Span Motor Development*. Champaign, IL.: Human Kinetics. 2nd edition.

Hennessy, S. and McCormick, R. (1994) The general problem solving process in technology education – myth or reality? in F. Banks (ed.) *Teaching Technology*. London: Routledge.

Her Majesty's Inspectorate (1992) *English Key Stages 1, 2 and 3: A Report by HM Inspectorate on the Second Year 1990–91*. London: Her Majesty's Stationery Office.

Hicks, D. and Holden, C. (1995) *Visions of the Future: Why We Need to Teach for Tomorrow*. Stoke-on-Trent: Trentham Books.

Hillier, Susan (1995) *After the Freud Museum*. London: Bookworks.

Hillman, M. (1993) *Children, Transport and the Quality of Life*. London: Policy Studies Institute.

Hirst, Paul H. (1974) *Knowledge and the Curriculum*. London: Routledge & Kegan Paul.

Holm, A. (1965) *I am David*. London: Methuen.

Holroyd, C. and Harlen, W. (1996) Primary teachers' confidence about teaching science and technology, *Research Papers in Education*, Vol. 11, no. 3, pp. 323–35.

Holt, David (1997) Hidden strengths: the case for the generalist teacher of art, in D. Holt (ed.) *Primary Arts Education: Contemporary Issues*. Lewes: Falmer.

Hoodless, P. (1996) *Time and Timelines in the Primary School*. Teaching of History No. 69. London: The Historical Association.

Hughes, Arthur (1998) Reconceptualizing the art curriculum, *Journal of Art and Design Education*, Vol. 17, no. 2, pp. 42–9.

Hughes, Carmel (1999) Unpublished MA assignment. University of London, Institute of Education.

Independent (1998a) Schools to reach creativity. 5 February.

Independent (1998b) More artists than artisans in Britain by year 2006. 16 April.

Independent (1998c) Hirst's sheep give Britain art failure. (14 September).

Independent ICT in Schools Commission (1997) *Information Technology in UK Schools: An Independent Inquiry* (the Stevenson Report). London: Her Majesty's Stationery Office.

Jackson, R. (1997) *Religious Education – An Interpretive Approach*. London: Hodder & Stoughton.

Jahoda, G. (1963) The development of children's ideas about country and nationality, *British Journal of Educational Psychology*, Vol. 33, pp. 47–60.

James, W. (1890) *The Principles of Psychology*. New York: Dover.

Johnsey, R. (1995) An analysis of the procedures used by primary school children as they design and make. MSc thesis, Warwick University.

Johnsey, R. (1998) *Exploring Primary Design and Technology*. London: Cassell.

Keogh, B. and Naylor, S. (1997) *Starting Points for Science*. Sandbach: Millgate House.

Kimbell, R. A. (1994) *Understanding Technological Approaches: Final Report of*

Research Activities and Results. London: Goldsmiths College, ESRC.

Kimbell, R., Stables, K., Wheeler, T. Wosniak A. and Kelly, V. (1991) *The Assessment of Performance in Design and Technology*. London: APU/SEAC.

Klineberg, O. and Lambert, W. E. (1967) *Children's Views of Foreign Peoples: A Cross National Study*. New York: Appleton-Century-Crofts.

Kress, G. (1997) *Before Writing: Rethinking the Paths into Literacy*. London: Routledge.

Langer, Susan (1957) Expressiveness, in *Problems of Art*. New York: Charles Scribner's Sons. pp. 15–30.

Langer, Susan (1978) *Philosophy in a New Key*. Cambridge, Mass: Harvard University Press. 3rd edition.

Lapointe, A. E., Mead, N. A. and Askew, J. M. (1992) *Learning Mathematics*. Princeton, NJ: Educational Testing Service.

Lee, M. (1993) Growing Up in Sport', in M. Lee (ed.) *Coaching Children in Sport – Principles and Practice*. London: E. & F. N. Spon. pp. 91–105.

Lee, P. J. (1984) Why learn history? in A. K. Dickinson, P. J. Lee and P. J. Rogers (eds), *Learning History*. London: Heinemann.

Lee, P. J., Dickinson, A. K. and Ashby, R. (1996) There were no facts in those days: children's ideas about historical explanation, in M. Hughes (ed.) *Teaching and Learning in Changing Times*. Oxford: Blackwell.

Leeson, E., Stanisstreet, M. and Boyes, E., (1997) Primary children's ideas about cars and the environment, *Education 3–13*, Vol. 25, no. 2, pp. 25–9.

Lehrer, T. (1965) 'New Math' in *That Was the Year that Was*. 6179-2 Reprise Records.

Lewis, M. and Wray, D. (1995) *Developing Children's Non-Fiction Writing: Working with Writing Frames*. Leamington Spa: Scholastic.

Light, P. (1993) Collaborative learning with computers, in P. Scrimshaw (ed.) *Language, Classrooms and Computers*. London: Routledge.

Liverpool Eight Children's Research Group (1996) *Children's Needs Survey*. Unpublished.

Martin, J. R. (1989) *Factual Writing: Exploring and Challenging Social Reality*. Oxford: Oxford University Press. 2nd edition.

Marwick, A. (1970) *The Nature of History*. London: Macmillan.

Mathematical Association (1956) *The Teaching of Mathematics in Primary Schools*. London: G. Bell & Sons.

Mathematical Association (1992) *Mental Methods in Mathematics: A First Resort*. Leicester: Mathematical Association.

Maude, P. (1996) Differentiation in physical education, in E. Bearne (ed.) *Differentiation and Diversity in the Primary School*. London: Routledge. pp. 126–37.

Maude, P. (1998) I like climbing, hopping and biking – the language of physical education, in E. Bearne (ed.) *Use of Language Across the Primary Curriculum*. London: Routledge. pp. 228–39.

McCormick R. *et al.* (1996) Research on student learning of designing and problem solving in technological activity in schools in England. Paper presented to American Educational Research Association Annual Meeting,

New York.

McFarlane, A. (ed.) (1997) *Information Technology and Authentic Learning*. London: Routledge.

McGettrick, B. (1995) *Values and Educating the Whole Person*. Dundee: Scottish CCC.

Meadows, S. (1993) *The Child as Thinker*. London: Routledge.

Mercer, N. (1995) *The Guided Construction of Knowledge: Talk Amongst Teachers and Learners*. Clevedon: Multilingual Matters.

Mercer, N. (1996) The quality of talk in children's collaborative activity in the classroom, *Learning and Instruction*, Vol. 6, pp. 359–79.

Mercer, N., Wegerif, R. and Dawes, L. (1999) Children's talk and the development of reasoning in the classroom, *British Educational Research Journal*, Vol. 25, no. 1, pp. 95–111.

Merry, R. (1997) Cognitive development 7–11, in N. Kitson, and R. Merry (eds) *Teaching in the Primary School: A Learning Relationship*. London: Routledge.

Merseth, K. (1993) How old is the shepherd? An essay about mathematics education, *Phi Delta Kappan*, Vol. 74, no. 7, pp. 548–54.

Millar, R. (1996) Towards a science curriculum for public understanding, *School Science Review*, Vol. 77, no. 280, pp. 7–18.

Millar, R. and Osborne, J. (eds) (1998) *Beyond 2000: Science Education for the Future*. London: King's College.

Millett, A. and Johnson, D. C. (1996) Solving teachers' problems? The role of the commercial mathematics scheme, in D. C. Johnson and A. Millett, (eds) *Implementing the Mathematics National Curriculum*. London: Paul Chapman. pp. 54–74.

Morse, B. (1995) Rhyming poetry for children, in R. Beard (ed.) *Rhyme, Reading and Writing*. London: Hodder & Stoughton.

Mortimore, P., Sammons, P., Stoll, L., Lewis, D. and Ecob, R. (1988) *School Matters: The Junior Years*. Wells: Open Books.

Murphy, P., Selinger, M., Bourne, J. and Briggs, M. (eds) (1995) *Subject Learning in the Primary Curriculum: Issues in English, Science and Mathematics*. London: Routledge.

Music Education Council, Music Industries Association, National Music Council (1998) *The Fourth 'R': the Case for Music in the School Curriculum*. Surrey: The Campaign for Music in the Curriculum.

National Curriculum Council (1989) *Mathematics Non-Statutory Guidance*. York: National Curriculum Council.

National Curriculum Council (1990) *Curriculum Guidance 3: The Whole Curriculum*. York: National Curriculum Council.

National Curriculum Council (1993a) *Spiritual and Moral Development: A Discussion Paper*. York: National Curriculum Council.

National Curriculum Council (1993b) *Teaching Science at Key Stages 1 and 2*. York: NCC.

National Foundation for Educational Research (1998) *The Effects and Effectiveness of Arts Education in Schools* (Summary of First Interim Report).

London: Royal Society of Arts.

National Numeracy Project (1998) *Framework for Teaching Mathematics*. Crown Copyright.

National Society for Education in Art and Design (1999) Direction (2): towards a new art education. Conference papers.

Newell, A. and Simon, H. A. (1972) *Human Problem-Solving*. Englewood Cliffs, NJ: Cambridge University Press.

Nicholls, J. (1984) Conceptions of ability and achievement motivation, in K. Ames and C. Ames (eds) *Research on Motivation in Education. Volume 1: Student Motivation*. New York: Academic Press. pp. 39–73.

Nisbet, J. and Shuckman, J. (1986) *Learning Strategies*. London: Routledge & Kegan Paul.

Norris Nicholson, H. (1993) *Inspirations for Geography*. Leamington Spa: Scholastic.

Novak, J. D. and Gowin, D. B. (1984) *Learning How to Learn*. Cambridge: Cambridge University Press.

Novak, M. (1967) *The Joy of Sports – End Zones, Bases, Baskets, Balls, and the Consecration of the American Spirit*. Lanham, MA: Madison.

Odam, George (1995) *The Sounding Symbol*. Cheltenham: Stanley Thornes.

Office for Standards in Education (1993) *English: Key Stages 1, 2, 3 and 4: Fourth Year 1992–3*. London: Her Majesty's Stationery Office.

Office for Standards in Education (1994a) *Geography. A Review of Inspection Findings 1993/94*. London: Her Majesty's Stationery Office.

Office for Standards in Education (1994b) *Spiritual, Moral, Social and Cultural Development*. A Discussion Paper London: OFSTED.

Office for Standards in Education (1995a) *English: A Review of Inspection Findings 1993/94*. London: Her Majesty's Stationery Office.

Office for Standards in Education (1995b) *Mathematics: A Review of Inspection Findings 1993/94*. London: Her Majesty's Stationary Office.

Office for Standards in Education (1996) *Subjects and Standards: Issues for School Development Arising from OFSTED Inspection Findings 1994–5: Key Stages 1 & 2*. London: Her Majesty's Stationery Office.

Office for Standards in Education (1997a) *Standards in English 1995–6: Primary Schools*. London: Ofsted.

Office for Standards in Education (1997b) *The Impact of New Agreed Syllabuses on the Teaching and Learning of Religious Education*. London: OFSTED.

Office for Standards in Education (1998a) *Inspecting Subjects 3–11*, Guidance for Inspectors. OFSTED, July.

Office for Standards in Education (1998b) *Primary Subjects and Standards: History*. London: Office for Standards in Education.

Office for Standards in Education (1998c) *Standards in Primary English*. London: OFSTED.

Office for Standards in Education (1998d) *Standards in the Primary Curriculum 1996–97*. London: OFSTED.

Office for Standards in Education (1998e) *The Arts Inspected* London: Heinemann.

Olson, D. (1994) *The World on Paper: The Conceptual and Cognitive Implications of Writing and Reading*. Cambridge: Cambridge University Press.

Osborne, J. and Simon, S. (1996) Primary science: past and future directions, *Studies in Science Education*, Vol. 27, pp. 99–147.

Osborne, J., Black, P., Smith, M. and Meadows, J. (1990) *Primary SPACE Project Research Report: Light*. Liverpool: Liverpool University Press.

Palmer, J. (1993) From Santa Claus to sustainability: emergent understanding of concepts and issues in environmental science, *International Journal of Science Education*, Vol. 15, no. 5, pp. 487–96.

Papert, S. (1981) *Mindstorms: Children, Computers and Powerful Ideas*. Brighton: Harvester Press.

Paynter, John (1970) *Sound and Silence*. Cambridge: Cambridge University Press.

Peters, R. S. (ed.) (1969) *Perspectives on Plowden*. London: Routledge & Kegan Paul.

Peters, R. S. (1996) *Ethics and Education*. London: George Allen and Unwin.

Phenix, Philip H. (1964) *Realms of Meaning*. New York: McGraw-Hill.

Phillips, R. (1998). *History Teaching, Nationhood and the State: A Study in Educational Politics*. London: Cassell.

Piaget, J. (1970) *Le structuralisme*. Paris: Presses Universitaires de France. 4th edition.

Piaget, J. and Weil, A. (1951) The development in children of the idea of homeland and of relations with other countries, *Institute of Social Science Bulletin*, Vol. 3, pp. 561–78.

Pike, N. (1998) Pupils plus calculators equal big nothing, *Times Educational Supplement*, 30 January.

Pimm, D. (1986) Beyond reference, *Mathematics Teaching*, Vol. 116, pp. 48–51.

Plunkett, S. (1979) Decomposition and all that rot, *Mathematics in School*, Vol. 8, no. 3, pp. 2–7.

Prentice, R. (ed.) (1995) *Teaching Art and Design*. London: Cassell.

Puttnam, D. (1998) *The Independent*. 10 April.

Qualifications and Curriculum Authority (1998a) *Design and Technology – An Exemplar Scheme of Work for Key Stages 1 and 2*. London: Qualifications and Curriculum Authority.

Qualifications and Curriculum Authority (1998b) *Geography, A Scheme of Work for Key Stages 1 and 2*. London: Qualifications and Curriculum Authority/Department for Education and Employment.

Qualifications and Curriculum Authority (1998c) *Maintaining Breadth and Balance at Key Stages 1 and 2*. London: Qualifications and Curriculum Authority 98/190.

Qualifications and Curriculum Authority (1998d) *Survey of the Implementation of the New Curriculum Guidance*. London: Qualifications and Curriculum Authority.

Raban, B., Clarke, C. and McIntyre, J. (1993) *Evaluation of the Implementation of English in the National Curriculum at Key Stages 1, 2 and 3 (1991–1993): Final Report*. York: National Curriculum Council.

Reid, L. A. (1986) *Ways of Understanding and Education*. London: Heinemann.

Richards, C. (ed.) (1982) *New Directions in Primary Education*. Lewes: Falmer.

Roberts, G. (1992) Motivation in sport and exercise: conceptual constraints and conceptual convergence, in G. Roberts (ed.) *Motivation in Sport and Exercise*. Champaign, IL.: Human Kinetics.

Roberts, G. and Treasure, D. (1993) The importance of the study of children in sport: an overview, in M. Lee (ed.) *Coaching Children in Sport – Principles and Practice*. London: E. & F. N. Spon. pp. 3–16.

Robitaille, D. F. and Garden, R. A. (eds) (1989) *The IEA Study of Mathematics II: Contexts and Outcomes of School Mathematics*. Oxford: Pergamon Press.

Rogers, Richard (1997) *Cities for a Small Planet* London: Faber.

Rogers, Rick (1998) *The Disappearing Arts?* London: Royal Society of Arts.

Ross, A. O. (1976) *Psychological Aspects of Learning Disabilities and Reading Disorders*. New York: McGraw-Hill.

Ross, Malcolm (1984) *The Aesthetic Impulse*. Oxford: Pergamon Press.

Rousham, L. and Rowland, T. (1996) Numeracy and calculators, in R. Merttens (ed.) *Teaching Numeracy*. Leamington Spa: Scholastic Press.

Rowland, T. (1991) Taking control, *Times Educational Supplement*, 18 January.

Rowland., T. (1994) *CAN in Suffolk – The First Six Months of a Calculator-Aware Number Curriculum*. Cambridge: Homerton College. 2nd edition.

Russell, T. and Watt, D. (1990a) *Primary SPACE Project Research Report: Evaporation and Condensation*. Liverpool: Liverpool University Press.

Russell, T. and Watt, D. (1990b) *Primary SPACE Project Research Report: Growth*. Liverpool: Liverpool University Press.

Sainsbury, M. (1998) *Evaluation of the National Literacy Project: Summary Report*. Slough: NFER.

Salmon, Phillida (1995) Experiential learning, in R. Prentice (ed.) *Teaching Art and Design*. London: Cassell.

Scheerens, J. (1992) *Effective Schooling: Research, Theory and Practice*. London: Cassell.

Schoeser, Mary (1999) *Decadence?* (Teachers' Notes). London: Crafts Council.

Schools Council (1965) *Curriculum Bulletin No.1*. London: Her Majesty's Stationery Office.

Schools Council 13–16 Project (1976) *A New Look at History*. Edinburgh: Holmes MacDougal.

Schools Curriculum and Assessment Authority. (1997) *Geography at Key Stage 2*. London: SCAA.

Scottish Consultative Council on the Curriculum (1996) Teaching for effective learning: a paper for discussion and development, Dundee: Scottish CCC.

Scruton, R. (1998) *On Hunting*. London: Yellow Jersey Press.

Seashore, C. E. (1967) *Psychology of Music*. New York: Dover.

Sharp, C. (1991) The exercise physiology of children, in V. Grisogono (ed.) *Children and Sport – Fitness, Injuries and Diet*. London: John Murray. pp. 32–71.

Shemilt, D. (1984) Beauty and the Philosopher: empathy in history and classroom, in A. K. Dickinson, P. J. Lee and P. J. Rogers (eds) *Learning History*. London: Heinemann.

Shulman, L. (1986) 'Those who understand: knowledge growth in teaching', *Educational Researcher*, Vol. 15, no. 2, pp. 4–14.

Shulman, L. (1987) Knowledge and teaching: foundations of the new reform, *Harvard Educational Review*, Vol. 57, no. 1, pp. 1–22.

Simpson, Kenneth (ed.) (1976) *Some Great Music Educators: A Collection of Essays*. Kent: Novello.

Slater, J. (1989) *The Politics of History Teaching: a Humanity Dehumanised?* Institute of Education, Special Professorial Lecture, London: Institute of Education.

Sleap, M. and Warburton, P. (1992) Physical activity levels of 5–11-year-old children in England determined by continuous observation, *Research Quarterly for Exercise and Sport*, Vol. 63, pp. 238–45.

Sleap, M. and Warburton, P. (1994) Physical activity levels of pre-adolescent children in England, *British Journal of Physical Education Research Supplement*, Vol. 14, pp. 2–6.

Small, Christopher (1998) Musicking: the meanings of performing and listening. Paper presented at the Conference of the National Association of Music Educators.

Smart, N. (1971) *The Religious Experience of Mankind*. London: Fontana.

Smart, N. (1996) *Dimensions of the Sacred*. London: HarperCollins.

Smith, Chris (1998) *Creative Britain*. London: Faber & Faber.

Smith, R. (1989a) Curricular developments in gymnastics, in L. Almond (ed.) *The Place of Physical Education in Schools*. London: Kogan Page. pp. 72–82.

Smith, R. (1989b) What's going on in their heads? *Mathematics in School*, Vol. 18, no. 5, pp. 33–5.

Sparrowhawk, A. (1995) *Report on Initial Findings from Schools Using the 'CD-ROM in the Primary School' Initiative*. National Council for Educational Technology.

Spencer, C. and Stillwell, R. (1974) Children's early preferences for other nations and their subsequent acquisition of knowledge about those nations, *European Journal of Social Psychology*, Vol. 3, no. 3, pp. 345–9.

Sports Council (1993) *Young People and Sport*. London: Sports Council.

Stannard, J. (1997) Raising standards through the National Literacy Project. Paper presented at the Literacy Task Force Conference, London, 27 February 1997.

Sternberg, R. J. (1985) *Beyond IQ: A Triarchic Theory of Human Intelligence*. New York: Cambridge University Press.

Storm, M. (1984) Teaching about minorities, in N. Fyson (ed.) *The Development Puzzle*. Sevenoaks: Hodder & Stoughton/CWDE.

Streefland, L. (ed.) (1991) *Realistic Mathematics Education in the Primary School*. Utrecht: Freudenthal Institute.

Swann, M. (1985) *Education for All: Final Report of the Committee of Inquiry into the Education of Children from Ethnic Minority Groups*, Cmnd 9453. London: Her Majesty's Stationery Office.

Swanwick, K. (1988) *Music, Mind and Education*. London: Routledge.

Swanwick, K. and Tillman. J. (1986) The sequence of musical development: a study of children's composition, *British Journal of Music Education*, Vol. 3, no. 3, pp. 305–39.

Swift, J. and Steers, J. (1998) *A Manifesto for Art in Schools*. http://www.nsead.org/html/issues.html

Sylvester, R. (1994) *How Emotions Affect Learning in Educational Leadership*. ASCD, Virginia: USA.

Tanner, R. (1989) *What I Believe: Lectures and other Writings*. Bath: Crafts Study Centre.

Taylor, R. (1986) *Educating for Art*. Harlow: Longman.

Taylor, S. (1998) Progression and gender differences in mapwork, in S. Scoffham (ed.) *Primary Sources: Research Findings in Primary Geography*. Sheffield: The Geographical Association.

Teddlie, C. and Reynolds, D. (eds) (1999) *The International Handbook of School Effectiveness Research*. Lewes: Falmer.

Threlfall, J. (1998) Mental calculation strategies, in L. Bills (ed.) *Proceedings of the Leeds Conference of the British Society for Research into Learning Mathematics*. Coventry: University of Warwick.

Underwood, J. (1994) *Computer Based Learning*. London: David Fulton.

Underwood, J. and Brown, J. (eds) (1997) *Integrated Learning Systems: Potential into Practice*. Oxford: Heinemann.

Underwood, J. D. and Underwood, G. (1990) *Computers and Learning: Helping Children Acquire Thinking Skills*. Oxford: Blackwell.

Vygotsky, L. (1962) *Thought and Language*. Cambridge, Mass: MIT Press.

Vygotsky, L. (1978) *Mind in Society: the Development of Higher Psychological Processes*. M. Cole, V. John-Steiner, S. Scribner and E. Souberman (eds). Cambridge, Mass: Harvard University Press.

Watt, D. (1997) Towards effective teaching in primary science: an analysis of the evolving contribution of the SPACE Project to understanding the role of the teacher. PhD thesis. University of Warwick.

Watt, D. and Simon, S. (in press) Textual support for primary science teaching? *The Curriculum Journal*, Vol. 10, no. 3.

Wegerif, R. and Scrimshaw, P. (1997) *Computers and Talk in the Primary Classroom*. Clevedon: Multilingual Matters Ltd.

Weigand, P. (1991a) The known world of the primary school, *Geography*, Vol. 76, no. 2, pp. 143–9.

Weigand, P. (1991b) 'Does travel broaden the mind?', *Education 3-13*, Vol. 19, no. 1, pp. 54–8.

Weigland, P. (1992) *Places in the Primary School*. London: Cassell.

Weiss, M. and Duncan, S. (1992) The relationship between physical competence and peer acceptance in the context of children's sports participation, *Journal of Sport and Exercise Psychology*, Vol. 14, no. 2, pp. 177–92.

Welch, G. (1986) A developmental view of children's singing, *British Journal of Music Education*, Vol. 3, no. 3, pp. 295–303.

Whitebread, D. (1997) Developing children's problem-solving, in A.

McFarlane, (ed) *Information Technology and Authentic Learning*. London: Routledge. pp. 13–37.

Wiggins, T. (1996) The world of music in music education, *British Journal of Music Education*, Vol. 13, no. 1, pp. 21–9.

Williams, A. (1989) The place of physical education in primary education, in A. Williams (ed.) *Issues in Physical Education for the Primary School*. London: Falmer. pp. 11–27.

Williams, A. (1996) Physical education at Key Stage 2, in N. Armstrong (ed.) *New Directions in Physical Education – Change and Innovation*. London: Cassell. pp. 11–27.

Wragg, E. C. (1997) *The Cubic Curriculum*. London: Routledge.

Wray, D. and Lewis, M. (1997) *Extending Literacy: Children Reading and Writing Non-Fiction*. London: Routledge.

Index